MW01044466

SCHOLARLY MAN OF FAITH

SCHOLARLY MAN OF FAITH

Studies in the Thought and Writings
of Rabbi Joseph B. Soloveitchik

Edited by

EPHRAIM KANARFOGEL *and* DOV SCHWARTZ

THE MICHAEL SCHARF PUBLICATION TRUST
OF THE YESHIVA UNIVERSITY PRESS
NEW YORK

KTAV Publishing House

URIM PUBLICATIONS
Jerusalem · New York

Published with the assistance of the
NATALIE and ISIDOR FRIEDMAN Chair
in the Teaching of the Thought of Rabbi Joseph B. Soloveitchik
at Bar-Ilan University

In Memory of ISIDOR FRIEDMAN,
a Devoted Admirer of Rabbi Soloveitchik

Scholarly Man of Faith: Studies in the Thought and Writings
of Rabbi Joseph B. Soloveitchik
Edited *by* Ephraim Kanarfogel and Dov Schwartz
Editorial board: Ephraim Kanarfogel, Avi Sagi, Dov Schwartz,
David Shatz
Copyright © 2018 Yeshiva University Press
Typeset by Ariel Walden
Printed in Israel
First Edition
ISBN 9789655242812
KTAV Publishing House
527 Empire Boulevard
Brooklyn, NY 11225
www.ktav.com
Urim Publications
P.O. Box 52287,
Jerusalem 9152102
Israel
www.UrimPublications.com

Library of Congress Cataloging-in-Publication Data
Names: Kanarfogel, Ephraim, editor. | Schwartz, Dov, editor.
Title: Scholarly man of faith : studies in the thought and writings of Rabbi
  Joseph B. Soloveitchik / edited by Ephraim Kanarfogel and Dov Schwartz.
Description: Brooklyn, NY : Urim Publications, [2018]
Identifiers: LCCN 2017058462 | ISBN 9789655242812 (hardcover : alk.
  paper)
Subjects: LCSH: Soloveitchik, Joseph Dov—Teachings.
Classification: LCC BM755.S6144 S336 2018 | DDC 296.8/32092—dc23
  LC record available at https://lccn.loc.gov/2017058462

CONTENTS

INTRODUCTION

The intellectual and spiritual lives of Rav Yosef Dov Soloveitchik contain a series of seeming paradoxes. He was a great Torah giant whose views on Zionism did not accord with those of others of his stature; he was the great leader of modern Orthodoxy who saw himself mainly as a teacher, a *melammed*; his Torah presence in Israel was such that he was offered the position of Chief Rabbi, but he visited there only once, before the founding of the State; he was a virtuoso of Jewish philosophy who wished to be known principally through his talmudic teachings; and he was a prolific writer who did not publish many of his writings, due to the rigorous demands that he placed upon himself. Rav Soloveitchik did not subscribe to the remonstration of Rabbenu Bahya ibn Paquda, "do not be overly cautious of the need for caution."

With respect to his thought, many talmudists and academics have attempted to reveal the essence of his personality and his brilliance. A number have dealt with the role or weight of modernity in the thought of the Rav. Others have sought to elucidate the sources of the Rav's thought. And still others have tried to clarify his system of ideas in order to discover consistent themes. The Rav, however, expressed his thought in a way that made it somewhat elusive. First, he employed a number of different writing styles. On occasion, such as in the essay *U-bikashtem mi-sham*, the Rav employed the accepted style for discussing religious phenomenology; in other instances, however, his presentation tended toward a more sermonic style, as in *The Lonely Man of Faith*. The doctoral dissertation that Rav Soloveitchik wrote on the thought of Hermann Cohen is highly technical and analytical, but it does not refer to a single one of Cohen's "Jewish" writings.

Second, the Rav relied on an extensive and variegated series of thinkers and sources. An extreme example of this is his work on halakhic knowledge, *The Halakhic Mind*. The sheer range and density of the sources makes it difficult to discern those that are most central. Finally, the Rav treated many significant issues without offering firm resolutions for at least some of them; two examples are his attitudes toward modernity and Zionism.

It is possible to suggest that the dynamism of the Rav's thought and the differing views that it embraces reflect the paradoxical nature of modern Orthodoxy as a whole. The intertwining of the intellectual freedom that characterizes modern thought on the one hand, and the unbending obligation to the requirements of the *halakhah* on the other, is itself a paradox, and it sheds much light on the search that modern Orthodoxy has undertaken. The influence of Rav Soloveitchik on modern Orthodoxy in North America is akin, in many ways, to the influence of Rav Kook on religious Zionism in Israel. Indeed, Rabbi Aharon Lichtenstein, the Rav's son-in-law, wrote: "The views of Rav Kook, with which the Rav agreed in many areas even as he strongly disagreed in some others, form a basis for comparison (in terms of the Rav's originality and breadth of ideas), even as the essential building blocks of their thought and the modes of their philosophical expression differed greatly" ("The Rav at Jubilee: an Appreciation," in *Leaves of Faith: the World of Jewish Learning* [Jersey City, N. J., 2003], vol. 1, 193).

In the past thirty years, the influence of the thought of Rav Soloveitchik on religious Zionism in Israel has increased, and the reason for that shift can be pinpointed. From the mid–1970s through the mid–1980s, religious Zionism in Israel became intertwined with the settlement of Yehuda and Shomron and Gaza. At that point, the philosophical writings of the Rav that deal so much with the alienation and existential loneliness endemic to modern man were not so influential. The strong sense of unity and purpose that permeated the religious Zionist camp did not allow for a deep understanding of the Rav's writings. However, from the late 1980s onward, in the face of social and political changes that affected religious Zionism, the Rav's writings were "re-discovered," and this time they spoke strongly to the young religious Zionist.

In recent years, modern Orthodoxy in North America has undergone a self-assessment as well. A number of rabbinic leaders decided to make 'aliyah,' and changes have also occurred at the flagship institution of modern Orthodoxy in North America, Yeshiva University. The writings of the Rav, which express the considerations and concerns of modern Orthodox Jewry, have never been more relevant.

These parallel developments impelled us to organize a joint conference, under the auspices of both the Friedman Chair for Teaching the Thought of Rav Soloveitchik at Bar-Ilan University and Yeshiva University in New York, at which scholars would discuss the thoughts of the Rav. The two volumes that have emerged, in English and in Hebrew, bring the fruits of those conference proceedings to the reader. We hope and trust that these studies of the Rav's words and teachings will constitute a meaningful intellectual experience, and will also contribute to a further understanding of the complex challenges that stand before his students, and their students.

Ephraim Kanarfogel
Dov Schwartz

"In Many Respects God was Closer to Abraham than He was to Moses": Themes in *Emergence of Ethical Man*

I

Four of R. Soloveitchik's main philosophical-theological works were published in his lifetime, and thus can be taken to be in a form satisfactory to him. In all four there is one identifiable primary theme. *Halakhic Man* announces itself as a descriptive study of an ideal type. *U-Vikkashtem mi-Sham*, drafted in the same period, is about the relationship of man and God. *Halakhic Mind*, also prepared in the 1940's, is devoted to the epistemology of religious cognition. *Lonely Man of Faith* articulates the life view of the man of faith in the secular modern world. Likewise the first two theological books published posthumously are dedicated to one theme: *The Family Redeemed* to the family; *Worship of the Heart*, where the author himself began to revise for publication, to prayer. The same is true of such medium-sized essays as "A Theory of Emotions."

The book entitled, by its posthumous editor, *The Emergence of Ethical Man*, is clearly a unified work, although it breaks off in the middle; the continuation apparently was intended to trace the course of human existence to its terminus. Perhaps R. Soloveitchik abandoned the project of completing the text, satisfied with the unity of the material we have before us, so that the summary at the end of the published book is indeed the stopping point. He was engaged in several writing projects in the 1950's, and may have decided that the unfinished chapters, if resumed, would find their place elsewhere.[1]

---

1. For example, there are passages in the lectures on prayer that comprise

11

Meanwhile, the book we have obviously deals with the nature of human beings. This, however, is a very general statement. Almost anything substantial the Rav wrote, outside the realm of Talmud, is about the human condition. Determining, if possible, the theme of the work is thus a priority for the reader.

One dimension of *Emergence* sets it apart from the rest of the Rav's extended thought. Alone among his works it approaches Judaism, and the Bible, from a diachronic perspective. Although *Halakhic Man* and *Halakhic Mind* depict complex personalities and types of inquiry, the fundamental themes are identifiably the same throughout. *U-Vikkashtem mi-Sham* describes a trajectory for the individual and the community, but one that is not alleged to differ from one generation to the next. *Lonely Man* places its protagonist in a particular historical context, that of mid-20th century Western culture: here too, the type portrayed oscillates between various experiences, while the impetus to that oscillation is unchanging. The conception of Judaism, like the social framework presumed in all these writings, is stable. Only *Emergence*, among the book-length essays, suggests that human nature, in its most significant religious-ethical dimensions, changes in crucial ways, in the course of the Biblical narrative.

R. Soloveitchik once told me that he had composed an important and substantial text discussing how Moses became Moses. His son-in-law, my revered teacher R. Aharon Lichtenstein, stated on one occasion that the Rav wrote a text comparable to *Lonely Man,* in which Abraham stood at the center, like Adam in *Lonely Man. Lonely Man* made it into print because R. Soloveitchik, when invited to lecture to a non-Jewish audience, preferred to deliver a paper working from the universal Adam rather than the more Jewish Abraham and therefore set aside the requisite time for polishing the former. If in either, or both of these cases the text referred to is identical with *Emergence,* this would place the emphasis on the element of evolution or emergence

---

Worship of the Heart that appear word for word in *Lonely Man.* When he began reviewing the former for publication in the late 1970's R. Soloveitchik was unsure whether he had "borrowed" this text from an early version of *Lonely Man* for lecture purposes, or whether he had extracted it from his manuscripts on prayer when writing *Lonely Man.* Either way he did not want duplication in his published works. Along similar lines, one may surmise that some material from the essay announced as "Loneliness and Boredom" but never published, was moved into the final version of *Lonely Man.*

whereby the charismatic patriarchal period (primarily Abraham) emerges from the first stage of Adam and Eve and then evolves into the apostolic community represented by Moses.

One may think the difference is not great between positing multiple perspectives in the Biblical text, as the Rav famously does in *Lonely Man*'s analysis of Genesis 1–2, distinguishing two synchronic aspects of the creation of man, and the picture presented in *Emergence*, in which the patriarchal experience diverges significantly from that of the community united in adherence to revealed Law. One may also compare the diachronic progression within the stories of Genesis-Exodus in *Emergence* with the contrast between the Judaism of the first temple period and that of the second, as is posited in *Lonely Man* and other essays,[2] although the change of atmosphere here is marked by the cessation of prophecy and is already noted by rabbinic tradition.[3] In any event, I believe that the originality of *Emergence* should not be minimized: it is an important experiment in the direction of diachronic theology and can thus provide a useful model for Orthodox Biblical theology.

To clarify what is at stake here, let us examine two elements in *Emergence*: the experience of death and the experience of law, noting parallels in the Rav's other writings. In *Emergence*, R. Soloveitchik explicitly states: "Abraham did not conquer death in the metaphysical, transcendental sense. His immortality is through and through *historical*."[4] Later, after reiterating the idea that immortality, for the charismatic personality, is defined in terms of the idea to the realization of which "he dedicated himself and his clan" (175), he writes:

> The first concept of immortality as coined by Judaism is the continuation of historical existence throughout the ages. It differs from transcendental immortality insofar as the deceased person does not lead an isolated, separate existence in a transcendental world. The identity persists on a level of

---

2. See, for example, "Mordecai and Esther," in *Days of Deliverance*, 70.
3. See my remarks on the place of diachronic analysis in Orthodox Biblical theology in the preface to Hayyim Angel, *Revealed Texts, Hidden Meanings: finding the Religious Significance of the Tanakh* (Jersey City, NJ: KTAV Publishing House, 2009).
4. *Emergence of Ethical Man*, 169. Further references to *Emergence* will be given in the text.

concrete reality disguised as a people. It asserts itself in the consciousness of the many, who trace their roots to the one. Yet metaphysical immortality is based upon historical immortality. Whoever does not identify himself with the historical ego and remains on the natural level cannot attain immortality. The first conquest of death takes place in the realm of history." (176)

An atemporal theology would begin by positing immortality as a principle of faith. It would be necessary to explicate this doctrine, to distinguish between immortality of the soul and the resurrection of the body and investigate the normative status of the two concepts. That the individual, in some sense, triumphs over death via the realization of the idea might be a comforting or inspiring notion, but it would not register as a principle of faith as such principles were enshrined in Jewish dogmatology, for example in Maimonides' list of thirteen principles. To say that the charismatic personality of Genesis conquers death only by identifying himself with the historical ego is tantamount to saying that the patriarchs did not work with the idea of "transcendental immortality."

From the point of view of later dogmatic debates, the term "transcendental immortality" is annoyingly ambiguous, because it does not distinguish between afterlife of the soul and that of the body, both of which would stand in contrast with the "historical" idea that the Rav ascribes to the charismatic personality. To be sure, he is not neutral as between these two traditional alternatives. Twentieth century religious thought witnessed a conflict between the "rationalists" who disdained resurrection of the body in favor of the more spiritual claim for continuation of the disembodied soul, as argued for in the philosophical tradition stretching from Plato through Descartes to Moses Mendelssohn, and those who insisted on corporeal resurrection as taught by Scripture in addition to (as for Maimonides) or instead of immortality of the soul.[5]

When R. Soloveitchik says that "metaphysical immortality is based upon historical immortality," and that the former is a prerequisite for the latter, he is stressing that the accepted Jewish teaching on meta-

---

5. The question mark in the title of Oscar Cullmann's 1956 monograph, *Immortality of the Soul or Resurrection of the Dead?*, and the agitated responses it provoked, as cited in his preface, capture the intensity of the conflict.

physical immortality must include bodily resurrection. If continued existence of the soul sufficed for metaphysical immortality it would make no sense to make it dependent on concrete social-historical identity. As an exegete of the book of Genesis, however, he abstains from making this point explicit. From the vantage point of the charismatic personality, who is not privy to the subsequent philosophical tradition, the full metaphysical implications of historical continuity through the nation are not the subject of consciousness.

"The first concept of immortality as coined by Judaism is the continuation of historical existence throughout the ages." R. Soloveitchik is very much aware that he is not here presenting a catechism of Jewish faith but rather a diachronic reconstruction of Biblical experience. The careless or agenda-driven revisionist might choose to misrepresent it as the former. To forestall such misinterpretation, the Rav reminds us that the historical concept is only the first stage in the unfolding of Jewish teaching. How he would have traced the further unfolding of doctrine cannot be discerned from the text before us.

The remarks on immortality in *Emergence* can be contrasted with the treatment of the subject in *Halakhic Man* and in many other writings. The discussion of immortality there is not diachronic but typological. R. Soloveitchik quotes a number of verses from Psalms and Isaiah that focus entirely on this-worldly existence, and accordingly characterize death as an unqualified evil. These verses buttress the claim that *halakhic man* is this-worldly and views death as a threat to his worldview. These biblical texts must be cited because many readers, influenced by popular religious ideas harmonious with the outlook of *homo religiosus*, consider traditional religion and Judaism in particular, as oriented to the other world. R. Soloveitchik could have referred to afterlife passages for the sake of expository completeness, but such completeness was unnecessary for his thesis. He could have investigated whether and why this-worldliness or other-worldliness predominates in different parts of the Bible. This too, however, was not part of his undertaking, and there is no reason to believe that such an exploration interested him at the time.[6]

---

6. Gerald Blidstein, "Death in the Writings of R. Joseph DovSoloveitchik" (*Tradition* Spring, 2011), reprinted in *Society and Self: On the Writings of Rabbi Joseph B. Soloveitchik* (Jersey City, 2012) is the most balanced and comprehensive treatment of the subject in all the Rav's publications to date.

There is no evidence that R. Soloveitchik was familiar with the ideas of R. Kook when he wrote *Halakhic Man* or that he studied R. Kook's *Orot* later on.[7] In the essay *L'Mahalakh ha-Ideot b'Yisrael*, R. Kook examined the role of belief in the afterlife from a diachronic point of view. In R. Kook's view, Judaism was this-worldly and collectivist through the First Temple period: it was the destiny of the Jewish people, rather than that of the individual, that mattered. Due to the exile and the weakening of the collective bond, Second Temple Judaism became more individualistic and highlighted reward and punishment beyond this world.[8] R. Kook does not speak of the appearance of individual reward and punishment and postmortem justice as entirely novel ideas. Rather, he offers the image of the "candle at noon" (*shraga b'tihara*), an idea that existed in the background but did not play an active role because other ideas commanded the foreground; with the eclipse of collective destiny in the exile, individualistic themes become more prominent.

R. Kook is implicitly responding to scholars who championed the hypothesis that the afterlife (and individual reward and punishment) "entered Judaism" only in the Second Temple age. He contests this view, even while taking into account the change in emphasis. Such views would surely have been known to R. Soloveitchik; one need range no further than Hermann Cohen's *Religion of Reason*. He is not concerned, within the text of *Emergence*, with the antiquity of belief in the afterlife before the Babylonian exile, as these historical eras are not the subject of the book.

It need hardly be noted that standard Talmudic teaching insists that resurrection of the dead is found in the Torah.[9] R. Soloveitchik, a staunch, and when the occasion called for it, a zealous, upholder of normative rabbinic tradition, could note its absence from the patriarchal narratives in Genesis. He would not have been impelled to adopt the Kookian principle of the daytime candle to explain the silence of

---

Blidstein does not consider the diachronic element noted here and omits reference to discussion of death in *Emergence*.

7. In conversation he mentioned studying *Orot haTeshuva* and parts of *Olat Reiyah*, not surprising in view of his own preoccupation with repentance and prayer.

8. See *Orot* 110.

9. Mishna *Sanhedrin* 10:1 and opening folios of *Sanhedrin* chapter 11 in Babylonian Talmud (*Perek Helek*).

Genesis. How he would have described its introduction after Genesis is impossible to determine based solely on the writing we have before us.[10]

II

The centrality of revealed law for Judaism is a ubiquitous theme in Rabbi Soloveitchik's work. Almost always he posits the Torah, and the Halakha, as unchanging institutions in Jewish life, without which Jewish ethics is unthinkable. *Emergence*, however, is the only one of the major works containing a definition of the ethical, and it is the only one that considers Halakha as a contingent, historical manifestation of the ethical, so that one could define or describe an ethical experience from which the formal features of revealed law are absent.

Here is the definition:

> An act is ethical when it is sponsored by two motives: the *imperativistic*, that is, under the pressure of a normative feeling, and the *idealistic*, namely, the fulfillment of the norm is experienced as redeeming, elevating and meaning-giving. The ethical need must be experienced by man in complete differentiation from the biological push. (77)

The first element in this definition distinguishes the ethical impulse from the fulfillment of desires. It entails that the ethical is experienced as compulsive in some sense, but not as determined by the calculus of natural interest. Without freedom to violate the norm, continues R. Soloveitchik, "man will not experience the moral gesture as an act filled with meaning that enriches his life." Furthermore, "the unique experience of duty and responsibility is only possible if the alternative of a non-ethical act is a live option." The second element denies the

---

10. See, however, notes on R. Soloveitchik's lecture on "Resurrection of the Dead," in *Morasha Kehillat Yaakov, Essays in Honour of Chief Rabbi Jonathan Sacks*, ed. Rabbi Michael Pollak, Dayan Shmuel Simons (Jerusalem 2014), 2-9. With all the caveats about relying on student notes, it is clear that the Rav finds several passages in the early books of the Bible, such as Hannah's prayer (I Samuel 2) important for defining and analyzing Jewish teaching on resurrection and for distinguishing the roots of the doctrine in the Bible from its Christian development.

name of ethical imperative from trivial or demeaning behavioral manifestations.[11]

It is noteworthy that this definition says nothing about the particular content of ethical obligation, or about its connection to God. Instead the focus is on the phenomenology of moral experience and on its metaphysical presuppositions, such as freedom and the possibility of violating one's duty. The general discussion is reminiscent of Kant, but only the Kantian structure of freedom and the attitude of respect for the moral law, not any of the formulations of the categorical imperative, referring to universality, human dignity, or the kingdom of ends. Nor is there anything about divine commands.

Contrast with the Rav's better known works. A well-known passage in *U-Vikkashtem mi-Sham* asserts that authentic moral experience must contain an element of divine command, and that the command must not always be compatible or appealing to the human logos. The ubiquity of divine command in moral experience, please note, does not entail the classic divine command theory of morality: it does not reduce the moral imperative to the experience of being commanded by God, nor does it imply that being commanded by God and being a moral imperative are analytically the same. Yet R. Soloveitchik, I believe, is saying something about the nature of moral experience: he is not making a merely pragmatic psychological claim about the need for divine command as a motivating factor for moral practice.[12] The definition in *Emergence* does not include divine command.

The tension between the two texts can be relieved if we recognize the diachronic structure of *Emergence*. The story of the Patriarchs

---

11. This definition was presupposed in my article "Pluralism and the Category of the Ethical" (*Tradition* 30:4, Summer 1996) 145–163, reprinted in Marc Angel, ed, *Exploring the Thought of Rabbi Joseph B. Soloveitchik* (Hoboken 1997). See also Shubert Spero, "Rabbi Joseph Dov Soloveitchik and the Role of the Ethical" (*Modern Judaism* 23:1, 12–31), who did not have access to *Emergence* and compare his revisions in the version he published in *Aspects of Rabbi Joseph Dov Soloveitchik's Philosophy of Judaism: an Analytic Approach* (Jersey City NJ, 2009).

12. In this I posit a "stronger" connection between God and morality, in the Rav's corpus than that ascribed to him by A. Sagi and D. Statman's *Dat u-Mussar* (Jerusalem 1993); but see their careful exegesis at 145 n.2. Their attribution to R. Soloveitchik of a weaker, more psychological analysis becomes more attractive, however, as an interpretation of the charismatic morality ascribed to the patriarchs in *Emergence*.

antedates the giving of the Torah. The morality of the patriarchs is defined in terms of imperativistic pressure, but not in terms of divine revealed command. The giving of the Torah comes to pass after the transition to the apostolic community. Once the relationship to the ethical is expressed via divine revelation, the commanding God becomes an essential ingredient in the moral experience: once God commands, no other voice, internal or external, provides the same normative pressure. Presumably, the idealistic element, too, is uniquely revealed through God's intervention. In most of the Rav's work, the phenomenological truths that count are invariant. Only in *Emergence* is it possible to speak of drastically differing modes of religious-ethical experience belonging to different stages of religious-ethical development, pre-Torah and post-Torah.

The Rav avoids relying on rabbinical statements implying that Abraham knew the Torah on his own, without benefit of divine revelation, although this would support his thesis, perhaps because this text was quoted by rationalists.[13] Nor does he cite the Talmudic statements ascribing to Abraham foreknowledge and conformity to the not yet revealed Torah, perhaps because these do not fit the plain sense of the Biblical text, perhaps because such statements downplay the gap between Genesis and Exodus, between the charismatic stage and the apostolic community. Instead he speaks of a revelation by God of a content consonant with the human being's own personality:

> The source of the law is the *mahazeh*, the prophetic vision, not the royal decree. The charismatic personality discovers the ethos himself. As a free personality, he goes out to meet the moral law with his full collected being; he chances to find it in himself and to consciously adopt it. (154)

Here is an insistence on an encounter with divine otherness, yet one that is not overpowering or restricting.

How coherent is this account with the narrative of Genesis? In Genesis 12, for example, God appears to Abram, out of nowhere, and

13. See *Avot d'Rabbi Nathan A*, chapter 33 and *Genesis Rabba* 42; see also *Tosefta Kiddushin* 5. On Hasidic use of this idea, see Arthur Green, *Devotion and Commandment: The Faith of Abraham in the Hasidic Imagination* (Cincinnati, 1989) 30–33.

summons him to leave his previous existence. Yet a few pages after
citing this verse (149), the Rav insists that there "is no imposition of
divine authority upon the charismatic person. Only a bilateral covenant, which binds both man and God, was concluded" (154). But a
little later he writes: "God came to man after the latter had sought and
found Him," (158) apparently relying on the rabbinic pre-history of
Abraham's quest for God. The next sentence alleviates the seeming tension between God's authoritative command and the thesis of bilateral
covenant: "God never derived His authority from the cosmic aspect,
or from His omnipotence, but from a historical factum: covenant,
redemption." Authority and kingship are compatible with the free
relationship, but only when the authority is grasped in a certain way.

We don't know how the Biblical exegesis would have been elaborated had the author presided over the final version. Overall, it
is consonant with Michael Wyschogrod's independently arrived at
insight that, unlike the time of Moses – "The theme of disobedience
seems muted with the patriarchs. One does not hear of sin in their
lives."[14] Genesis 18:23ff, where Abraham asks about divine justice
regarding God's plan to destroy Sodom, could be employed to support
his thesis, because the passage presupposes the Abraham's confidence
and solidarity with God. Or, to the contrary, it could imply that
Abraham's conception of justice potentially conflicts with God's and
leads him to challenge God's plan. R. Soloveitchik, however, omits
discussion of this passage.[15]

He does devote analysis to the story most apparently in conflict
with the thesis of *Emergence* about Abraham, namely the *akeda*.
Here God appears to be making a demand that runs counter to
the moral consciousness of Abraham himself. The Akeda is first
mentioned in the book when, in listing deleterious consequences
of sin, the Rav suggests that God is called *pahad Yitzhak* – the
"horror of Isaac" because "the latter's destiny was interwoven
with that of divine 'animosity' at the *Akedah*." And he continues:

---

14. Michael Wyschogrod, *The Body of Faith* (Harper & Row, 1989) 120.
15. He does mention the awesome or numinous aspects of the vision in Gen-
    esis 15, and his treatment is consistent with that found in *U-Vikkashtem
    mi-Sham*, where it reflects the *havaya gilluyit*, the unsought confrontation
    with God.

"Why did God act this way? Because many a time Abraham erred and forfeited his privileged position" (130).

In this paragraph, R. Soloveitchik is not interested in locating the specific fault for which Abraham is afflicted, though he is no doubt aware of rabbinic commentaries that identify such sins, in particular Rashbam's view about the backdrop to the Akeda. Nor is it accidental that he is not quick to use the word "sin" to categorize Abraham's failings. The point is that the effects of Adam's sin are not eliminated from the lives of the patriarchs. The thesis about the harmony and friendship between Abraham and God does not exclude the dark, frightening element in religious experience.

In a long footnote that is probably his most sustained treatment of the Akeda, the Rav confronts the apparent counter-evidence to his thesis about Abraham's moral bond with God. He begins by continuing the theme mentioned a moment ago:

> The strict legalistic relationship between lord and tenant comes to the surface. There is a demand on the part of the master for absolute surrender of the servant. God takes complete possession of his friend to whom He addressed Himself. The breach between God and man has apparently not been healed; there is still tension and conflict. Divine terror supersedes divine grace and love. Confederate turns into foe, "lover "into "pursuer." The Bible never tried to eliminate the tremor moment which was introduced by Adam. (156 n.2)

This opening statement echoes the idea of divine mastery and authority frequent in R. Soloveitchik's writing. In oral discourse he habitually resorted to the Akeda as a religious paradigm, and in that context often commended Kierkegaard's treatment in *Fear and Trembling*. According to this common reading of Kierkegaard, the message of the Akeda is that there is an occasional clash between the ethical and the religious, and in that extraordinary situation the knight of faith responds via the "teleological suspension of the ethical." Here, however, the Rav goes on to develop a more harmonious sense in the story by emphasizing Abraham's response, namely that he did not argue with God:

> We marvel at Abraham's sedateness, complacency and peace
> of mind. The enormous feat of the knight of faith was demon-
> strated not in his actual compliance with the divine order but
> in the manner in which he behaved in the face of the most
> puzzling divine absurdity. The blood-chilling fear of meeting
> the nonsensical did not overcome Abraham. Abraham's per-
> formance is not to be equated with a compulsory submission
> to a tyrannical power who overwhelmed him; nor should it
> be understood as an act of fatalistic despair, resignation to a
> fate which he cannot alter and which encounters man with
> animosity and malice. Abraham's deed was not born out of
> despair and anguish. Far from it. Abraham did not realize the
> absurdity and paradoxality of the divine order . . . He carried
> it out as if it were another means leading to the realization of
> the eternal covenant. . . . (156–7)

Yehuda Gellman distinguished felicitously between two kinds of
"double-mindedness."[16] On both models Abraham's faith (as opposed
to resignation) is characterized by the ability to obey God without
evaluating the contradiction between the ethical (the prohibition of
murder or God's undermining His promise of Isaac) and the religious
command. One type of double-mindedness is called "heavy" and highlights the painful, sacrificial aspect implicit in Abraham's obedience.
The other is "light": Abraham obeys without being burdened by the
absurdity of the contradiction.

I submit that most of R. Soloveitchik's remarks about the Akeda
are "heavy." He dwells on the inconsolability of the father who has
lost the child of promise, the grief that can never be assuaged.[17] He
points to the Kierkegaardian idea that religious commitment, in its
particularity, is incommunicable, also prominent in "Confrontation"
and "Lonely Man of Faith."[18] In *Emergence*, by contrast, the element

---

16. Jerome I. Gellman, *The Fear, the Trembling and the Fire: Kierkegaard and Hasidic Masters on the Binding of Isaac* (Lanham, MD, 1994), chapter 4. I am not certain that my use of the distinction is identical with Gellman's.
17. See for example, "*Al Ahavat ha-Torah u-Geullat Nefesh ha-Dor,*" in *Be-Sod ha-Yahid ve-ha-Yahad* (Jerusalem 1976), 401–432, 427ff, or the Yiddish transcription by Hillel Zeidman, "A Jew is Compared to a Torah Scroll," in *Bet Yosef Shaul* 4 (1994) with Hebrew translation by S. Carmy.
18. See *Ma Dodekh mi-Dod*, in *Be-Sod ha-Yahid ve-ha-Yahad* 189–253, 195. On

of contradiction and absurdity is posited, but Abraham's distinction is his "sedateness, complacency and peace of mind." This presentation fits and furthers the thesis of *Emergence* about the patriarchs. Hence it does not call attention to the sacrificial aspect of the Akeda and it pays no attention to Abraham's inability to communicate with others.

III

The tenor of the discussion in *Emergence*, including the references to absurdity and the knight of faith, clearly points to Kierkegaard and, as noted, the Rav freely acknowledged his indebtedness to *Fear and Trembling*. Yet Kierkegaard's name is not mentioned here. This raises the question of R. Soloveitchik's use of philosophical sources both in the works he published himself and in those produced from his manuscripts.

The major works published in the Rav's lifetime—*Halakhic Man*, *Lonely Man of Faith*, *U-Vikkashtem mi-Sham*, *Halakhic Mind* – are replete with philosophical allusions. The primary function of these references is to situate the Rav's writing within the history of philosophy and theology. Typically he presents a variety of approaches and then argues pluralistically for a position that incorporates the virtues and insights of each, or he notes the flaws of each.

R. Soloveitchik does not engage in textual interpretation of these philosophical sources. Evidently it is not his purpose to add to the exegetical literature. He also fails to identify the names of philosophers and terms even when such mentions would be routine. For example, the way of life arising from "natural experience" in *U-Vikkashtem*, with its emphasis on the human fulfillment of human drives and

---

this theme, and for an enumeration of others important for contemporary interpretation of the Akeda, see my "Paradox, Paradigm and the Birth of Inwardness: on R. Kook and the Akedah" in Ḥazon Naḥum: Studies in Jewish Law, Thought, and History Presented to Dr. Norman Lamm on the Occasion of his Seventieth Birthday, edited by Yaakov Elman and Jeffrey S. Gurock (Hoboken, NJ, 1997), 459–478, 470 n.22, noting that the other side of incommunicability is Abraham's return to the universal. As to the salience of the Kierkegaardian problemata for straightforward interpretation of the Biblical story, see S. Carmy and David Shatz, "The Bible as Source for Philosophical Reflection" in *Routledge History of Jewish Philosophy*, edited Daniel Frank and Oliver Leaman (London, 1997), 13–37, 17f.

desire, has clear affinities to the notion of autonomy associated with
Kant. Yet, the Rav carefully defers using the word "autonomy" until
fairly late in the essay, when he has reached the idea of *imitatio,* and
the applicability of the concept is unmistakable. Even then, he does
not identify Kant as the foremost exponent of autonomy in modern
ethics. When mapping the intellectual history, it seems to me, names
and common terminology are summoned to communicate the frame
of reference; when developing the ideas themselves, the Rav prefers
to formulate them in his own manner, rather than to facilitate the
intellectual short cut afforded by name-dropping.

This could be the Rav's reason for not mentioning Kierkegaard in
Emergence. The superficial reader would be liable to impose his or her
interpretation of *Fear and Trembling* on the Rav's discussion of the
Akeda. Furthermore, how to understand Kierkegaard is itself a vexed
question, complicated by the literary form of the book and its place
within Kierkegaard's pseudonymous authorship. Usually, as noted, the
Rav used Kierkegaard's book to illustrate the possibility of sacrificial
clash between conventional ethics and divine command as a feature
of religious life. In *Emergence* he is more occupied with the contrast
between resignation and faith, with Abraham's faith manifesting the
opposite of despair. In this respect the Rav's discussion here comes
intriguingly close to some recent readings of *Fear and Trembling* that
highlight Abraham's trust in God rather than the conflict of ethics
and religion.[19]

When dealing with works not finalized by the author, in particular
texts initially prepared for oral delivery, one cannot dismiss the possibility or even the likelihood that the presence or absence of references
is accidental. Facing a deadline, one uses a quote because it is available
at hand and defers the optimal reference for an.editorial moment
that may never arrive, or one borrows a phrase or passage and, for
the same reason, fails to inscribe its genealogy in the notebook. For
instance, we have noted the absence of direct allusion to Kant's idea
of the categorical imperative in *Emergence.* The two citations of Kant
are from passages that are not especially illustrative of Kantian ethics.
Rabbi Meir Tribeitz has pointed out that both are found in Ernst

---

19. See, for example, Robert Adams, "The Knight of Faith," *Faith and Philosophy,* 1990, and Sharon Krishek, *Kierkegaard on Faith and Love* (Cambridge,
2009).

Cassirer's *Essay on Man*.[20] This may be symptomatic of the influence exerted by this book, or it may indicate no more than its presence on his desk as he jotted down the text for his class. Conversely, when we come across mention of specific phrases in Emil Brunner or Buber's *Moses* it probably is a sign of serious engagement with the works in question, especially, given the frequency, regarding the latter, but there is no assurance that these works are inherently more central than others not so specified.

The last point brings us to cases like Max Scheler's *Man's Place in Nature*. Neither this book nor other writings from Scheler's last, post-Catholic stage are explicitly mentioned in the Rav's texts. However, as Alex Ozar has demonstrated, the opening paragraph of *Emergence* is a rewriting of Scheler's opening with changes reflecting substantially different emphases in their conceptions.[21] Here the deliberate reworking is clearly a clue to R. Soloveitchik's intent.

IV

The above is a partial engagement with *Emergence*. I chose to focus exclusively on its distinctive methodological character, namely its diachronic structure. When comparing R. Soloveitchik's work with that of R. Kook or those close to his approach, on the one hand, or with academic studies of Jewish thought, on the other hand, R. Soloveitchik appears to be relatively indifferent to historical evolution, more committed to discerning continuity and permanence in the experience of different generations. In *Emergence*, too, his analysis of the different historical stages should not be taken to imply that experiences of the past are irrelevant or totally unavailable to us, though, as R. Hayyim of Volozhin would be quick to point out, the kind of freedom in the observance of the divine law ascribed to Abraham is superseded with the giving of the Torah. Not only does this open up a new aspect of the Rav's thought, it also encourages the possibility of a theology oriented to him that incorporates elements of R. Kook's historical

---

20. Rabbi Tribeitz's lectures on *Emergence* are available at www.hashkafacircle .com. I thank Erich Kauffman, who brought this site to my attention.
21. See Alex Ozar, "The Emergence of Max Scheler: Understanding Rabbi Joseph Soloveitchik's Philosophical Anthropology" (*Harvard Theological Review 109(02)*: 178–206 April 2016).

orientation and offers opportunities to annex academic insights and methods as well.

Further study of *Emergence* cannot be confined to the themes accented here. Much of the book can be detached from the historical aspect. The opening sections follow the order of Genesis but place the human being in a naturalistic biological context that is, in effect, timeless, and the bulk of the supporting evidence is halakhic rather than narrative. The analysis of the primal sin comes after, as it does in Genesis. Although it is, I believe, the most thorough and ambitious treatment in the published corpus, going beyond what is found in *Lonely Man, Family Redeemed* and "Confrontation," its distinctiveness is not connected to the historical reach of the work in which it is embedded. Likewise the important formulation of a "halakhic philosophy of miracle" that highlights the experience of wonder rather than the suspension of a putative natural law does not depend on the diachronic structure of the book.[22] Not least, the analysis of the apostolic community, the question of "how Moses became Moses" opens rich perspectives on the post-Genesis books of the Torah. To take only one example within R. Soloveitchik's oeuvre: the nature and implications of Moses' role as mediator – is he God's messenger to Israel, or Israel's representative before God? – receive fuller attention in *Emergence* than in *Lonely Man*.

The order in which an author's works are published is often fateful to their reputation. Within the scope of his lifelong religious preoccupations, R. Soloveitchik's creativity exhibits remarkable variety of approach and accent, and therefore retains its capacity to surprise readers who have not studied it in the round. The late publication of *Emergence*, half a lifetime after its composition and a lifetime after the Rav's first major essay, makes this especially true. The uncertainty about the ultimate shape and nuance of the book, had it been brought to editorial completion by the author, compounds the challenge. I have not undertaken to finish this job, but I am not free to exempt myself from it.

---

22. The idea of a distinctive halakhic outlook on miracle alludes to Blidstein's exploratory essay in *Daat50-52*.

SHIRA WEISS

Biblical Hermeneutics in the Thought of R. Soloveitchik: A Preliminary Appraisal of the Influence of R. Yehudah Halevi

Much has been written about the influence of Maimonides on the philosophy of R. Soloveitchik. By contrast, the influence of R. Yehudah Halevi, often perceived to be at the opposite end of the philosophical spectrum from Maimonides, has been largely overlooked by scholars. However, in a significant letter to Prof. Simon Rawidowicz in 1954, R. Soloveitchik expresses his preference for Halevi's experiential conception over Maimonides' rationalistic approach:

> I am inclined to accept the perspective of R Yehudah Halevi regarding the issue of the intellectual religious experience [advocated by Maimonides] in contrast to the "concrete" transcendental religious experience [advocated by Halevi]. However, our great teacher [Maimonides] was dedicated to his perspective with all his heart and soul, though it cannot be maintained in day-to-day religious life.[1]

R. Soloveitchik himself writes that his philosophic approach is, in an important respect, closer to Halevi than to Maimonides! This focus on the experiential dimension of religion is pervasive throughout many of R. Soloveitchik's philosophical works,[2] and in numerous instances,

---

1. Joseph B. Soloveitchik, *Community, Covenant and Commitment; Selected Letters and Communications*, Edited by Nathaniel Helfgot, (NY: KTAV Publishing House, 2005), 286.
2. R. Soloveitchik's focus on the experiential over the intellectual pervaded his

27

he cites the *Kuzari* explicitly. Since such references are beyond the scope of this paper,[3] I have chosen to concentrate on Halevi's influence upon R. Soloveitchik's biblical hermeneutics which the Rav utilized to illustrate his preference for the concrete religious experience.[4]

In *Kol Dodi Dofek*[5] and *The Lonely Man of Faith*,[6] two existen-

---

thought and religious attitude. As he reflects upon the nature of Talmud Torah, the perpetuation of the revelatory experience, he distinguishes between an intellectual and experiential encounter with the Divine.

"Halakha is two-sided . . . the first is intellectual, but ultimately it is experiential . . . When a person delves into God's Torah and reveals its inner light and splendor . . . and enjoys the pleasure of creativity and innovation, he merits communion with the Giver of the Torah. The ideal of clinging to God is realized by means of the coupling of the intellect with the Divine Idea which is embodied in rules, laws and traditions . . . However, halakhic knowing does not remain sealed off in the realm of the intellect. It bursts forth into one's existential consciousness and merges with it . . . The idea turns into an impassioning and arousing experience; knowledge into a divine fire; strict and exacting halakhic discipline turns into a passionate love burning with a holy flame. Myriads of black letters, into which have been gathered reams of laws, explanations, questions, problems, concepts and measures, descend from the cold and placid intellect, which calmly rests on its subtle abstractions and its systematic frameworks, to the heart full of trembling, fear and yearning, and turn into sparks of the flame of a great experience which sweeps man to his Creator." (Soloveitchik, "Al Ahavat haTorah veGeulat Nefesh haDor," *BeSod haYahid ve-ha-Yahad*), 410.

R. Soloveitchik laments over students' approach to Torah through exclusively intellectual and abstract means, as they fail to achieve the living and invigorating experience of Torah study. They encounter Torah as an idea, but not as a reality, "perceptible to taste, sight and touch".

3.   Additional instances in which Halevi's influence is apparent are included in footnotes.

4.   Both R. Yehudah Halevi and R. Soloveitchik focus on the "experiential," as opposed to the cognitive aspect of religion (stressed by Maimonides), albeit in different ways. Halevi emphasizes the experience of mass revelation and the transmission of tradition which he equates with experience; Soloveitchik highlights the personal, existential experience of religious worship.

5.   Originally delivered at Yeshiva University on Yom Ha'atzmaut 5716 (1956) and first published in Simon Federbush, ed., *Torah u-Melukha: Al Mekom ha-Medina ba-Yahadut* (Jerusalem: Mosad ha-Rav Kook, 1961), 11–44. JB Soloveitchik, "Kol Dodi Dofek: It is the Voice of My Beloeved That Knocketh," Trans. L. Kaplan, *Theological and Halakhic Reflections on the Holocaust*, Ed. B. Rosenberg, F. Heuman, (NJ: Ktav, 1992), 51– 117.

6.   Originally delivered to an interfaith audience at St. John's Catholic Seminary in Brighton, MA in 1964 and then published one year later, JB Soloveitchik,

tialist works which he constructed around readings of a biblical text, R. Soloveitchik adapts Halevi's exegetical interpretation to address contemporary challenges. R. Soloveitchik and Halevi both acknowledge the limits of metaphysical understanding, and instead find meaning and value in the human experience, as exemplified in biblical interpretation. From the very inception of his work, Halevi iterates the importance of the experiential realm. The premise of the *Kuzari* which motivated the Khazar King's entire quest for the true religion was the repeated divine message that while his intentions were pleasing to God, his actions were not. (*Kuzari* I:1) Halevi demonstrates to the King the superiority of man's experiential relationship with the personal God of Abraham, over the purely cognitive apprehension of the abstract God of Aristotle.[7] In *Kol Dodi Dofek*, R. Soloveitchik offers a modernized version of Halevi's interpretation of *Song of Songs*, which serves as the underlying allegory for his entire essay in which he encourages his generation to actively heed the divine call and cautions his coreligionists not to miss their historical opportunity, as the Shulammite maiden did in the biblical text. Similarly, in *The Lonely Man of Faith*, R. Soloveitchik's core analysis of the nature of man's relationship with God focuses upon the experiential aspect of religion and the inadequacy of a purely cognitive relation, as illustrated by Halevi's exegetical distinction of divine names described in Genesis' two accounts of creation. While scholarship has demonstrated the clear impact that other medieval and contemporary philosophers had on R. Soloveitchik, it appears that Halevi had a more significant influence upon the Rav than has previously been ascertained.

R. Soloveitchik begins *Kol Dodi Dofek* with a juxtaposition of two responses to suffering. He describes the compelled, passive and mute existence of fate as one of shock and confusion in which the sufferer

---

"The Lonely Man of Faith", *Tradition*, 1965, 5–67. (See Walter Wurzburger, "Rav Joseph B. Soloveitchik as Posek of Post-Modern Orthodoxy" *Tradition* 29:1, Fall 1994 p. 16. While Wurzburger neglects to identify the seminary, Eugene Korn writes that Rav Soloveitchik's daughter, Dr. Atarah Twersky, has verified that it was St. John's, which was the only Catholic seminary in Brighton at that time. Eugene Korn, The Man of Faith and Religious Dialogue: Revisiting "Confrontation" After Forty Years http://www.bc.edu/dam/files /research_sites/cjl/texts/center/conferences/soloveitchik/Korn_23Nov03.htm)

7.   Judah Halevi. *The Kuzari: In Defense of the Despised Faith*, Trans. N. Korobkin. (NY: Feldheim, 2009).

asks the metaphysical 'why' question regarding his encounter with evil. Due to man's inability to understand his afflictions with speculative thought, R. Soloveitchik instead encourages the sufferer to ask the functional 'how' question in order to actively confront evil in an existence of destiny.[8] R. Soloveitchik applies the fate/destiny distinction to his generation, as he discourages the search for a metaphysical understanding of the Holocaust, but rather encourages a halakhic response of action on behalf of the spiritual and physical well-being of the State of Israel. R. Soloveitchik further illustrates the superiority of the experiential existence of destiny through an allegorical biblical interpretation which reflects Halevi's similar sentiments. In his discussion of the obligation of Torah Jewry to the Land of Israel, R. Soloveitchik makes an explicit reference to Halevi. Even though only a brief passage from the *Kuzari* is quoted in *Kol Dodi Dofek*, Halevi's influence is pervasive throughout R. Soloveitchik's interpretation of *Song of Songs*. The biblical narrative of the Shulammite maiden who indolently hesitates to respond to the knock of her beloved is interpreted by R. Soloveitchik to refer to the Jews' neglect to heed God's call to return to the Jewish homeland after His *hester panim* during the Holocaust. Just as the maiden articulates excuses for why she cannot open the door for her beloved (*Song of Songs* 5:3), so too modern Jews rationalize their behavior to remain in the Diaspora. R. Soloveitchik offers a modern application of the biblical text and concludes with a very pithy paraphrase from Halevi's *Kuzari*:

> When the Beloved . . . knocked on the doors of His love, the maiden – we religious Jews – did not rush to descend from her couch and let in the Beloved . . . I am afraid that we Orthodox Jews are, even today, still sunk in a very pleasant slumber . . . I have put off my coat; how shall I put it on? I have washed my feet; how shall I soil them?" (*Song of Songs* 5:3). If one telephones a rich Jew and asks that he contribute to a worthy cause, he replies: "I am going to Florida, and this year have decided to stay in a luxury hotel. I am, therefore, unable to

---

8.   "Man's task in the world, according to Judaism, is to transform fate into destiny; a passive existence into an active existence; an existence of compulsion, perplexity, and muteness, into an existence replete with a powerful will, with resourcefulness, daring and imagination." *Kol Dodi Dofek*, 54.

give the amount requested of me." What did the Rabbi say to
the King of the Khazars? "This is a justified reproach, O king
of the Khazars! . . . and that which we say, 'Bow to His holy
hill' (*Psalms* 99:9), . . . is but as the chattering of the starling
and the nightingale." (*Kuzari* II:24)[9]

R. Soloveitchik here, with great brevity, reminds his reader of the
Rabbi's response to the King of the Khazars by paraphrasing from
the opening and closing passage of *Kuzari* II:24.

R. Soloveitchik's use of the paraphrased quote from the *Kuzari*
can best be understood in its context within the medieval work. In
the preceding chapters of the *Kuzari* (II:8–12), the Rabbi stresses the
importance for Jews to settle in the land of Israel, a major theme
within the text. [10] He offers an analogy of a vineyard; in order to yield
fruitful vintage, choice vines, choice land, and proper cultivation are
necessary. Similarly, in order for a people to achieve divinity [prophe-
cy],[11] a chosen people, a choice land, and proper cultivation through
deeds and laws of the Torah in that land, are required (II:12).[12] Such
teachings motivate the Khazar King to question why the Rabbi had
not settled in Israel and suggests that the Rabbi's bowing towards
Israel's direction is "mere flattery or some insincere custom" (II:23).
R. Soloveitchik, in his own modern allegorical interpretation of *Song
of Songs*, quotes the opening and closing passages from the Rabbi's
response to the King's accusation within which Halevi elaborates upon

---

9. *Kol Dodi Dofek*, 78–80.
10. In his explanation of the *Kinot* on *Tzion*, the first of which was authored
    by Halevi, Soloveitchik also refers to Halevi's emotional love for the Holy
    Land (*The Lord is Righteous in all of His Ways*, 302–11).
11. Silman, *Philosopher and Prophet*, 156, referencing *Kuzari* II:8–24.
12. While Soloveitchik was influenced by Halevi's biblical interpretation which
    called for the return to Israel, he did not share Halevi's attribution of *kedu-
    shah* to the Land. "For [R. Yehudah Halevi and the Ramban], the attribute
    of *kedushah*, holiness, ascribed to the Land of Israel is an objective meta-
    physical quality inherent in the land. With all my respect for the Rishonim,
    I must disagree with such an opinion. I do not believe that it is halakhically
    cogent. *Kedushah*, under a halakhic aspect, is man-made; more accurately,
    it is a historical category. A soil is sanctified by historical deeds performed
    by a sacred people, never by any primordial superiority." (*The Emergence of
    Ethical Man*, 150) See also, *Family Redeemed*, 64 and Ziegler, *Majesty and
    Humility*, 295.

his medieval exposition of the biblical text. By quoting the opening
and closing lines of *Kuzari* II:24, R. Soloveitchik seems to be endorsing
Halevi's entire biblical interpretation.[13] After the Rabbi acknowledges
the legitimacy of the King's accusation, Halevi offers an interpretation
of *Song of Songs*[14] through which he explains that God's Presence did
not fully return to the Second Temple because, like the Shulammite
maiden, Israel was reluctant to respond to God's beckoning and return
from the Babylonian exile to rebuild the Temple:[15]

> The Rabbi said: "This is a justified reproach, O king of the
> Khazars. It is this very sin which prevented us from achieving
> that which God promised us for the Second Temple . . . the
> Divinity was prepared to dwell [in the Second Temple] as It
> had previously [in the First Temple], provided that the Jewish
> people would all agree to return to Israel eagerly. However,
> they preferred subservience in the Diaspora, so that they would
> not have to part from their homes and affairs. Perhaps this is
> what Solomon meant when he said, 'I am asleep but my heart
> is awake' (*Song of Songs* V:2) – likening Diaspora Jewry to one
> who is asleep. Although one is sleeping, the heart is still awake
> and beating, and this represents the constancy of prophecy that
> was still among them.[16] 'A voice! My beloved knocks!' which
> refers to God's beckoning call to return to Israel. When it later
> says, 'I have removed my robe,' this refers to the sluggishness
> of the Jewish people to return. But their consent to return was
> not whole-hearted. God in turn repaid them in accordance
> with what was in their hearts, so that all the holiness that
> returned was in a diminished state, commensurate with their
> diminished state . . . "And therefore our recitations of such

---

13. David Gordon, "A Note on the Title of Kol Dodi Dofek," *Tradition*, 39:3,
    2006.
14. Halevi's interpretation of *Song of Songs*, his only allegorical interpretation of
    Scripture in the *Kuzari*, alludes to *Midrash Rabbah* and BT Yoma 9b which
    suggest that had the exiled Jews heeded Ezra and Nehemiah's calls to return
    to Israel, the second Temple would not have been destroyed.
15. *Nehemiah* 7:66, *Ezra* 8:15.
16. R. Soloveitchik describes the constancy of prophecy, "From the day that God
    revealed Himself to man, the prophetic vision has not ceased, and God has
    not departed from man." (*U-vikkashtem Mi-sham*), 135.

phrases as 'Bow to His holy hill,' (Ps. 99:9) 'bow down to
His footstool,' (Ps. 99:5) 'Who returns His Divine Presence to
Zion,' and the like, are merely like the chattering of the starling
and the nightingale.[17]

The end of the *Kuzari* chapter quoted by R. Soloveitchik reflects the
Rabbi's reproach that Jews pay liturgical lip service regarding the value
of the restoration of God's Presence to Israel, but lack meaningful
intent as demonstrated through their action. If one says "Bow to His
holy hill . . . Blessed are You Who returns His Divine Presence to
Zion" [when he himself does not return to Zion, then his words are
like] the chattering of the starling and the nightingale." By the end of
the *Kuzari*, the Rabbi realizes that the desire or intention to approach
God in any place is insufficient; rather God requires every Jew to take
action and settle in the Land of Israel. The Rabbi deems his teachings
valueless unless he practices what he preaches. Thus the Rabbi, no
longer willing to be subject to the king's justified reproach or for his
prayers to be as empty as the "chattering of the nightingale," departs
for the Holy Land.[18] Similarly, R. Soloveitchik calls his audience to

---

17. *Kuzari* II:24.
18. *Kuzari* V:23,27 Thus the conclusion of the *Kuzari* connects back with its
    introduction in which the Khazar King was told that his intentions were
    pleasing to God, but his actions were not (*Kuzari* I:1), demonstrating that
    his discussion in II:24 forms the climax of the text in which he discovered
    how to improve his ways. Scholars have debated over the motivation and
    meaning of Halevi's journey to the Land of Israel. Ezra Fliescher argues
    that Halevi immigrated not due to political dangers in Spain, but because
    he feared the risk of his coreligionists' assimilation into Arabic civilization.
    He felt that immigration to the Land of Israel would create a new Jewish
    culture in which Judaism would be a source of national pride. Thus, his
    goal was not personal-religious, but rather, a political and educational
    ideology for others to follow, perhaps comparable to R. Soloveitchik's call
    to American Torah Jewry. (Ezra Fleischer, '"The Essence of Our Land and
    Its Meaning" – Towards a Portrait of Judah Halevi on the Basis of Geniza
    Documents' (Hebrew). *Pe'amim* 68 (1996):4–15.) Scheindlin, however,
    considers Halevi's "personal piety and individual religious vision as the chief
    motivation for his pilgrimage." Scheindlin agrees with Fleischer's view that
    Halevi's perception of violence and acculturation threatened the future of
    Spanish Jewry, however, he argues that Fleischer's conception of Halevi's
    motivation of Jewish pride – similar to the Zionist ideal – his aspiration to
    replace the weak and afflicted Diaspora Jew with a strong and proud Jew

action and bemoans the insufficiency of American Jewry's intentions and empty gestures on behalf of Israel. His depiction of the reluctance of modern Jewry to give up their amenities in order to support the Jewish State, reflects the influence of Halevi's lament regarding the majority of Israel who "preferred subservience in the Diaspora, so that they would not have to part from their homes and affairs." R. Soloveitchik blames the precariousness of the political situation on one and only one fact: American Jewry's failure to actively settle Israel.[19]

R. Soloveitchik, in *Kol Dodi Dofek*, offers a modernized version of Halevi's biblical interpretation.[20] By quoting the Rabbi's response to

---

in Israel, is anachronistic and more characteristic of historical literature of the modern era. (Raymond Scheindlin, *The Song of the Distant Dove: Judah Halevi's Pilgrimage*, Oxford: Oxford University Press, 2008, 156, 277.) Fleischer's opinion of Halevi's nationalist vision, however, was earlier argued by Michael Sachs in his work on the religious poetry of Spanish Jewry in which he described Halevi as nationalistic and patriotic in his solution to the problem of a dispersed people without a homeland. (Michael Sachs, *Die Religiose Poesie der Juden in Spaien*. Berlin, 1845.) (Ben-Zion Dinaburg also argues that Halevi's motivation was to awaken Spanish Jewry to return home. He, however, additionally views Halevi's journey as encouraging his coreligionists to anticipate the final redemption with the voluntary return to Zion. Such a Messianic motivation is absent from R. Soloveitchik's writing. Ben-Zion Dinaburg, 'Rabbi Judah Halevi's Aliyah to Palestine and the Messianic Tension of his Time' (Hebrew). In *Minhah le-David*, 152–82. Jerusalem: Reuven Mass Publishing, 1935.) David Malkiel offers a synthesis by arguing that since Halevi was well-known in Spain, even a personal-religious motivation would have public/nationalistic ramifications. (David Malkiel, "Three Perspectives on Judah Halevi's Voyage to Palestine," *Mediterranean Historical Review* 25:1, 2010, 1–15.) (For further discussion, see: Ross Brann, *The Compunctious Poet: Cultural Ambiguity and Hebrew Poetry in Muslim Spain* (Baltimore, Md., 1991), 108–9; Aaron Hughes, *The Art of Dialogue in Jewish Philosophy* (Bloomington, Ind., 2008), 32, 49; Yochanan Silman, *Philosopher and Prophet*. (Albany: SUNY Press, 1995), 269; Joseph Yahalom, *Yehuda Halevi: Poetry and Pilgrimage*, trans. Gabriel Levin. Jerusalem: Magnes Press, 2009.)

19. *Kol Dodi Dofek*, 76–77.
20. R. Soloveitchik was not the first modern Jewish thinker to offer such an application to Halevi's interpretation.

    David Gordon cites R. Abraham Isaac haKohen Kook who commented on the Balfour Declaration in 1917: "Happily, the thick darkness is now pierced by the radiant glow of Divine Providence. Our task is to illuminate, elevate, and exalt these developments. Evidently, "the voice of my beloved knocketh" (*Song of Songs* 5:2) as the mighty, omniscient and merciful Architect of

the Khazar King following his contemporary interpretation of *Song of Songs*, R. Soloveitchik is rebuking modern Jewry for praying for Zion when they have the ability to actualize their prayers. The *Kuzari*, thus, seems to be the source for the entire section of *Kol Dodi Dofek*.[21]

R. Soloveitchik extends the introductory approach of *Kol Dodi Dofek*, which demonstrates the supremacy of concrete action over metaphysical speculation, from the personal-individual realm to the national-historical sphere. He applies his original distinction between the fate and destiny of the sufferer to Israel's covenants in Egypt and at Sinai, respectively. The fate-laden existence of Egypt leads to the incomprehensible loneliness and irrational alienation of the Jew, explanations of which are purely speculative and in vain. The covenantal relationship at Sinai, however, is achieved in the realm of destiny when man passionately yearns for the God of Israel, manifested in concrete actions.[22] Such an experiential covenantal encounter is elaborated upon in *The Lonely Man of Faith*.

As in *Kol Dodi Dofek*, R. Soloveitchik is influenced by Halevi's biblical illustration of the supremacy of the experiential over the cognitive dimension of religion in *The Lonely Man of Faith*. R. Soloveitchik begins his essay with a creative interpretation of Genesis 1–2 in which

---

history . . . illuminates the darkness." (*Iggerot HaRe'iyah*, vol. 3, Jerusalem: Mosad ha-Rav Kook, 1985, 138,155.)

Tsevi Yehudah Kook cites *Kuzari* II:24 in the context of his father's comments. (Tsevi Yaron, *The Philosophy of Rabbi Kook*, trans. A. Tomaschoff, (Jerusalem: Eliner Library, 1991), 359 n59) (D. Gordon, "A Note on the Title of Kol Dodi Dofek," *Tradition*, 39:3, 2006) Gordon also argues that Soloveitchik would endorse the translation of the title of *Kol Dodi Dofek* to mean *Listen! My Beloved Calls*, which reflects the imperative to heed the Divine call to return to Israel as depicted in the *Kuzari*. He surmises Soloveitchik would advocate for such a translation based on his endorsement of Ibn Ezra's interpretation of Gen 4:10 *kol demei ahikhatso'akim elai min ha-adama* (*Listen! The Blood of your brother is crying out to Me*) where Ibn Ezra mentions his consistent interpretation of *Song of Songs* 2:8 *kol dodi hinei zeh ba* [*Listen! My Beloved is coming*]. (Gordon, D. "A Note on the Title of Kol Dodi Dofek," *Tradition*, 39:3, 2006).

21. "Substitute America for "Babylon," eight years after the founding of the State of Israel for "after the destruction of the First Temple," and R. Soloveitchik for "Ezra, Nehemiah, and the Prophets," and you have an uncanny formulation of the Rav's argument expressed in this essay." (JJ Schacter, "Religious Zionism and the Meanings of Redemption," *Tradition* 39,3, 2006).

22. *Kol Dodi Dofek* ,92.

he distinguishes between the dual natures within the existentially
lonely, religious individual who experiences tension between worldly
engagement and traditional religious commitment. In a footnote,[23]
R. Soloveitchik merely references Halevi's awareness of the discrep-
ancies between the two accounts of the creation of man, which he
elaborates upon later in the essay, in his development of the cosmic
and covenantal dialectic. Halevi's influence is most pronounced in
chapter seven amidst R. Soloveitchik's discussion of Adam the second
and his covenantal faith community. R. Soloveitchik begins the section
by describing how, like Adam the first, the man of faith is inquisitive
about the cosmos, but quickly clarifies that the "covenant, not the
cosmos, provides him with an answer to his questions. The covenantal
confrontation is indispensable for the man of faith."[24]

R. Soloveitchik explains that the man of faith must encounter God
on a personal covenantal level, as opposed to in an impersonal cosmic
manner, in order to redeem himself from his existential loneliness.[25]
Abraham, referred to in Kierkegaardian terminology as "the knight
of faith," is described by R. Soloveitchik as the paradigm who sought
God in the star filled cosmos, but was only able to achieve redemption
when he encountered God in a personal experiential way. Referencing
Genesis Rabbah 59 and Rashi Gen. 24:7,[26] R. Soloveitchik supports
this distinction between the impersonal cosmic and the personal covenantal connection to the divine. "Our sages said that before Abraham
appeared *majestas dei* was reflected only by the distant heavens and it

---

23. "The Lonely Man of Faith," 10. In a footnote, Soloveitchik references to
    Kuzari IV and elaborates upon Halevi's interpretation of the discrepancy
    of the divine names used in Gen. 1–2 in chapter 7 of "The Lonely Man of
    Faith."
24. "The Lonely Man of Faith," 30. Though he does not reference Halevi, R.
    Soloveitchik implicitly reflects the influence of the *Kuzari,* as Halevi demon-
    strates the empirical certainty of God's mass revelation at Sinai experienced
    by all of Israel. (*Kuzari* I:87). In a later passage, Halevi interprets Psalms 19
    to demonstrate the significance of the cosmic encounter, yet the supremacy
    of the revelational experience. (*Kuzari* II:56).
25. While both Soloveitchik and Halevi emphasize the significance of the reve-
    latory experience for the religious individual, Halevi refers to the historical/
    traditional experience while Soloveitchik describes the personal/ emotional
    experience.
26. "The Lonely Man of Faith," 32.

was a mute nature which "spoke" of the glory of God.[27] It was Abra-

---

27. In *Worship of the Heart*, Soloveitchik begins his discussion of The Intellectual Medium of religious experience as one would expect by referencing Maimonides (MT Laws of Repentance 10:6). When he proceeds to The Emotional Medium, he turns to Halevi to elaborate upon how man can transcend the bounds of the finite through religious emotionality. Soloveitchik quotes the Rabbi's explanation to the Khazar King regarding the inadequacy of intellectual philosophical abstraction and the advocacy of direct emotional apprehension and communication:

"Experience of the human soul shows that it fears when it experiences frightening sensations, and not when one is simply told about something, that it loves a beautiful form that is present, which it does not love when told about it. Do not believe the clever person who says that his thought attaches itself in an orderly manner, so that he attains what is requisite to knowing God through his intellect alone without relying on sensation" (*Kuzari* 4:5).

Soloveitchik concludes his discussion of Halevi by acknowledging that even Maimonides recognized that an exclusively cognitive approach is insufficient and requires love to engage in communion with God. "According to the knowledge, so is the love" (MT Laws of Repentance 10:6).

Soloveitchik understands the distinction between Maimonides and Halevi "in terms of philosophical order rather than of essence" (*Worship of the Heart*, 8). Maimonides begins man's connection to God with the intellect followed by love while Halevi commences with the emotional response to encountering the Infinite which man then seeks to understand in rational terms.

Soloveitchik brings up Halevi's distinction between the God of Aristotle and the God of Abraham later in *Worship of the Heart*.

There is a contrast between indirect, inferential and abstract discovery of God and the immediate living encounter with Him. In the cognitive and the ethical act one approaches God by the process of deduction. There is no direct apprehension of the Creator. One arrives at the conclusion of governing cosmic intelligence by studying the universal drama and by reaching the fringes of the coherent causal nexus . . . The absolute of the logos and the ethos is more idea than fact, more mathematical boundary than reality, more postulate than living personal God, more abstraction than apprehension. If we speak of experiencing God, and if by this we understand the ecstatic encounter of a man quivering with passion and tenseness, then one cannot consider the ethical or noetical act as capable of engendering such an experience. For the ethical and the cognitive, the rendezvous with the Creator is a quiet sedate one. There is, in fact, no actual meeting. A real encounter is never achieved by the scientist or the ethicist. For them, there is only, if we may use a metaphor of Yehudah Halevi (*Kuzari* I:109), an exchange of epistles; the contact is established in an impersonal way,

ham who "crowned" Him the God of earth, i.e., the God of men."[28]

In a note on chapter seven of *The Lonely Man of Faith*,[29] R. Solove-itchik explicitly utilizes the *Kuzari* to make an important clarification within his dialectic. He explains his intentional use of the term "cosmic" and not "cosmological" in his description of Adam the first's relationship with the divine. R. Soloveitchik distinguishes between the experiential cosmic confrontation, which he understands as man's direct apprehension of God in nature,[30] as opposed to man's purely intellectual cosmological encounter with God which he conceives of

---

through correspondence. (Soloveitchik, JB. *Worship of the Heart*, Ed. S. Carmy, Ktav, 2003, 58–9).

Soloveitchik extracts Halevi's aforementioned metaphor from his parable about a king in India which Halevi uses to illustrate to the Khazar King that only with direct proof, in contrast to hearsay, can one be convinced of the truth.

28. "The Lonely Man of Faith," 32. In *Genesis Rabbah* 59 and Rashi Gen. 24:7, cited by R. Soloveitchik, Abraham refers to God as the 'God of the heavens' who took him from his father's house and only later as the 'God of heavens and earth', once humans personally experienced and accepted Him as God. In *Kuzari* IV:17, Halevi similarly describes Abraham's progression, "Abraham had to scoff at his earlier pursuits in logic. Our Sages discussed this in their explanation of the verse, 'God took him outside (Gen 15:5): 'God said to him, "Leave your astrology!" (BT Shabbat 156a). In other words, God commanded Abraham to leave behind all logical wisdom based on astrology and the like, and instead devote himself to serving the God Whom Abraham had tasted. This is the meaning of 'Taste and see that God is good' (Ps. 34:9)."

29. "The Lonely Man of Faith," 32.

30. R. Soloveitchik's experiential cosmic encounter seems similar to the cosmic religious experience described by Albert Einstein. "[The scientist's] religious feeling takes the form of a rapturous amazement at the harmony of natural law, which reveals an intelligence of such superiority that, compared with it, all the systematic thinking and acting of human beings is an utterly insignificant reflection. This feeling is the guiding principle of his life and work, insofar as he succeeds in keeping himself from the shackles of selfish desire. It is beyond question closely akin to that which has possessed the religious geniuses of all ages." (Albert Einstein, *The World as I See It*, NY: Covici, Friede, 1934, 268).

"The Jewish tradition . . . contains . . . something which finds splendid expression in many of the Psalms, namely a sort of intoxicated joy and amazement at the beauty and grandeur of this world, of which man can just form just a faint notion. This joy is the feeling from which true scientific research draws its spiritual sustenance." (Einstein, A. *The World as I See It*), 145.

as an abstract comprehension of God through nature. Even though he recognizes that the cosmic experience is inadequate to ameliorate existential loneliness, it still has a place within the patriarchial tradition and is recognized by Halakha.[31] R. Soloveitchik does not want the reader to misunderstand such an experience and equate it with the Aristotelian philosophical tradition that he refers to as "Halevi's God of Aristotle" (which is contrasted to the "God of Abraham" in the *Kuzari*).[32] R. Soloveitchik follows Halevi's criticism of the Philosopher's overintellectualized quest for God through philosophical proofs which, unlike prophetic revelation, are subject to doubts and incapable of being proven.[33] Furthermore, Halevi renounces such abstract arguments since they do not lead to experiencing God, but rather to heresy, whereas the God encountered through witness and taste commands real love and obedience.[34] Reflecting a modernized

---

31. Adam I was commanded by God (Gen. 1:28) to use his creative capacity with which he was created in the Image of God to make sense of how the cosmos function in order to dominate the world around him.

32. Halevi demonstrates the superiority of the God of Abraham through the King's realization of the truth of the Rabbi's teachings in *Kuzari* IV:16 as opposed to his rejection of the philosopher's articulation of his impersonal conceptions of God in I:1.

33. "Religion arrived at through logic and analysis is subject to much ambiguity . . . Philosophers base their religion on logical arguments, some of which are based on absolute facts, others seem reasonable and others that are not even intellectually satisfying, let alone based on fact." (*Kuzari* I:13) The Rabbi later explains his reply to the King that he believes in the 'God who has led his ancestors out of Egypt' and not the 'God who created the world', since such creation is beyond the realm of demonstrable proof. (*Kuzari* I:25) Halevi writes, "This belief of the philosophers was disproved by the great event at Sinai." (*Kuzari* I:87) Halevi considers the challenge posed by the Philosophers to Judaism as that between reason and revelation and, therefore, demonstrates the empirical truth of God's mass revelation at Sinai and explains how reason need not conflict with, but rather can bolster and explicate, the contents of revelation. Halevi viewed any contradiction between reason and revelation as the result of the philosophers' acceptance of conclusions that were not proven by reason. Halevi insists upon approaching God rationally, "God forbid me from [accepting] . . . anything the intellect denies and posits as impossible." (*Kuzari* I:89). (Kreisel, H. "Judah Halevi's Kuzari: Between the God of Abraham and the God of Aristotle", in *Joodse Filosofie tussen Rede en Traditie*, ed. R. Munk and E. J. Hoogewoud, Kampen, 1993, 25).

34. Halevi argues that while man can reach the Prime Mover through his intellect, he can never reach the living God that "souls yearn for" *(Kuzari*

version of Halevi's medieval criticism, R. Soloveitchik argues that
philosophers' attempts to rationally demonstrate God's existence
in abstract, logical arguments, such as the 'cosmological' proof are
deficient since they are devoid of any experiential component. Thus, he
refers to Hume and Kant's objection to such theoretical philosophical
proofs, relegating them only appropriate in the scientific realm. In
U-Vikkashtem mi-Sham,[35] R. Soloveitchik even explicitly references
Halevi in this regard:

> Rational cosmic religiosity devolves into pantheism . . . but a
> single step away from atheism. In a word, if religiosity derives
> its substance only from the intellect and cultural conscious-
> ness, it leads to denial of God. This truth was known to R
> Judah Halevi when he said that the God of Aristotle was to be
> found in the abstraction and generalization, and apprehended
> via syllogism. (*Kuzari* IV:15) " . . . He who relies only on the
> cosmological approach will end up ruined and faithless.[36]

Rather, R. Soloveitchik conceives of such proofs experientially.[37] In
U-Vikkashtem mi-Sham, he writes,

> But instead of abolishing all of these proofs, it accepted them
> anew as immediate experiences that are not based on logical
> inferences, but rather are manifested in sudden revelations
> and insights. These experiences have nothing in common with
> indirect inference or logical deduction. Just as consciousness
> of the world in general, and of the self in particular, do not

---

IV:16). Reliance on philosophical proof can lead the individual, at most, to
an intellectual recognition of an entirely abstract notion of "God."

"[Philosophical] Demonstration can lead astray. Demonstration was the
mother of heresy and destructive ideas . . . Those who go to the utmost length
are the philosophers, and the ways of their arguments led them to teach of
a Supreme Being which neither benefits nor injures, and knows nothing of
our prayers, offerings, obedience or disobedience, and that the world is as
eternal as He Himself." (*Kuzari*, IV:3) (Lobel, 177–8).

35. Originally drafted in the 1940's as a companion to *Halakhic Man*, and first
published in the rabbinic journal *Hadarom* in 1978. JB Soloveitchik, *And
From There You Shall Seek*, Trans. N. Goldblum, (NJ: Ktav, 2008).
36. *U-vikkashtem Mi-sham*, 24.
37. Reuven Ziegler, *Majesty and Humility*, (NY: Urim, 2012), 137.

involve logical demonstrations but constitute the spiritual essence of man, so too with the experience of the divine.[38]

Man does not rationally deduce, but rather experiences the divine ontologically. R. Soloveitchik quotes Ps. 34:9, "Taste and see how good is the Lord; happy is the man who takes refuge in Him,"[39] and uses it in the same manner as Halevi applied to Abraham in *Kuzari* IV:17 upon his personal covenantal experience,[40] for once man directly apprehends God, there is no need for abstract proof. In *The Lonely Man of Faith*, as well as in *U-vikkashtem Mi-sham*,[41] R. Soloveitchik quotes Kierkegaard's sarcastic remark when he was told that Anselm of Canterbury, who had developed the abstract ontological proof, prayed for rational evidence of the existence of God, thereby demonstrating commitment based on experience and emotion, and not cognition:

> Does the loving bride in the embrace of her beloved ask for proof that he is alive and real? Must the prayerful soul clinging in passionate love and ecstasy to her Beloved demonstrate that He exists?[42]

R. Soloveitchik concludes his discussion within the note by referencing Maimonides' term *Leida* [לידע שיש שם מצוי ראשון][43] for support, which he interprets as transcending abstract logos and including experience. R. Soloveitchik similarly interprets the Maimonidean reference in the fourth footnote of *U-vikkashtem Mi-sham*, explaining that such

---

38. *U-vikkashtem Mi-sham*, 12.
39. *U-vikkashtem Mi-sham*, 13.
40. See note 28.
41. In *U-vikkashtem Mi-sham*, 16, Soloveitchik makes a similar point that the consciousness of the transcendent being cannot be logically deduced. He quotes Kierkegaard's ridicule of Anselm's supplication to God: "You fool, does a baby in his father's arms need proof or signs that the father exists? Does a person who feels the need to pray to God require a philosophical demonstration?" (1853 Journal Entry, "Curious, Self-Contradiction").
42. "The Lonely Man of Faith," 32.
43. Maimonides, *Mishneh Torah*, Laws of Foundation of Torah 1:1. In the first paragraph of the *Mishneh Torah*, Maimonides establishes the experience of God as a firm reality and only later in the fifth paragraph does he mention the Aristotelian cognitive cosmological proof of the unmoved mover.

knowledge is "not based on logical inference, but is, rather immediate:
the knowledge of reality as divine reality." R. Soloveitchik clarifies
that even though Maimonides presents indirect philosophical proofs
of God's existence which he believed comprise all that man can know
about God, the "essence of his view is nevertheless that this knowledge
is based on the immediate ontological cognition that there is no reality
but God."[44] While Maimonides and Halevi are often juxtaposed at
opposite ends of the philosophical spectrum, R. Soloveitchik narrows
the gap between their respective approaches, thereby reflecting the
conflation prevalent in an earlier period.[45] As Adam Shear demon-

---

44. *U-vikkashtem Mi-sham*, p158–9.
45. R. Soloveitchik's interpretation of "leida" in "The Lonely Man of Faith"
and *U-vikkashtem Mi-sham*, are consistent with Prof. Simon Rawidowicz's
suggestion that Maimonides' "madda" should be understood as belief, not
knowledge.

This suggested interpretation of "madda" and its connection with "de'ah"
may help tighten in some respect the bonds connecting Maimonides with
his predecessors in the field of Jewish philosophy, to whom this "pair" of
"notions" and "beliefs" was both philosophically and theologically a kind
of inseparable combination of fundamental ideas. Yehuda Halevi (*Kuzari*
II:81), e.g. used here the same terminology: *ara* and *I'tiqadat* – which is so
often to be found in Maimonides' Arabic written works (*Guide* Intro; III,
II, 36, Commentary on last *Mishnah* of *Berakoth*). It should not be inferred
from here that Maimonides never used "madda" in the general and more
intellectualistic way, (i.e. for pure knowledge), but whenever problems of
theology are concerned, especially when man's "madda" is related to God – it
seems never to mean intellectual cognition. Here "madda" is always nearer –
to say the least – to belief than to rationalistically colored knowledge. It can
certainly be stated that in this respect in the Sefer ha-Madda, Maimonides
never uses "madda" for "knowledge." And Maimonides did not even deviate
from the traditional path while he made use of "yada" as far as the first
commandment – namely to believe in the existence of God – is concerned.
(On Maimonides' "Sefer Ha-Madda" in *Essays in honour of the Very Rev.
Dr J.H.Hertz*, Ed. Epstein, Levine, Roth., London: E. Goldson, 1944, 337–8).

It is noteworthy, however, that in two letters to Prof. Rawidowicz in
1954, Soloveitchik suggests a more rationalistic reading of Maimonides than
he does in "The Lonely Man of Faith" or *U-vikkashtem Mi-sham*, which
demands for the individual to understand divine revelation according to
his capacity. "We are well aware that Maimonides maintains that the commandment to affirm God's existence and unity contains both an obligation
of complete faith as well as maximal intellectual effort which translates this
faith into rational concepts. Indeed, this is how he began [the Code]: "It is
a positive commandment to know that there is a first being, etc." ... Our

strates, up until the late nineteenth century, a tendency prevailed which treated Halevi's and Maimonides' philosophical works as belonging to the same discourse and presenting compatible messages. "Indeed, most Jewish intellectuals saw the *Kuzari* and the *Guide* as belonging to more or less the same genre and as sharing the common purpose of proving the revealed truths of Judaism in the face of the rationalist doctrine of philosophy."[46] However, the late modern period, reflecting the various ideological rifts within modern Jewry, tended towards a more polarized view of Halevi and Maimonindes. R. Soloveitchik renewed the conflation between their views as he assimilated each of their approaches into his unified philosophy.

After clarifying the difference between the cosmic and cosmological, R. Soloveitchik returns to his discussion in *Lonely Man* and reiterates the value (though ultimately insufficient) of majestic man's cosmic encounter with God, since he is only capable of understanding transcendence in cosmic terms.[47] Here, again, R. Soloveitchik reflects Halevi's exegetical influence, as he grounds his dialectic in a profound interpretation of the two biblical names of God.[48] He suggests that the Bible uses the divine name *Elohim*, connoting God as the creator of

---

master never tired of repeating this fundamental idea." Commensurate with the level of knowledge of God is the corresponding level of God's favor and thus, His closeness to man. Soloveitchik expresses his preference for Halevi's experiential conception over Maimonides rationalistic approach as quoted in the Introduction to this paper (*Community, Covenant and Commitment*, 284–6). Since in this conflicting text, R. Soloveitchik attributes both the experiential and cognitive dimensions to Maimonides' conception, perhaps he is highlighting the affective realm in his existentialist works in which he advocates for experience over theory.

46. Adam Shear, *The Kuzari and the Shaping of Jewish Identity, 1167–1900*, (NY: Cambridge University Press, 2008), 120.

47. "Majestic man, even when he belongs to the group of *homines religiosi* and feels a distinct need for transcendental experiences, is gratified by his encounter with God within the framework of the cosmic drama. Since majestic man is incapable of breaking out of the cosmic cycle, he cannot interpret his transcendental adventure in anything but cosmic categories." ("The Lonely Man of Faith,"), 33.

48. In *Guide of the Perplexed* I:61, Maimonides also distinguishes between the Tetragrammaton and other divine names in a manner similar to that of Halevi, thus further reflecting the conflation of their philosophic views.

the cosmos, in the description of Adam I's encounter with the Deity
in the first account of the creation of man in chapter one of Genesis:[49]

> Therefore, the divine name of *Elohim*, which denotes God
> being the source of the cosmic dynamics, sufficed to charac-
> terize the relationship prevailing between majestic man and
> his Creator addressing Himself to him through the cosmic
> occurrence.[50]

Adam II sought a closer relationship with His Creator, signified by the
Tetragrammaton in the narrative of the creation of man in the second
chapter of Genesis.[51]

> However, covenantal man of faith, craving for a personal and
> intimate relation with God, could not find it in the cosmic *Elo-
> him* encounter and had to shift his transcendental experience
> to a different level at which the finite "I" meets the infinite
> He "face-to-face." This strange communal relation between
> man and God is symbolized by the Tetragrammaton, which
> therefore appears in the Biblical account of Adam the second.[52]

R. Soloveitchik notes here that this distinction between the two divine names was developed by Halevi in *Kuzari* IV, in which Halevi

---

49. **בראשית פרק א**

(כז) וַיִּבְרָא **אֱלֹהִים** אֶת הָאָדָם בְּצַלְמוֹ בְּצֶלֶם אֱלֹהִים בָּרָא אֹתוֹ זָכָר וּנְקֵבָה בָּרָא אֹתָם:

50. "The Lonely Man of Faith," 33.

51. **בראשית פרק ב**

(ז) וַיִּיצֶר **יְקֹוָק** אֱלֹהִים אֶת הָאָדָם עָפָר מִן הָאֲדָמָה וַיִּפַּח בְּאַפָּיו נִשְׁמַת חַיִּים וַיְהִי הָאָדָם לְנֶפֶשׁ חַיָּה:

52. "The Lonely Man of Faith," 33. A similar reference by Soloveitchik to
the distinction between the universal *Elohim* and the personal, purposive
Tetragrammaton:

Halevi and Nahmanides of old emphasized time and again the unique
character of the Jewish historical occurrence by placing it directly under
divine protection and vigilance. The historico-coincidental forces are superseded by transcendental-purposive motives. While the universal historical
process is completely dominated by the *Elohim* aspect – uniformity and
regularity, similar to the monotony in the cosmic drama, are characteristics
of the historical occurrence – the charismatic historical emergence is guided
by the Tetragrammaton idea . . . Covenant history connotes the involvement
of God in the historical occurrence (*Emergence of Ethical Man*, Ch 8), 159.

distinguishes between the common noun, *Elohim*, God's generic name descriptive of God's manifestations in this world, and the proper noun, the Tetragrammaton, God's personal name.[53] In IV:15, Halevi argues that the meaning of *Elohim* can be understood through reason, whereas the Tetragrammaton can only be understood by prophetic experience.[54] In *U-Vikkashtem mi-Sham*, R. Soloveitchik further supports his argument by quoting *Kuzari* IV:11[15] (as merely referenced in *Lonely Man*). After quoting the *Kuzari*, R. Soloveitchik summarizes, "In Halevi's opinion the divine name *Elohim* denotes the cosmic

---

53. *Kuzari* IV:1
54. Halevi explains: "The idea conveyed by *Elohim* is something grasped by logic; the intellect dictates that the universe has a ruler and organizer . . . The insight of the Tetragrammaton, however, is not something perceivable by logic, but by prophetic vision . . . When a person reaches this level, all prior doubts that he may have had about God fall away. He scoffs at the logical arguments that he used in the past to apprehend God's mastery and unity. He becomes a servant who craves the One he serves." *(Kuzari* IV:15)

In the following section, *Kuzari* 4:16, the Khazar King summarizes the Rabbi's teaching:

"The difference between *Elohim* and the Tetragrammaton is now clear to me, and I understand the difference between the God of Abraham and the God of Aristotle. I see that the Tetragrammaton is the Entity Whom souls desire to taste and witness, and that *Elohim* can be arrived at through logic. And this tasting brings one who experiences it to be consumed in love for him even unto death, whereas that reasoning only demonstrates that giving him priority is (logically) necessary, so long as it causes no pain or hardship."

D. Lobel argues that Halevi's use of the term *ta'am* [taste] reflects sufi mystical language, in which God is known in a "quasi-sensory way, all human facets, intellect, imagination, emotions, body, participate in seeking a relationship with God." ("'Taste and See that the Lord is Good': Ha-Levi's God Re-Visited", in *Be'erot Yitzhak:Studies in Memory of Isadore Twersky*, ed. J. Harris (Cambridge, Mass., 2005), 161–78).

This *Kuzari* excerpt is quoted by Soloveitchik in *Out of the Whirlwind*, 121–2, in a discussion about revelational experience. Soloveitchik describes the shock felt by finite man when confronted with infinity, as he becomes aware of the ontic void. Man is then able to rise above himself in the apocalyptic experience, surpassing the cosmic level. Soloveitchik here describes the paradoxical nature of the revelational experience, entailing shock and mental anguish, as well as a feeling of grace. In similar terms to "The Lonely Man of Faith," he distinguishes between cosmic man's intellectual encounter with God and covenantal man's experiential reality. He supports his conclusion by quoting Halevi's distinct definitions of *Elohim* and the Tetragrammaton (Kuzari IV:16) as referenced by Soloveitchik in "The Lonely Man of Faith."

revelation of God, whereas the Tetragrammaton denotes the prophetic revelation. The divine revelation assumes a sensory wrapping . . . While the intellect abstracts, the prophet's eye beholds a vision of God, and he feels Him with all his senses."[55] In *U-Vikkashtem mi-Sham*, R. Soloveitchik attributes the association of *Elohim* with the cosmic experience to Halevi, consistent with his own interpretation that he later distinguishes in *Lonely Man* from Halevi's cosmological encounter that was associated with the God of Aristotle. R. Soloveitchik adopts Halevi's association of the Tetragrammaton, apprehended through prophecy, with the covenantal experience, or that which Halevi refers to as the God of Abraham. However, R. Soloveitchik does not adopt Halevi's model fully; he is creative with the fundamental building blocks that Halevi provides and associates *Elohim*, experienced in nature, with the cosmic encounter, which differs from Halevi's association of the divine name with the God of Aristotle, conceived of through reason. Halevi contrasts Abraham with Aristotle, noting how Abraham was able to withstand his trials because he apprehended God through experience and not through logic, thereby, recognizing that nothing is hidden from God Who rewards man for his righteousness and guides him along the proper path.[56] R. Soloveitchik and Halevi both emphasize the supremacy of the personal experience with God through Abraham's progression.[57]

Alluding to an earlier discussion of divine names in the *Kuzari*, in *U-Vikkashtem mi-Sham,* R. Soloveitchik adds that God's personal name, the Tetragrammaton, was not only used in the creation of covenantal man in Genesis 2, as described in *Lonely Man*, but also in God's revelation on Sinai (*Kuzari* II:4), which Halevi argues was experienced by Jews with all of their senses:

> One who does not encounter God cannot be liberated from the gloomy, mute[58] world that has not been illuminated with

55. *U-Vikkashtem mi-Sham*, 171.
56. J. Rembaum, "Kuzari: A Study in Theological Exegesis." *Threescore and Ten*, (NJ: Ktav, 1991), 154–55.
57. Though R. Soloveitchik refers to Abraham's journey from the cosmic to the covenantal, as opposed to from the cosmological to the covenantal.
58. In *Redemption, Prayer, and Talmud Torah*, R. Soloveitchik similarly describes the transition from a mute existence to a redemptive existence. "Redemption, we have stated, is identical with communing, or with the revelation of the

the light of spiritual uniqueness. Personal reality is the reality of revelation. R Judah Halevi, the poet-philosopher, discovered this fundamental principle. (Kuzari, IV) . . . As R. Judah Halevi expressed it, the Creator reveals Himself with the name *Elohim* as the possessor of powers relating to the natural world (*Kuzari* IV:1), a world which is nothing but [an impersonal] system of mechanical forces, and to closed-off natural man, who constitutes an infinitesimal fraction of this world. The Creator reveals Himself to spiritual man with His special name, the Tetragrammaton, as the "I" at Mount Sinai. When the infinite "I" connects with man, man is redeemed from a closed-off natural existence and is raised to a unique personal level of existence.[59]

---

word, i.e. the emergence of speech. When a people leaves a mute world and enters a world of sound, speech and song, it becomes a redeemed people~ a free people." R. Soloveitchik explains that man was commanded to redeem himself through calling out to God in prayer in order to achieve full being, thus renewing the revelational confrontation between man and God. Prayer merges with another redemptive experience, *Talmud Torah*, the perpetuation of the Sinai experience, as man finds himself and realizes redemption (Soloveitchik, *"Redemption, Prayer, and Talmud Torah," Tradition* 17(2), 1978).

R. Soloveitchik describes the prayerful experience elsewhere, in "The Community," further reflecting Halevi's influence. In an explanation of the plural form of prayer, R. Soloveitchik refers to man's existential awareness of others on whose behalf he must pray. He quotes Halevi: "The people of Israel among the nations is like the heart in the body . . . the heart . . . is sensitive to the slightest trauma" (*Kuzari* II:36–41). Thus, the community-oriented experience is an extension of the experiential emphasis found in both Soloveitchik and Halevi (Soloveitchik, "The Community," *Tradition* 17(2), 1978).

That same reference to the *Kuzari* is also quoted by Soloveitchik in *Days of Deliverance* amidst a discussion about the universal historical role of the individual as a representative of the masses. In *Kuzari* II:36, the Rabbi compares "the people of Israel among the nations is like the heart amidst the organs. It is the most sick and the most healthy of them all," since its sensibility and feeling expose it to all sorts of diseases, such as sadness, love, hate and fear. Soloveitchik explains that God intended for the Jews to feel the pain and share in the suffering of humanity. (JB Soloveitchik, *Days of Deliverance*, NJ: Ktav, 2007, 75–76).

59. *U-vikkashtem Mi-sham*, 135–6, In a lengthy discussion of divine names in n.15, Soloveitchik quotes *Kuzari* II:2 in which the Tetragrammaton is described as depicting God's essence, whereas all other names of God reflect

This reference to the Tetragrammaton at Sinai from *Kuzari* II precedes and serves as a springboard for Halevi's discussion of God's land, where the Jewish people can realize their intimate connection with their personal God and achieve prophecy, as connoted in Halevi's interpretation of *Song of Songs*.[60]

This preliminary appraisal of some of R. Soloveitchik's works suggests that R. Yehuda Halevi had a far more profound impact upon R. Soloveitchik's philosophy than has previously been demonstrated. Both concentrate on experience and action over pure theory, illustrated through Scriptural readings. R. Soloveitchik's use of biblical hermeneutics, such as his interpretation of *Song of Songs* and the Genesis narrative, clearly reflect Halevi's thought. An initial analysis of the explicit, as well as implicit, influence of his medieval predecessor elucidates important themes and nuances within R. Soloveitchik's philosophy that have yet to be fully explored.

His acts (*U-vikkashtem Mi-sham*), 185.

60. M. Berger, Toward a New Understanding of Judah Halevi's Kuzari. *The Journal of Religion*, 72(2), 1992, 210–28.

The Identity of Love and Cognition in the Thought of R. Joseph Soloveitchik

"Halakhic man is not a man of words . . . every jot and tittle
of Rashi's commentary in the Talmud and Rambam's*Mishneh
Torah* allude to heaps and heaps of *halachoth* . . . Each and
every sentence in the writings of R. Chaim constitutes a flow-
ing spring of creative insight and cognition."
— R. Joseph Soloveitchik, *Halakhic Man*, 86–7.

"There is an identity of love and cognition."
— R. Joseph Soloveitchik, footnote in *U'bikashtem
mi-Sham*, 156.

In the Western philosophical tradition, there is a standard view of
the relationship between emotion and reason that runs roughly as
follows. Emotions are biased, subjective, and irrational attitudes that
people express, while reason is cold, objective, dispassionate, and able
to ascertain the truth. Emotions are:

"nonreasoning movements," unthinking energies that simply
push the person around and do not relate to conscious perceptions. Like gusts of wind or the currents of the sea, they move,
and move the person, but obtusely, without vision of an object
or beliefs about it . . . This view is connected with the idea that
emotions derive from the "animal" part of our nature . . .[1]

---

1. Martha Nussbaum, "Emotions as Judgments of Value and Importance,"
    in *Thinking about Feeling: Contemporary Philosophers on Emotions*, ed.

Rabbi Joseph B. Solovetichik, however, rejected the false dichotomy between reason and emotion. For R. Soloveitchik, emotions are not just subjective outpourings of the heart. They can, and do, reveal an objective world to us. In *The Halakhic Mind*, R. Soloveitchik states that emotions are cognitive - they should be seen as making claims about the way the world is.[2] And in *U'bikashtem Mi-Sham*, R. Soloveitchik goes even further and asserts that there is an identity between love and cognition.[3]

This essay is an attempt to understand the meaning of this identity. In particular, I argue that R. Soloveitchik's claim of an identity between love and cognition must be understood in light of his broader epistemological doctrines with respect to the relationship between subjectivity and objectivity, most prominently spelled out in *The Halakhic Mind*. This claim has substantial implications for how we are to conceive of that primary activity of halakhic man – the construction and cognition of the theoretical law (*lomdus*), and of the centrality of emotion and subjectivity to such activity. But before we can elaborate on the distinctive nature of R. Soloveitchik's identity thesis, it is essential to begin with a summary of Maimonides' views, for it is clear that R. Soloveitchik is heavily indebted to Maimonides' formulations on the relationship between love and knowledge. Only after placing R. Soloveitchik's views in such historical context will we be able to better appreciate the distinctively modern nature of R. Soloveitchik's far-reaching claim of an identity between love and cognition, an identity that plays such a crucial role in R. Soloveitchik's overall epistemology.

*

In a footnote found in *U'bikashtem mi-Sham*, R. Soloveitchik asserts his identity thesis between love and cognition, which is immediately preceded by this background:[4]

Robert C. Solomon (Oxford: Oxford University Press, 2004), 186.

2. Joseph B. Soloveitchik, *The Halakhic Mind* (London: Seth Press, 1986), 42–43.

3. Joseph B. Soloveitchik, *And From There You Shall Seek (U'bikashtem mi-Sham)*, trans. Naomi Goldblum (Jersey City: TorasHoRav Foundation, 2008), 156.

4. On the importance of the footnotes in *U'bikashtem mi-Sham* see the Introduction by David Shatz and Reven Ziegler, xxxiv.

What Maimonides wanted to do was establish an enduring conjunction of the psyche with the intellect. Reason conjoins with emotion and is enriched by it. Reason supports emotion but is also nourished by it; there is reciprocity here. On the one hand, when the affects blend with the intellect, their nature changes, and they become less passive. In place of involuntary impressions, free activity blooms. When cognition absorbs emotion, it converts it and subsumes it under free action and creation. Cognition bestows some of its glory onto emotion – the glory of free action and the desire for accomplishment. On the other hand, cognition too is elevated through its melding with emotionality.[5]

In the passage above, R. Soloveitchik points out that there is a reciprocal relationship between reason and emotion, and introduces us to the Kantian theme of acting freely - that is - acting in accordance with reason. R. Soloveitchik continues:

The unity of the knower and the known ... occurs only in a cognition imbued with love and desire ... Maimonides set forth love as the goal of divine worship. **There is an identity of love and cognition** [emphasis added] ...[6]

R. Soloveitchik's claim of identity is cryptic, as it is not clear how love and cognition are to form an identity. We might understand how love can *accompany*, *motivate*, or *arise out of*, an act of cognition, but that does not establish a relation of identity.

In order to help unlock the meaning of this identity, it will be helpful to separate out what seem to be three distinctive approaches to such an identity, each of which is signaled by R. Soloveitchik in the surrounding passages that help to clarify the meaning of the identity. Below I elaborate on these three approaches: a) borrowing from Maimonides, R. Soloveitchik asserts a 'strong' identity, whereby love is *collapsed* into knowledge; b) R. Soloveitchik does not completely reduce emotion into knowledge, for he also recognizes that there is a sense in which emotions run *alongside* cognition, and are not reduc-

---

5.   *U'bikashtem mi-Sham*, 156.
6.   *U'bikashtem mi-Sham*, 156.

ible to it; and c) finally, the central piece of R. Soloveitchik's thesis is that subjectivity forms the essential core of the act of cognition, a prominent theme developed by R. Soloveitchik in *The Halakhic Mind*. I elaborate on this three-fold schema below.

I.   'STRONG' IDENTITY – LOVE AND
      KNOWLEDGE IN MAIMONIDES' *GUIDE*

Throughout the passage in which R. Soloveitchik asserts his identity thesis, he continually refers to Maimonides. As we have seen, R. Soloveitchik refers to the Maimonidean doctrine of the unity of the knower and the known (to which we shall return), and further, R. Soloveitchik writes that, "There is an identity of love and cognition: "One only loves God with the knowledge with which one knows Him . . .(Laws of Repentance 10:6)."[7] It is clear, then, that R. Soloveitchik means to closely connect his understanding of the relationship between love and cognition with that of Maimonides.

In Part III, Ch. 51 of his *Guide*, Maimonides writes:

> [I]t says, *To love the Lord your God, and to serve Him with all your heart and with all your soul* [Deut. xi. 13]. Now we have made it clear several times that love is proportionate to apprehension. After *love* comes this worship to which attention has also been drawn by [the Sages] . . . who said: *This is the worship of the heart*. **In my opinion it consists in setting thought to work on the first intelligible and in devoting oneself exclusively to this as far as this is within one's capacity.** . . . Thus it is clear that after apprehension, total devotion to Him and the employment of intellectual thought in constantly loving Him should be aimed at. Mostly this is achieved in solitude and isolation. [bolded emphasis added.][8]

It would seem that for Maimonides, there are three interrelated terms: love, worship of the heart, and knowledge. Worship of the heart subsumes both love and knowledge into a unified whole. But we

---

7.   *U'bikashtem mi-Sham*, 156.
8.   Maimonides, *The Guide for the Perplexed*, trans. Shlomo Pines, Vol. II (Univ. of Chicago Press, 1963), Part III, ch. 51.

should not be mistaken in thinking that once love is taken up into worship of the heart (as opposed to the initial stage when he writes "after love comes this worship . . .") that this love retains its usual affective quality. That is not what Maimonides has in mind, for he immediately explains what he means by this worship of the heart: that "it consists in setting thought to work on the first intelligible and in devoting oneself exclusively to this as far as this is within one's capacity." In other words, to engage in *worship of the heart just is to be continuously engaged in thinking of Him*. Maimonides writes in the same chapter:

> There are those who set their thought to work after having attained perfection in the divine science, turn wholly toward God . . . renounce what is other than He, and direct all the acts of their intellect toward an examination of the beings with a view towards drawing from them proof with regard to Him . . . This is the rank of the prophets.

As he continues in the paragraph, it is clear that this worship consists exclusively in thinking of Him. This is another way of saying that love of God, or more precisely, worship of the heart, is made identical to what Maimonides later on refers to as continuous "knowledge in actuality,"[9] the ever-present awareness in thought of God. This is certainly a very robust or 'strong' conception of the relationship between love and cognition. In this account, the identity should be taken very seriously, for to love God (the love subsumed in worship) *just is* to be constantly thinking of Him in the right ways.

That R. Soloveitchik also has in mind something like this 'strong,' or reductive, conception of the relationship between the two terms is clear from R. Soloveitchik's introduction of the unity of the knower and the known in his explication of the identity. As Aviezer Ravitzky has shown, this unity of the knower and the known is a highly-intellectualist approach to the unity of God and human beings, a unity

---

9. Part III, Ch. 51, Friedlander translation: "it is in this case less intense, because when a person perfect in his knowledge [of God] is busy with worldly matters, he has not knowledge in actuality, but only knowledge in potentiality [though ready to become actual]. This person is then like a trained scribe when he is not writing."

predicated exclusively along the cognition of the same forms by both God and humans.[10] Thus, this doctrine of the unity of the knower and the known essentially reduces or collapses what might apparently be a highly-charged emotional relationship between humans and the divine into a relationship based on cognition.

Yet this understanding of the relationship between love and cognition is not all that is found in Maimonides' *Guide*, for we can isolate at least two other aspects to the relationship between love and knowledge as described by Maimonides.[11] To be sure, the primary mode that the relationship between worship-love and knowledge takes here in the *Guide* is one of identity. Nevertheless, Maimonides also notes that the continual intellectual contemplation of God will result in one's "rejoicing" in the knowledge of God.[12] This "rejoicing" is surely also part of what it means to love God and cannot be reduced to knowing Him,

---

10. See *U'bikashtem mi-Sham* 94–96 for R. Soloveitchik's discussion and Aviezer Ravitzky, "Rabbi J. B. Soloveitchik on Human Knowledge: Between Maimonidean and Neo-Kantian Philosophy," *Modern Judaism* (6:2, May 1986) 157–188, particularly 161–168. In his summary of this doctrine as found in Maimonides, Ravitzky writes that this unity of knower and known is accomplished by the mind's thinking of the form of an object. Since what is essential to an object is its form (in Aristotelian philosophy), it turns out that if one has in mind the form of an object, one's mind becomes identical with the essence of that object, i.e., its form. And moreover, God is also thinking of this form (since God contains all knowledge in His mind), and since God is also thinking of the form of an object, it follows that God's mind, as it were, also becomes identical with the form of that object being thought. And by deduction, it follows that one's mind and God's mind become unified through their each thinking of the same forms, i.e. of the forms of the objects in the world. As Ravitzky writes: "And now to the final step: the Creator knows His world and this implies a unity of subject and object. Man knows God's world, and this implies a unity of subject and object. It follows that Creator and creature are united via their common object of knowledge – the cosmos." (162). Note how radically, in this account, the unity of God and man assumes a purely intellectualist form. This unity, which many mystics imagine in highly-charged emotional terms, is here reduced to an intellectual union of God and human beings exclusively through their apprehension of the same forms.
11. Worship of God *through acts* also plays an important role in Maimonides' account. The acts can either be preparatory, or they can be post-knowledge, that is, natural by-products of knowledge of God, as Maimonides describes them in the final chapters of the Guide.
12. Maimonides, *Guide*, Part III, ch. 51.

as it results *from* knowing Him. It is the joy that accompanies one's knowledge of God. Second, as humans are, by their nature, incapable of maintaining a permanent intellectual connection to God by always thinking of Him, such a limitation necessitates that even if we cannot keep the intellectual bond 'active' at all times, we nevertheless should possess an intense *desire* for continuous knowledge in actuality, to have our hearts constantly filled with longing after Him.[13]

So it turns out that in addition to the almost complete reduction of 'love-worship of God' into cognition of God by Maimonides, 'love of God' also connotes: (1) *rejoicing* in our knowledge of Him; and (2) possessing *an intense desire* to be in a continuous state of knowledge in actuality. And neither the rejoicing nor the desire are reducible to knowledge, for the former results *from* knowledge and accompanies it, while the latter results from an absence of continuous occurent knowledge. We can, therefore, say that while Maimonides espouses a quite robust identity thesis, he also recognizes that the relationship between love and knowledge is not one of 'absolute' identity.

For Maimonides then, the identity between love and knowledge amounts to the following set of interlocking claims: that 'loving God' means to be: (i) continuously *thinking* of Him, which thinking is accompanied by (ii) *rejoicing* in such thought, and which inevitable lack of continuous thought of Him due to human incapacity leads to (iii) an intense *desire* or longing to be always thinking of Him.

While (i) is that of a strong identity, (ii) and (iii) point us in the opposite direction. That is, as against an understanding of love and knowledge that would reduce one term to another, we might say that Maimonides also includes elements of a 'weak' identity, whereby love and desire *accompany* knowledge, but are not constitutive of it. In this account, subjective experience, emotions and desires are external to, or run *alongside,* the cognitive act, but they are not part of it. When emotion runs alongside or accompanies the act of cognition, we should recognize that the claim of identity is somewhat hyperbolic, and we might be entitled to only refer to this relationship as a 'weak' version of an identity. R. Soloveitchik also has this version in mind in his own understanding of the identity thesis, as we shall see in the following section.

---

13. Maimonides, *Guide*, Part III, ch. 51.

II.   'WEAK' IDENTITY – SUBJECTIVITY
EXTERNAL TO COGNITION

(a)   Emotions precede cognition
People get ideas from everywhere. Sometimes, mysterious inspiration
hits them like a flash of lightning. Other times, they may struggle
endlessly for a solution to a problem, only to find that the solution
appears to them in a dream. "In the context of discovery, we get
ideas, no matter how – dreams or drugs will do."[14] R. Soloveitchik
also believes that halakhic man has pre-intellectual 'visions' of the
halakhic truth:

> Occasionally the Torah marries and unites with an individual
> . . . The Torah is thus absorbed into the innermost recesses of
> his being and bonds with him . . . Logical halakhic reasoning
> draws on the pre-intellectual vision tempestuously breaking
> through from the depths of his personality . . . This mysterious
> intuition is the source of halakhic creativity and innovation.
> Rigorous intellect. . . . thinks only what it has been furnished
> by the visionary soul. The halakhic man that Torah has wed
> "sees" halakhic contents, *"feels"* halakhic ideas as if they had
> been tones, sights, or smells.[15]

What is important to point out here is that subjectivity *precedes* cognition and may lead to the "discovery" of objective halakhic constructs,
but the source of an idea cannot be considered an essential aspect of
the content of the idea. In this sense then, emotions or "pre-intellectual" visions may provide what the philosopher Timothy Williamson
calls the "context of discovery," but they are not essential in the way
needed to establish an identity between emotion and cognition. How
someone arrives at an idea is irrelevant to its truth-content. On this
view, emotions precede cognition; but they do not help to constitute it.

---

14. Timothy Williamson, "Reclaiming the Imagination" accessible at http://
    opinionator.blogs.nytimes.com/2010/08/15/reclaiming-the-imagination/.
15. *Mah Dodekh mi-Dod*, 74-75, cited in Dov Schwartz, *Religion or Halakha:
    The Philosophy of Rabbi Joseph B. Soloveitchik, Volume 1*, trans. Batya Stein
    (Leiden: Brill, 2007), 334.

(b) Emotions accompany cognition

In an essay on study and action, R. Aharon Lichtenstein claims that when one is engaged in the cognition of the law, one must also have a desire to actualize or fulfill that law.[16] Here, the desire is extrinsic to cognition and merely accompanies it. If we were to take away the simultaneous desire, nothing would be lost from a cognitive perspective. There may be other defects of a person who experiences no desire to fulfill the law while cognizing it, but the defect is not a cognitive one. Emotions or desires which accompany cognition are separable from it and therefore cannot be said to provide an example of an 'identity.'[17]

Similarly, it may be thought that Spinoza's *amor Dei intellectualis*, the intellectual love of God, which R. Soloveitchik cites in *Halakhic Man* (85), may serve as a model for the identity of cognition and love. But it does not, since according to Spinoza, this intellectual love is the feeling of pleasure which accompanies the act of cognizing God as the First Cause. Here, the affect doesn't do any of the cognitive lifting; it simply arises out of, or accompanies, the act of cognition. Without the love, nothing cognitively is lost.[18]

(c) Emotions follow cognition

In *Halakhic Man*, R. Soloveitchik writes that:

> Halakhic Man is worthy and fit to devote himself to a majestic religious experience . . . However, for him, such a powerful, exalted experience only follows upon cognition, only occurs after he has acquired knowledge of the a priori, ideal Halakhah and its reflected image in the real world. But since

---

16. Aharon Lichtenstein, "Talmud and Ma'aseh in Pirkei Avot," in *Rav Chesed: Essays in Honor of Rabbi Dr. Haskel Lookstein, Vol. 2*, ed. Rafael Medoff (New York, 2009).
17. See also the chapter by Reuven Ziegler on experience and intellect. Ziegler's approach highlights how emotions run alongside cognition. See Reuven Ziegler, *Majesty and Humility: The Thought of Rabbi Joseph Soloveitchik* (Boston: Urim Publications, 2012), 334–342.
18. See Jonathan Bennett, *A Study of Spinoza's Ethics* (Cambridge: Press Syndicate of the Univ. of Cambridge, 1984), 370.

this experience occurs after rigorous criticism and profound penetrating reflection, it is that much more intensive. (83–4)

The passage above clearly displays the centrality of subjective experience and emotion for halakhic man – to be sure, not a sentimental or ecstatic and uncontrolled emotion – but an emotion which arises from cognition. Nevertheless, it does not show, on its own, that emotions are a constitutive part of cognition. In the passage, emotions "top off" or follow cognition, but they do not increase understanding, nor do they help to shape or direct what halakhic man cognizes.

Similarly, consider the following famous passage from Maimonides:

> What is the path [to attain] love and fear of Him? When a person contemplates His wondrous and great deeds and creations and appreciates His infinite wisdom that surpasses all comparison, he will immediately love, praise, and glorify [Him].[19]

In the passage above, no relationship of identity is established. Rather, according to Maimonides, love follows cognition. It is the end result of a cognitive process (and may accompany it), but it is separable from it.[20] While we may not experience appropriate love of God without knowledge, the two terms in no way stand in a relation of identity, one merely follows from the other. Emotion, in this reading, is not a constitutive part of cognition.[21]

So on the understanding presented above, there is a sense in which talk of an identity between love and cognition is somewhat exaggerated. According to the 'weak' identity thesis, emotions run alongside cognition, but they are not essential to it. Yet neither the strong or weak version of the identity thesis capture the unique and defining features of what R. Soloveitchik means by the identity between love

---

19. *Mishneh Torah*, Hilchot Yesodei Torah, Perek 2, Halakha 2.
20. And as Maimonides continues in the same passage, such love, engendered by knowledge, may then lead one to yearn to attain even more knowledge, so that love first follows cognition, and then precedes it by serving as motivation to cognize even more. But an identity is never established.
21. Even if the relationship is one of necessity, where love necessarily follows from knowledge, it is a *causal* necessity, and this relationship still does not rise to the level of an identity.

and cognition. To be sure, both of those understandings play a role in rounding out the meaning of the identity, but they do not capture perhaps the most significant element in that identity as understood by R. Soloveitchik, who was after a *non-reductive, yet deep and conceptual*, relationship between love and cognition, a relationship which in part arises out of his modern, general epistemological sensibilities. A clarification of this non-reductive, yet essential relationship between emotion and cognition will complete our sketch of the meaning of the identity thesis for R. Soloveitchik.

III.   NON-REDUCTIVE IDENTITY – SUBJECTIVITY ESSENTIAL TO COGNITION

As we have seen, there are many ways in which emotion and cognition can be related to one another, but if those ways depict emotion's relationship to cognition along *temporal* dimensions, whereby emotions precede, accompany, or follow, the act of cognition (as in 'weak' identity), we would not be warranted in claiming that there is an identity between love and cognition. R. Soloveitchik's language then, would seem to be an instance of hyperbole.

But is there another way to understand the relationship between love and cognition such that we can take R. Soloveitchik's claim of identity seriously, yet non-reductively? Is there a way to understand how love and other emotional and experiential states can play an *essential, yet non-reductive,* role in the act of cognition, whereby subjectivity helps to shape the very content of cognition? There is, and the argument is found in *The Halakhic Mind*, which R. Soloveitchik connects to his identity thesis.

(a) The Cognitive Status of Emotions

In *The Halakhic Mind*, R. Soloveitchik endorses the view that emotions are not just irrational outpourings of the heart, but that they are cognitive; that is, an examination of the structure of an emotion would reveal that those emotions contain within them evaluative claims about the nature of the world.[22] For R. Soloveitchik, the world

---

22. *The Halakhic Mind*, 41–5.

of values is in fact opened up by our emotions: "Emotions are the media through which the value-universe opens up to us."[23]

How do our emotions open up the world of values in a way that 'reason' alone cannot? The contemporary philosopher Martha Nussbaum, who has played a leading role in helping to establish the cognitive nature of emotions in the general philosophical literature, provides an example:

> The agent who discerns intellectually that a friend is in need or that a loved one has died, but who fails to respond to these facts with appropriate sympathy or grief . . . a part of discernment or perception is lacking. This person doesn't really, or doesn't fully *see* what has happened, doesn't recognize it in a full-blooded way or take it in . . . [The agent] doesn't yet fully *know* it, because the emotional part of cognition is lacking. And it isn't just that sometimes we need emotions to *get to* the right (intellectual) view of the situation . . . Neither is it just that the emotions supply extra praiseworthy elements external to cognition . . . *[Rather], the emotions are themselves modes of vision, of recognition.* [Emphasis added.][24]

So it is through our emotional responses that we come into contact with certain ways of viewing and understanding the world of values. And for R. Soloveitchik, this world of values is not to be restricted to the world of everyday or common values, for his use of the term 'values' or 'norms' is an expansive one. As he writes in *Halakhic Man*:

> But what is the tale of the heavens, if not the proclamation of the norm? . . . All of existence declares the glory of God – man's obligation to order his life according to the will of the Almighty.[25]

---

23. Joseph B. Soloveitchik, *Out of the Whirlwind*, ed. David Shatz, Joel B. Wolowelsky, and Reuven Ziegler (New York: Toras HaRav Foundation, 2003), xliv.
24. Martha C. Nussbaum, *Love's Knowledge: Essays on Philosophy and Literature* (New York: Oxford University Press, 1990), 79.
25. *Halakhic Man*, 64.

For halakhic man, to see the world under its normative, value-laden aspect is to see the world through the prism of Halakha, so the entirety of the Halakha constitutes, for R. Soloveitchik, a detailed exploration and elaboration of the world of values, of norms, broadly conceived. [26]It follows then, if emotions are the media by which the value-universe opens up to us, that if we are to truly cognize the value-laden universe, we must involve our emotions in the act of such cognition. And so part of the meaning of the identity of love and cognition is that it is only through love – or emotions and subjectivity more broadly – that we can fully come to know and understand the world *as a world replete with value*. That R. Soloveitchik wanted to connect his identity thesis with his broader claim regarding the cognitive nature of emotions is evidenced by his claim that "many aspects of this view influenced the modern theory of affects . . . and which draws upon the idea of the "logic of the heart" . . ."[27] R. Soloveitchik here reveals that he wants to connect his identity thesis with modern understandings of the role of emotion in the cognitive act. So for R. Soloveitchik, full and proper cognition must involve 'the logic of the heart.'

(b) The Emotional Heart of Logic

Yet R. Soloveitchik means to signal much more with his assertion of the identity between love and cognition, for immediately after R. Soloveitchik presents this claim of identity, he provides us with a crucial remark that changes how we are to understand Pascal: "Instead of discussing the logic of the heart, Maimonides focuses on the emotional heart of logic."[28] These lines are no doubt meant to expand on the identity thesis, but their meaning is not entirely clear.

What does R. Soloveitchik mean by the distinction between 'the logic of the heart' and 'the emotional heart of logic'? In *The Halakhic Mind*, R. Soloveitchik refers to Pascal and the reasons of the heart, and there he offers not one, but *two* interpretations of this phrase, interpretations that nicely correspond to the distinction between the

---

26. The meaning of values here is more closely related to that which we most care about, which can be a very broad category. For halakhic man, that which he most cares about is the theoretical law.
27. *U'bikashtem mi-Sham*, 156.
28. *U'bikashtem mi-Sham*, 156.

'logic of heart' and the 'emotional heart of logic' found in *U'bikashtem mi-Sham.*

According to R. Soloveitchik, there are two ways to understand Pascal's phrase that there are reasons of the heart. In the first way, which doesn't concern R. Soloveitchik much, a person immediately apprehends that which is true. This version simply states that the 'heart' can sometimes arrive at truth immediately, without the need for inferences. R. Soloveitchik writes:

> Nothing new or exciting is revealed in this passage [of Pascal]. The fact that first postulates are somehow immediately apprehended was already known . . . Pascal only substitutes the heart for immediate knowledge not subject to demonstration.[29]

But there is a second, more exciting and revealing meaning to Pascal's famous phrase in which:

> The reason is the instrument of the will and the theoretical is subordinated to the volitional. . . . In such a context, "reason of the heart" is not a mere metaphor denoting rational immediate knowledge . . . for this type follows upon the volitional decision and is not antecedent to the will. . . .[30]

This version of what it means for there to be reasons of the heart, according to R. Soloveitchik, is not simply that the heart immediately apprehends the truth in an act of intuition, but that the 'heart' *helps to shape* and mold the very content of the truth being discovered. This far-reaching claim is elaborated upon by Daniel Rynhold in his article on R. Soloveitchik and Nietzsche.[31] According to Rynhold, R. Soloveitchik affirmed the modern epistemological doctrine that "non-cognitive" aspects of the person affect and even help to guide and direct the human intellect. As Rynhold writes:

---

29. *The Halakhic Mind*, 108–09. I thank David Shatz for pointing out this passage in another context.
30. *The Halakhic Mind*, 108–09.
31. See Daniel Rynhold and Michael J. Harris, *Nietzsche, Soloveitchik, and Contemporary Jewish Philosophy* (Cambridge: Cambridge University Press, forthcoming 2018), ch. 1.

Soloveitchik therefore emphasizes the volitional element in all acts of cognition. As noted before, cognitive claims are made against an evaluative background. They are informed by the (non-cognitive) interests that we are pursuing. Thus, for both Soloveitchik and Nietzsche there is a very important sense in which the affective side of human nature drives our knowledge claims, and indeed appear *necessary* for them to be considered as knowledge claims at all. Devoid of such affective and evaluative perspectives, we would simply be unable to formulate knowledge claims at all.[32]

So for R. Soloveitchik, the claim that there is an identity between cognition and love, which is followed almost immediately by his invocation of Pascal's phrase, in part amounts to the claim that there is no such thing as "disinterested" knowing. There is, as R. Soloveitchik writes, "an emotional heart of logic" whereby our subjectivity and emotions are central to cognition and in which subjectivity helps to direct the content of our objective constructs.

What might be an example of how subjectivity helps to shape the very content of cognition? We can get a better sense of the interrelationship between subjectivity and cognition when we examine R. Soloveitchik's treatment of the proofs of God's existence.

In *U-Bikashtem mi-Sham*, the Rav writes that the main problem with the cosmological and ontological arguments is that they have devolved into logical constructs divorced from the foundational experience which gives rise to a sense of God's reality.[33] It is the subjective experience of God's reality that matters, and the logical arguments cannot be divorced from such experiences. If they are, they will be barren and empty and devolve into casuistry. Here, experience/subjectivity is doing more than merely serving as the contingent means of discovering certain truths. With respects to 'proofs' of God's existence,

---

32. See Daniel Rynhold and Michael J. Harris, *Nietzsche, Soloveitchik, and Contemporary Jewish Philosophy* (Cambridge: Cambridge University Press, forthcoming 2018), ch. 1.

33. See *U'bikashtem mi-Sham*, 13 and 157. On the relationship between the ontological argument and religious experience, see Ermanno Bencivenga, *Logic and Other Nonsense: The Case of Anselm and His God* (Princeton: Princeton University Press, 1993).

it is clear that *experience and subjectivity are essential to knowledge* as R. Soloveitchik portrays it.

In this account, love, emotions and subjectivity are primary modes of knowledge, and the objective constructs, like the cosmological argument, are derivative.[34] The identity of love and cognition essentially amounts to the claim that subjectivity, emotion and experience form the core of the objective constructs that are derived from them.

IV.   SCOPE AND IMPLICATIONS

That R. Soloveitchik had in mind the *theoretical* law when he writes of the identity between love and cognition and of "the emotional heart of logic" is evidenced from his insertion of the doctrine of the unity of the knower and the known in the very same paragraph. That doctrine, as used by R. Soloveitchik, refers to the *theoretical* law, as Aviezer Ravitzky has convincingly shown. Ravitzky has argued that in many places where R. Soloveitchik is interpreting Maimonides, R. Soloveitchik switches the focus of Maimonides's discussion on cognition of the world to cognition of the law.[35] In this case, whereas Maimonides uses the doctrine of the unity of the knower and the known to refer to cognition of the world by both God and man,[36] R. Soloveitchik switches the focus to a unity derived from cognition of the *theoretical* law.[37] So when R. Soloveitchik writes that he is after "the emotional heart of logic," he is, above all, after the emotional heart of *halakhic* logic – that is, he is after the subjectivity lying behind and helping to shape the objective halakhic constructs derived from

---

34. The section on the identity of love and cognition groups together three different terms – subjective experience, emotion and love. Each term is actually a sub-set of the previous term. What really matters is the cognitive value of subjective experience, broadly conceived. Emotion is a central component of subjectivity, and love is the paradigmatic emotion.

35. See, Ravitzky, 161–68.

36. See note 10.

37. Ravitzky argues that R. Soloveitchik, operating with modern, Kantian assumptions regarding the limitations of knowledge, could not have availed himself of an unadulterated version of the doctrine of the unity of the knower and the known as utilized by Maimonides, which depends on access to the world as it really is. Therefore, the same "forms" that both God and man cognize are *halakhic* forms.

such subjectivity.[38] This has some striking implications for how we are to conceive of the centrality of subjectivity to the enterprise of the construction and cognition of the theoretical law. To clarify this point, it is worth exploring what R. Soloveitchik writes about subjectivity in *The Halakhic Mind*. If *The Halakhic Mind* means to include the *theoretical* law within its purview, this would mean that for R. Soloveitchik, *lomdus* – the primary activity of halakhic man – is shot through with emotion and subjectivity.

In *The Halakhic Mind*, one of the primary themes that R. Soloveitchik develops is that Jewish law is to be seen as an elaboration, concretization, objectification and expression of more fundamental *subjective,* religious states. As R. Soloveitchik writes:

> Religion, which is perhaps more deeply rooted in subjectivity than any other manifestation of the spirit, is also reflected in externalized phenomena. . . .[39]

What is the scope of this claim? Does this mean that *the entirety* of Jewish law, of the objective Halakha, can be described on the basis of the presentation in *The Halakhic Mind*, where all of the Halakha is to be viewed as an exemplification of subjectivity rushing to "externalize" and objectify itself?[40]

We can isolate three possibilities regarding the scope of the objective Halakha that is to be reconstructed in order to find subjectivity. In the first option, the scope is: (1) limited to what R. Soloveitchik has elsewhere termed "experiential" commandments; (2) in the second option, the scope includes the "practical" commandments, even those not properly classified as "experiential"; and lastly, (3) in addition

---

38. The word "logic" here is not to be understood *exclusively* as 'halakhic' logic. R. Soloveitchik is certainly making a more general epistemological claim. My point is rather that, for R. Soloveitchik, halakhic logic is the highest expression of 'logic' and is therefore his ultimate focal point of concern in this passage.
39. *The Halakhic Mind,* 67.
40. My focus here is on the scope of the *laws* that form the subject matter of *The Halakhic Mind*. But it should be clear that the non-legal aspects of Jewish tradition, including Jewish philosophy, mystical writings, the narrative parts of the Bible, and *Aggada* would also certainly fall under the scope of *The Halakhic Mind*. See in particular 91 of *The Halakhic Mind*.

to #1) and #2), we can include the entirety of the *theoretical* law as well – that is – *The Halakhic Mind*'s discussion of subjectivity moving outwards towards objectivity and the related discussion of reconstruction would also be applicable to *lomdus*.

I believe that position #3 most accurately depicts the scope of the Halakha ripe for reconstruction, and significant implications follow from this claim regarding the nature of the theoretical law as conceived by R. Soloveitchik. To see this, we need to briefly examine these three possibilities.

(1) In his *Worship of the Heart* and in various other writings, R. Soloveitchik carves out a special category of commandments that he labels "experiential", whose fulfillment lies in an internal, experiential state, and the corresponding acts serve merely to trigger or express those internal states. As R. Soloveitchik writes:

> In contradistinction to the actional *mitzvot*, which form a single objective series, the experiential mitzvot refer to a spiritual act, a state of mind, an inner attitude or outlook. . . .
> In contrast to the actional *mitzvot*, the experiential *mitzvot* postulate a way not only of doing but of experiencing as well. The *Halakhah* attempts to regulate not only the body but also the soul.[41]

R. Soloveitchik then discusses two subcategories of experiential mitzvot, one of which contain both outer and inner aspects:

> For instance, the precept of rejoicing on a festival, *simhat Yom Tov*, is realized through a double activity-experiencing and redeeming, uplifting and inspiring joy on the one hand, and conforming to the external cultic standard of bringing shelamim sacrifices . . . and feasting, on the other . . . in each *mitzvah* we must carefully discriminate between the *ma'aseh ha-mitzvah* (the piecemeal process of actual execution) and *kiyyum ha-mitzvah*, compliance with the norm. . . . These

---

41. See Joseph Soloveitchik, *Worship of the Heart*, ed. Shalom Carmy (New York: Ktav Publishing House, 2003), *15*.

> actions are antecedent to the fulfillment, the *kiyyum* . . . which
> is attained in the depths of a great experience. . . .[42]

This subcategory of experiential commandments described above are known, as the passage above indicates, as those commands subject to R. Soloveitchik's well-known *ma'aseh/kiyyum* distinction, where the act (*ma'aseh*) is severed from the proper fulfillment (*kiyyum*) of the mitzvah. In his review of *Worship of the Hea*rt, Lawrence Kaplan points out that there is a striking similarity between these experiential commandments, that is, the commandments subject to the *ma'aseh/kiyyum* distinction, and the language in *The Halakhic Mind*.[43] If Kaplan is correct, this would suggest that the discussion of the re-construction of subjectivity out of objective laws in *The Halakhic Mind* refers to (and is limited to) the dozen or so 'experiential' commandments to which R. Soloveitchik applied the *ma'aseh/kiyyum* distinction.[44] And this would make eminent sense, given that the whole point of the discussion of *The Halakhic Mind* is to trace the subjective/experiential states of religious commandments, and what better category of commands can there be to locate those states than in the commands which R. Soloveitchik explicitly claimed are 'experiential' in nature?

(2) Nevertheless, that R. Soloveitchik did not intend to limit the application of reconstruction in *The Halakhic Mind* to the dozen or so experiential commandments is clear from his ensuing discussion, where he hints at the experiential states of the Sabbath laws as an example of the process of reconstruction. Now the Sabbath laws are not, technically, subject to the *ma'aseh/kiyyum* distinction. R. Soloveitchik never claims that the fulfillment of the commandment to keep the Sabbath lies in the internal state of 'creation-consciousness' or in any other internal state.[45] This expansion of the application of *The Hal-*

---

42. See Joseph Soloveitchik, *Worship of the Heart,* ed. Shalom Carmy (New York: Ktav Publishing House, 2003), 17–18.

43. Lawrence Kaplan, Review Essay – "Worship of the Heart: Essays on Prayer", *Hakirah,* Vol. 5 (2007) 80–81.

44. It should be noted that Kaplan himself merely notes the connection and does not state that *The Halakhic Mind* is limited to the experiential commands. That is merely one implication of his connection, so position #1 is not, strictly speaking, Kaplan's position.

45. This should be distinguished from the commandments to honor and delight

akhic Mind to the Sabbath laws suggests that R. Soloveitchik intended, at the very least, to include not only the experiential commandments, but the practical laws more generally. This is precisely the position advocated by Dov Schwartz. For Schwartz, the argument regarding reconstruction in *The Halakhic Mind* is limited in its application to the practical laws, such as repentance, prayer and the Sabbath. But it is not applicable to the realm of the theoretical laws. As Schwartz writes: "*The Halakhic Mind* makes no reference to *lomdus*."[46]

(3) But is it true that *The Halakhic Mind* makes no reference to *lomdus*? Consider the following passage:

> Religion, which is perhaps more deeply rooted in subjectivity than any other manifestation of the spirit, is also reflected in externalized phenomena . . . The aggregate of religious objective constructs is comprised of ethico-religious norms, ritual, dogmas, ***theoretical postulates***, etc.[47] [emphasis added.]

R. Soloveitchik's inclusion of "theoretical postulates" signals that the theoretical law – *lomdus* – is also subject to the reconstruction of the 'subjectivity' lying behind such laws.

Moreover, as added evidence that the construction of the theoretical law is infused with subjectivity, in *Halakhic Man*, the Rav, with unmistakeable clarity, indicates that the two works are closely linked, when he writes that, "Halakhah is the objectification of religion . . . It translates subjectivity into objectivity . . . The Halakhah wishes to objectify religiosity . . . through the structuring and ordering of the inner correlative in the realm of man's spirit."[48] The language and substance of subjectivity forming the inner correlative of objectivity

---

in the Sabbath, which are in part, internal states.

46. Dov Schwartz, *Religion or Halakhah? The Philosophy of Rabbi Joseph B. Soloveitchik*, trans. Batya Stein (Leiden: Brill Academic Publishers, 2007). Evidence of Schwartz's position can be seen from R. Soloveitchik's frequent discussion of action in *The Halakhic Mind*. The theoretical law seems unrelated to action. This is true, but only shows that the *focus* of the discussion in *The Halakhic Mind* is on the practical norms, and not that the discussion is meant to *exclude* the application of reconstruction to the theoretical law.

47. *The Halakhic Mind*, 67.

48. *Halakhic Man*, 59.

bears a striking resemblance to the language and substance of *The Halakhic Mind*. This sentence in *Halakhic Man*, which describes the *theoretical* halakha,[49] demonstrates that subjectivity is not erased from *Halakhic Man*, even if it is not emphasized in the way that it is in *The Halakhic Mind*.

R. Soloveitchik is in fact describing a two-fold movement in *The Halakhic Mind*. The first is one of *construction*, where the objective laws are built out of, and are in part expressive of, underlying subjectivity/experiential states. And the second is one of *re-construction*.[50] After the laws have been constructed, philosophers of religion are to reconstruct, or attempt to extract, the underlying subjectivity that gave rise to those objective laws.[51] And If I am right that the process of reconstruction as described in *The Halakhic Mind* is applicable to the theoretical law as well, this would mean that lurking behind the entirety of the seemingly cold, objective and dispassionate models that make up the bulk of the theoretical law, lies *subjectivity*. And this is what R. Soloveitchik asserts in *U'bikashtem mi-Sham*:

> [T]he soul, seized by vision and agitated by beauty, travels through existence following the footsteps of the lover hiding inside the crannies of the symbolic mind.[52]

To say that the lover is hiding inside the crannies of the symbolic mind is essentially to recapitulate the entire theme of reconstruction in *The*

---

49. R. Soloveitchik compares it to mathematics and science.
50. The first is the movement outward, from subjectivity to objectivity. The second is the reverse – we start with the objectivity and work our way backwards – to subjectivity. The movement outward eventually results in action, that is, in the performance of a religious command. Insofar as the consummation of this outward movement is an action, it is clear that in this respect, *The Halakhic Mind* is limited in application to the practical laws, as Schwartz writes.
51. Halakhic man engages in construction. The philosopher of religion engages in reconstruction. R. Soloveitchik himself engages in both. Further evidence that R. Soloveitchik did not intend to limit the application of reconstruction to the practical laws comes from an essay published in *Out of the Whirlwind*, where he attempts to reconstruct the subjectivity lying behind the laws of the red heifer, hardly an area of practical concern. See *Out of the Whirlwind*, 42–45. Ziegler also makes this point, see *Majesty and Humility*, 339.
52. *U'bikashtem mi-Sham*, 15. See also n. 36.

Halakhic Mind. In other words, this sentence is a poetic restatement of the task of reconstruction, which is to find the love, emotion and subjectivity buried inside the constructs of the symbolic mind, by extracting it from those constructs, i.e. from the theoretical law, which constitutes the highest expression of the symbolic mind.[53] So for R. Soloveitchik, the identity of love and cognition amounts to a claim that lying behind the constructs of the symbolic, halakhic mind – lies love, emotion and subjectivity. The identity thesis is in large part to be understood as a claim regarding centrality of subjectivity and emotion to the *theoretical* law.

We can now better understand R. Soloveitchik's claim in *Mah Dodekh mi-Dod* that halakhic man 'sees' halakhic ideas and 'feels' halakhic contents. Earlier, we had cited this passage as an instance of how emotion and subjectivity *precede* cognition, and therefore cannot rise to the level of an identity with cognition. Subjectivity served merely as the context for the discovery of halakhic ideas. But now we can understand the passage better in light of R. Soloveitchik's identity thesis and of his description of subjectivity moving outward towards objectivity in *The Halakhic Mind*. When R. Soloveitchik writes in *Ma-dodech mi-Dod* that "Logical halakhic reasoning draws on the pre-intellectual vision tempestuously breaking through from the depths of his personality" he is essentially recapitulating his claim in *The Halakhic Mind* that subjectivity rushes outward towards objectification and and to express itself in concepts.[54] And this subjectivity isn't merely what precedes cognition, but it is that which shapes and directs it, as we have shown, for there is an emotional-subjective heart to halakhic logic. And if subjective-experiential states "from the depths of one's personality" form the core of the eventual constructs which are objectified expressions of that subjectivity, we can understand why R. Soloveitchik writes that halakhic man *feels* and *sees* halakhic ideas and contents, for those "ideas" and "contents" are, at their core – *subjective-experiential* ideas and concepts in much the same way that the color red is, at its core, a subjective-experiential concept. Just as color has both a subjective and an objective dimension, and the subjective dimension constitutes the core of the

---

53. Ziegler also connects the task of reconstruction to the theoretical law. See his *Majesty and Humility*, 340–43.
54. And eventually actions also, but my focus here is on concepts.

concept, so too halakhic-theoretic models have both subjective and objective dimensions, but the subjective dimension is primary, as it forms "the heart" of halakhic logic. In *Ma-dodech mi-dod* then, we encounter a striking passage where the theme of the identity of love and cognition, of the emotional-subjective heart of logic, and of the centrality of subjectivity to the cognition of the theoretical law is given prominent voice by R. Soloveitchik.

V. THE MYSTERIOUS RELATIONSHIP BETWEEN SUBJECTIVITY AND OBJECTIVITY

We have, up until this point, argued that for the relationship between love and cognition to rise to the level of an identity, we have to show how subjectivity and emotion are essential to the cognitive task of constructing, directing and making sense of the theoretical law. But can we really think that this relationship amounts to an identity when so much of what R. Soloveitchik writes actually *cautions* us *not* to delude ourselves into believing that we can plumb the depths of the law and understand it, even when engaged in the task of reconstruction?

Consider the example of color, which recurs in R. Soloveitchik's writings as an apt analogy for discussing the relationship between subjectivity and objectivity as he conceives it. According to R. Soloveitchik, color can be examined from two perspectives. There is an objective-quantitative dimension to color, that is, color can be described in terms of the science of optics, wavelengths, etc., and there is a subjective-qualitative dimension to color, whereby color is seen as what a person experiences, the actual phenomenology of color perception. But there is a problem with the analogy if we were to apply it to the task of reconstruction. For R. Soloveitchik, it is clear that these parallel dimensions somehow interact with one another, but the precise nature of their interaction is completely mysterious to us:

> For example, when I perceive a color, the qualitative riddle, the question, emerges. But what is the answer? The wavelength, a mathematical quantity. The answer does not explain the qualitative content. There is a parallelism here between the two series, the qualitative and the quantitative. But there is no explanation. We know precisely that the objective, quan-

titative order matches the subjective, qualitative one. But this match does not answer or solve the question. . . .[55]

We would *not* be able to reconstruct the subjective dimensions of color – what it is like to see red – by examining the objective aspects of color. The scientific exploration of color can *in no way* furnish any clues as to what the color red looks like. This brief description of the parallel ways of understanding color and of the problem of sensation and knowledge that it implies, is mentioned by R. Soloveitchik in both *The Halakhic Mind* and *U'bikashtem mi-Sham*. And what this implies is that the relationship between subjectivity and objectivity is mysterious and highly tentative. That is why R. Soloveitchik repeatedly uses phrases such as "hints at" or "points to" when he describes the reconstruction of subjectivity out of objectivity.[56]

If this is the case – if the relationship between subjectivity and objectivity is so mysterious and tentative – how can we talk about an "identity" between love and cognition, between subjectivity and objectivity, and of the deep conceptual connections that such an identity implies? In order to meet the objection above, we need to distinguish between the claim that there is an identity between subjectivity and *specific or individual* theoretic models and laws on the one hand, and the claim of a deep, conceptual *general* connection between subjective states and objective constructs, on the other. That is to say, it is true that according to R. Soloveitchik, we cannot *definitively* trace a *particular* halakhic practice or theoretic construct to its underlying *particular* subjective states, but that does not mean that in general terms subjectivity doesn't form the backdrop for those constructs. As an analogy, there is a deep conceptual connection between color's phe-

---

55. *U'bikashtem mi-Sham*, 160–61.
56. See *The Halakhic Mind*, 93–98. See also *Worship of the Heart*, 51. The color analogy, taken too far, would *altogether preclude* any benefit to reconstruction. Just as we can't *at all* glean the nature of color as qualia from the study of color's objective features, we would not be able to reconstruct *any* subjectivity from an examination of the objective halakhic constructs. This consideration points to an important dis-analogy. While color might be a 'pure' impression, uncluttered or mediated by concepts, religious experience is always mediated by concepts. There is no such thing as 'pure' subjectivity with respect to religious experience, as there may be with colors. Or at least, the latter certainly is less mediated.

nomenal properties and its objective properties, even though we might not be in a position to spell out those specific connections, and in fact we may never be able to understand them. This inherent limitation of our capacity to understand how individual subjective experiences of color conceptually link up to color's objective-quantitative aspects in no way undermines the claim that, in general terms, color's phenomenological properties are essential to understanding what color is and, that in some way, the objective properties conceptually link up to those experiential properties. This is what R. Soloveitchik means by his claim that, "We know precisely that the objective, quantitative order matches the subjective, qualitative one."[57]

Yes, for R. Soloveitchik, the objective and the subjective do match somehow, even if they will match up differently for different people on account of our uniqueness, and even if we cannot definitively understand how each specific law matches up with specific subjective states. That is why R. Soloveitchik discusses the relationship between subjectivity and objectivity by invoking such tentative language. So in this account, ultimately the "identity of love and cognition" must be understood in general and tentative terms, on account of our uniqueness and on account of our epistemological limitations.

VI. THE IDENTITY THESIS REVISITED

R. Soloveitchik's summary assertion that there is an identity between love and cognition, buried in a footnote in *U'bikashtem mi-Sham*, serves as a marker for a cluster of interconnected ideas which R. Soloveitchik espouses regarding the relationship between emotion and thought, between subjectivity and objectivity. And further, this set of interlocking ideas has far-reaching consequences for how we are to conceive of the nature of the theoretical law as R. Soloveitchik

---

57. There will be variations in my phenomenology of different shades of blue and yours. We do not see exactly the same. This will also be true for the religious subjectivity we can each extract from the objective laws, even more so. Because we are all unique, the subjectivity we reconstruct will not be identical. That is why Rav Soloveitchik, in the opening of *Worship of the Heart*, writes that he is describing only what certain laws mean to him, without any claims to eternal, universal applicability. Although note that the binding nature of certain experiences in the *maaseh/kiyyum* laws would need to be explored in this context.

conceived of it. So when R. Soloveitchik writes that there is an identity between love and cognition he has in mind:

(i) following Maimonides, a strong claim of identity wherein to love God means to be "continuously thinking of Him" and, as per Ravitzky, for R. Soloveitchik, thinking of Him actually consists of being engaged in the cognition of the theoretical law;

(ii) that such cognition is accompanied by: (a) a unique joy that results from continuous thought of Him; (b) and an intense desire to always be thinking of Him;[58]

(iii) and as other parts of R. Soloveitchik's corpus make clear, that the affective feelings of love and other emotions precede, accompany and follow upon the act of cognition; and

(iv) that those emotions which accompany the act of cognition are cognitive, and help to orient ourselves to, and connect us with, a *value-laden* world; and

(v) that emotions and subjectivity play an essential role in both guiding our theoretical-cognitive reason and shaping the very content of our cognition; and finally,

(vi) that the relationship between subjectivity and objectivity remains, at the specific-particular level, full of mystery.

It turns out then, that this identity between love and cognition encapsulates an entire orientation of R. Soloveitchik as to how he conceives of the act of cognition in general, of the act of cognition of the theoretical law in particular, and of the centrality of emotion and subjectivity to such enterprises. When R. Soloveitchik writes that Maimonides was trying to focus on the "emotional heart of logic" he is not being hyperbolic. Subjective experience and emotions are central to the cognition of the man of God. 'There is an identity of love and cognition.'

---

58. See also note 11.

Ephraim Kanarfogel

The History of the Tosafists and their Literary Corpus According to Rav Soloveitchik's Interpretations of the *Qinot* for *Tishah B'av*

I

Although Rav Soloveitchik was well aware of the events of his day and of important events from both the Jewish past and from the broader history of the world, he evinced little interest, at least in his published works and public lectures, in pursuing the details of history with any depth. Historical events were sometimes used to flavor his discourses, but his main interaction with them (and with historical theory more broadly) was to incorporate them into his philosophical and theological teachings and categories, in order to learn from them about the human condition and obligations, in both the halakhic and philosophical realms.[1]

A telling model for this type of engagement with history is Maimonides' treatment of the development of monotheism at the beginning of *hilkhot 'avodah zarah* in *Mishneh Torah*. Even as Maimonides, in his *Introduction to Pereq Ḥeleq*, openly declares his lack of interest in (if not disdain for) "the history of the kings and how and when

1. See Jeffrey Woolf, "Time Awareness as a Source of Spirituality in the Thought of Rabbi Joseph B. Soloveitchik," *Modern Judaism* 32 (2012), 54–75 [="Historiyyah ve-Toda'ah Historit be-Mishnato ha-Hilkhatit shel ha-Rav Soloveitchik," *Rav ba-'Olam he-Ḥadash*, ed. A. Rozenak and N. Rothenburg (Jerusalem, 2010), 324–38.] I am grateful to my friends and colleagues, Professors Charles Raffel (*z"l*), Jacob J. Schacter and David Shatz, who were kind enough to read a draft of this study and offer a number of helpful comments and suggestions.

they were succeeded," he deftly mobilizes details about the life and career of Avraham *Avinu,* as found in biblical, talmudic and midrashic sources, in order to form a historical picture whose goal is not to teach or analyze history, but rather to speak to the intellectual and spiritual development of Judaism and mankind.[2]

In terms of the history of talmudic studies and interpretation, the Rav would relate, on occasion, to the methodology of a particular *rishon* in some kind of historical context. He might note, for example, the way that Ri Migash, the main teacher of Rambam's father and thus a very important influence on Maimonides as well, adumbrated Rambam's thinking about or formulation of a particular interpretation or approach. At the same time, however, the well-known description presented by the Rav about how various *rishonim* and *'aharonim* – from Rashi and *Tosafot* to Rambam and Rabad, to his grandfather R. Hayyim Soloveitchik and his father R. Moshe – would metaphysically enter the *beit midrash* as he unfolded their teachings in the course of developing his own shiur, while chronologically accurate, was intended to make the point that the continuum of talmudic study represented by this progression of rabbinic scholars (the *hakhmei ha-masorah*) transcended history, and is not inherently affected by the historical process.[3]

Indeed, the Rav did not often discuss, in the course of his talmudic discourses, the provenance, history or historical context of a particular *rishon.* At least in my day in the Rav's shiur, R. Menahem *ha-Mei'ri* of Perpignan alone came in for special mention – more for criticism than for anything else – which was centered on Meiri's "congenital inability" to maintain consistency in the sobriquets that he developed for citing his various predecessors (rather than referring to them by name). The Rav certainly knew that Meiri (ca. 1249-1316) was among the last of the *rishonim* and that his work of summation (in which his Provencal background afforded him a commanding overview of what had come before him in Sefarad, Ashkenaz and southern France, even

2. I first heard this insight many years ago from my distinguished teacher and colleague, Prof. Arthur Hyman. See also Isadore Twersky, *Introduction to the Code of Maimonides* (New Haven, 1980), 153–54, 220–28, 389–91; and Y. H. Yerushalmi, *Zakhor: Jewish History and Jewish Memory* (Seattle, 1982), 32–33, and 114–115 (n. 5).
3. See A. R. Besdin, *Man of Faith in the Modern World: Reflections of the Rav,* vol. 2 (Hoboken, 1989), 21–23.

as Maimonides played a particularly significant role in Meiri's work) had potentially important implications.[4] At the same time, however, the relatively late publication of Meiri's corpus meant that his work had not been properly evaluated or utilized in a significant way by the greatest among the 'aharonim, a point that was very important for the Rav, and one to which we shall return.[5]

Some have suggested that the Rav's dismissal of the Meiri actually had more to do with Meiri's broad method of summation. Well before the advent of Rabbi Adin Steinsaltz's commentaries to the *Gemara*, or the Schottenstein Artscroll Talmud, the Rav did not want his students to rely on Meiri's gathering and analysis of the various *rishonim* who were available on a particular *sugya*. Rather, he wanted to ensure that the students discovered and discussed these interpretations on their own, so that they would be better prepared to understand and to interact with his own analysis that would follow. In any case, while the Rav was acutely aware of the provenance of the various *rishonim*, and occasionally framed disputes between them in terms of geographic differences (such as *Hakhmei Ashkenaz* versus *Hakhmei Sefarad* and the like), he did not typically focus on the historical development (or spread) of their positions.

One area or realm of endeavor in which the Rav does appear to have been more interested in and open to pursuing the *sitz im leben* as well as the methods of various *rishonim*, was that of *hespedim* and other testimonies about the rabbinic figures with whom he had meaningful contact. I recall, for example, that in his 1982 *hesped* for Rabbi Professor Michael Bernstein – who had served for a number of years as a Rosh Yeshiva at the Rabbi Isaac Elchanan Theological Seminary until the onset of a degenerative illness that compelled him to forego giving a daily shiur and instead to teach Semitics, biblical interpretation, and other courses in the languages and texts of the ancient Near East at the Bernard Revel Graduate School, which he taught at his home for quite a number of years, and even from his

---

4.　See e.g., Israel Ta-Shma, *Ha-Sifrut ha-Parshanit la-Talmud*, vol. 2 (Jerusalem, 2000), 158–73.

5.　See e.g., *Igrot ha-Grid ha-Levi* (Jerusalem, 2001), fol. 57a; and below, n. 15. The Rav also noted that the method and content of the *Beit ha-Behirah* (including the lack of clear citations and its relative verbosity) suggest that its author was not as highly regarded as someone such as the contemporary Rashba.

sick-bed – the Rav invoked the image and achievements of R. Sa'adyah Gaon, whose commanding expertise was evident not only in the study and interpretation of Talmud and *halakhah*, but also in the areas of grammar and syntax and scriptural exegesis and analysis, among other linguistic and literary fields. Once the Rav had briefly described the protean achievements of Sa'adyah, he started to quickly and effusively list a series of like-minded and oriented scholars such as Menaḥem ben Saruq, Dunash Ibn Labrat, Judah Ibn Ḥayyuj and Jonah Ibn Janaḥ, and what they had written,[6] as paradigms for the exceptionally high-level and variegated categories of Torah study and mastery that characterized the accomplishments of Rabbi Bernstein as well.

The Rav clearly knew all of these figures and their works, and their ability to achieve greatness in multiple disciplines surely impressed him. In this instance, he allowed himself to recount their schools and their achievements, in proper historical order and with sensitivity to what each individual had accomplished mainly because he wanted to thereby highlight what the *niftar* who lay before him had also aspired to and had taught. As we shall see in a moment when I turn to the main focus of this study, the Rav's interpretations of the *Qinot*, the Rav often stressed that it was necessary to describe in very specific and loving terms the beauty and spiritual greatness of Jerusalem and the Temple prior to their destruction, in order to understand and appreciate more fully what had in fact been lost with their destruction. In commenting on R. Yehudah *ha-Levi*'s *qinah*, ציון הלא תשאלי לשלום אסיריך, which is the first of several such Zionide poems extolling the virtues of Zion that are included in the standard *Qinot le-Tishah B'Av* (and *Ha-Levi* is acknowledged by subsequent Ashkenazic authors as the initiator of and inspiration for this genre),[7] the Rav posited that there are two elements to the observance of Tishah B'Av and the recitation of the *qinot*. The first is to remember Zion in its state of destruction, while the second is to remember Zion in its magnificence prior to its destruction (as ירושלים של מטה ששם היתה השכינה שרויה, ושהיתה מכוונת כנגד שערי השמים העליונים). Both of these aspects emerge from the verse in *Eikhah*

---

6. On these figures and their works, see e.g., Nahum Sarna, "Hebrew and Bible Studies in Mediaeval Spain," *The Sephardi Heritage* I (1971), 323–66.

7. See Ezra Fleisher, *Ha-Yoẓerot be-Hithavvutam ve-Hitpathutan* (Jerusalem, 1984), 681, 704–07; and my *The Intellectual History and Rabbinic Culture of Medieval Ashkenaz* (Detroit, 2013), 418, 438–40.

זכרה ירושלים ימי עניה ומרודיה כל מחמדיה אשר היו מימי קדם (1:7), "Jerusalem remembers the days of her affliction and her anguish, all her treasures that she had from the days of old." In order to appreciate the magnitude of the *hurban* and the losses associated with it, one needed to be familiar with the beauty of the *Beit ha-Miqdash* and of Jerusalem *before* the disasters had occurred. Indeed with this *qinah*, the standard Tishah B'Av liturgy from Ashkenaz/Eastern Europe transitions to remembering Jerusalem before the *hurban*.[8]

To return to the Rav's *hesped* for R. Michael Bernstein, although the Rav was surely aware that R. Sa'adyah Gaon was by far the most outstanding talmudist among this group of rabbinic scholars – his placing R. Sa'adyah at the head of the list and giving him the most attention was not simply a matter of chronology – he did not pause at that time to consider the talmudic levels of the other great grammarians and biblical exegetes, or to reflect upon any of the differences and difficulties that they had with their patrons or with the rabbinic establishment more broadly.[9] The Rav's working assumption was that all of these figures were Torah scholars by virtue of their trenchant contributions to our deeper understanding of the biblical corpus, and they could serve as appropriate paradigms for the *niftar* – there was not only the singular R. Sa'adyah Gaon, but also a larger cadre of elite rabbinic scholars with whom the *niftar* was to be identified. Specific historical details about the lives and careers of each figure were not significant in this context, but their basic orientations and major achievements most certainly were.

II

In similar fashion but to an even greater extent, the Rav felt the need to comment about the history and achievements of leading medieval rabbinic scholars in the course of his interpretations of and discourses

---

8. See *The Koren Mesorat HaRav Kinot*, ed. S. Posner (Jerusalem, 2010) [hereafter cited as KMHK], 558–59; *The Lord is Righteous in All His Ways: Reflections on the Tish'ah be-Av Kinot by Rabbi Joseph B. Soloveitchik*, ed. J. J. Schacter (New York, 2006), 305–06; *Harerei Qedem: Me-Hiddushei Torato shel Rav Yosef Dov ha-Levi Soloveitchik*, ed. M. Shurkin vol. 2 (Jerusalem, 2010), 311; and below, n. 23.
9. See e.g., *The Book of Tradition by Abraham Ibn Daud*, ed. G. D. Cohen (Philadelphia, 1967), xlvii, 101–02, 267, 280–81.

on the *qinot* of *Tishah B'Av*, just as he undertook to outline and to highlight the background of the *payyetanim* themselves. Given the weighty notion described above of retrieving and carefully describing the former glory of the religious institutions, as well as the leaders of Torah scholarship and comportment that had been lost during the *ḥurban* and other persecutions from both the ancient and medieval periods (in accordance with the talmudic and rabbinic dictum found initially in *Rosh ha-Shanah* 18b, שקולה/קשה מיתתן של צדיקים כשריפת בית א-לוהינו), the Rav felt that this imperative also included placing the authors of the various *qinot* in their historical and literary contexts.

Thus, for example, the Rav spent a great deal of time discussing and characterizing both the period and the literary achievements of Eleazar *ha-Qallir*. The Rav noted the view of *Tosafot* and other *rishonim* that Qallir was the Tanna R. Eleazar (or Eli'ezer) ben Simeon (a view that was associated with no less a figure than Rabbenu Tam), but he quickly shifted to the opinion of other *rishonim* that Qallir was more likely an Amora or one of the post-talmudic *qadmonim*, and that he lived in the sixth or seventh century CE. The Rav further noted that a number of *Tosafot* (and other passages in the literature of the *rishonim*) cite the *piyyutim* of Qallir in order to arrive at halakhic conclusions or to interpret a midrash, which indicates that Qallir was not only considered to be a great *payyetan* but also an authoritative rabbinic scholar whose *piyyutim* were to be examined quite closely in all of their literary and content aspects: "*Tosafot* quote R. Eleazar ha-Qallir many times when halakhic problems arise. Qallir was not simply a *payyetan*; he was one of the *Ḥakhmei ha-Masorah*."[10]

Indeed, the Rav pointed to a passage within one of Qallir's *qinot*, לך ה' הצדקה (that is recited toward to end of the opening unit of the *qinot* according to *minhag Ashkenaz*, all of which were composed by Qallir), which seems to suggest that Qallir lived during the tenth century, nine hundred years after the *ḥurban*. The Rav followed this proof with an even more explicit passage, found in a *qerovah* by Qallir for the חזרת

---

10. See *KMHK*, 198, 388; *The Lord is Righteous in All His Ways*, 137–38, 299; Perez Tarshish, *Ishim u-Sefarim ba-Tosafot*, ed. H. S. Neuhausen (New York, 1942), 110–12; Ruth Langer, "Kalir was a Tanna," *Hebrew Union College Annual* 67 (1996), 99–100; I. Ta-Shma, *Knesset Meḥqarim*, vol. 1 (Jerusalem, 2004), 105, 262 (n. 8), 292; vol. 3 (Jerusalem, 2005), 257–58, 290–91; and my *The Intellectual History*, 454.

הש"ץ on the morning of Tisha B'Av (אאביך ביום מביך), in which Qallir notes that nine hundred years have passed since the *ḥurban* (אאנין תשע מאות שנה), and yet the משיח has still not yet arrived. The Rav is then said to have remarked, "I do not know why historians have to explore when Qallir lived, when he himself states that nine hundred years have passed and the Messiah has not yet arrived. It means that Qallir lived in the tenth century."[11] Further historical evidence or investigation is not needed here since we have, in effect, a case of הודאת בעל דין.

The Rav perhaps preferred to locate Qallir early in the period of the *rishonim* (or just prior to that period) because this would further explain the steadfast reliance of the *rishonim* on his compositions as sources of *halakhah* on the one hand, and because Qallir then becomes, in addition, a kind of model for their own *piyyutim* and *qinot*. Qallir could be trusted to maintain absolute fealty to established halakhic practices in all of his compositions. Even as there are *halakhot* and *midrashim* reflected in Qallir's work that are seemingly unknown to us, and even though we do not always fully understand his poetic and literary constructions, the Rav's conclusion is that "there is a hardly a sentence of R. Eleazar ha-Kallir that does not reflect *halakhot* or *'aggadot* of Ḥazal." In addition, the Rav felt that Qallir "was certainly well-acquainted with the Christian arguments against Judaism especially as indicated in the *qinah* beginning הטה א‐להי אזנך, and he clearly knew the so-called Byzantine theology very well." Moreover, Qallir understood that pagans were more tolerant than

---

11. *The Lord is Righteous in All His Ways*, 138. See also *KMHK*, 386–88. Prof. J. J. Schacter drew my attention to related passages by R. Ezekiel Landau (d. 1793) and R. Solomon Judah Leib Rapoport (Shi"R, d. 1867, both of whom coincidentally served as chief rabbi of Prague). In his commentary to *Berakhot* 34a (ציון לנפש חיה [צל"ח], ד"ה דע), R. Landau asserts that the phrase in Qallir's *qerovah* for the morning of the ninth of Av, which maintained that nine hundred years had passed since the *ḥurban*, must have been inserted by a later rabbinic scholar as a means of sharpening the mourning in his own day, since in R. Landau's view (which he presents at some length), Qallir undoubtedly lived during the talmudic period. Shi"R, in a note on "the time and place" of Qallir that appeared in the periodical *Bikkurei ha-'Ittim* (1830), 100–01, contests the textual suggestion made by the בעל הצל"ח, noting that this phrase is an integral part of the literary fabric of the *qerovah* in question (and thus could not have been a later addendum), and pointing to the confirmation of the (later) period in which Qallir lived from the *qinah* לך ה' הצדקה (as the Rav did).

the Christians, which explains why the study of Torah was exiled to Babylonia after the destruction of the Temple and beyond, rather than allowing it to remain in Israel under Christian or Byzantine control (which reflected the beliefs of the Roman empire in that region). In short, whether Qallir actually lived in Israel or not, he was quite familiar with Jewish life in the Diaspora.[12]

Part of this initiative, to identify and extrapolate the historical status and religious awareness of Qallir, stems from the fact that the Rav held, as a given, that any accepted *piyyut* or *qinah* from the medieval period must have been authored by a rabbinic scholar of some note, whether or not we posses further information about the author. The deep knowledge of the biblical corpus and the larger bodies of talmudic and rabbinic teachings that the Rav often found embedded in these liturgical compositions, as he elucidated them in his comments and observations, meant that their authors had to be significant Torah scholars by definition. Only such authors were capable and worthy of composing liturgical poems – well after the period of *Anshei Knesset ha-Gedolah* – that could be included in the standard yearly liturgy of the various Jewish communities. "Later *piyyutim* were written by *Ḥakhmei Ashkenaz* and *Ḥakhmei Ẓarefat*. There is no doubt that the authors of the *piyyutim* mourning the destruction during the Crusades were of the *Ba'alei ha-Tosafot*. But the *Ḥakhmei Ashkenaz* and *Ḥakhmei Ẓarefat* were [also] the *Ḥakhmei ha-Masorah*. They were responsible not only for the *piyyutim* but also for the *shalshelet ha-qabbalah*." Thus, for example, the Rav suggested that the medieval *qinah* about the brother and sister (the son and daughter of R. Yishma'el *Kohen Gadol*) who were taken as

---

12. *The Lord is Righteous in All His Ways*, 139–41. See also *KMHK*, 266–67, 366, 378, 410–12. The Rav also felt that the language in Qallir's *qinot* for the ninth of Av became simpler as they unfolded (even within the first section of the standard Ashkenazic rite in which all of the *qinot* were composed by Qallir himself), and was surely simpler than the language of his *piyyutim* for other occasions (and in other liturgical genres), a concession perhaps to allow those who recited the *qinot* to understand them more easily. Of the *qinot* by Qallir that appeared later in the Tisha B'Av liturgy, the Rav asserted that "one would think that R. Yehudah *ha-Levi* wrote some of them, or maybe Ibn Ezra or Qalonymus or the *payyetanim* of Germany and France." It is not surprising that here again, the Rav sought to delineate an element of similarity between Qallir and other leading medieval *payyetanim*

slaves, ואת נוי חטאתי השמימה – which is attributed in one manuscript to
יחיאל – may have been composed by the Tosafist R. Yeḥi'el b. Joseph of
Paris.[13] Similarly, the Rav remarked that "the authorship of this *qinah*
[אש תוקד בקרבי בצאתי ממצרים] is unknown, but it is fairly certain that the
author was a *Rishon*."[14]

And so, in order to bring these authors alive and to recognize and
underscore their worthiness, and even more importantly, to properly
eulogize and learn from those rabbinic scholars who lived (and perished) during and after the First Crusade, along with those who were
present during other medieval persecutions and traumatic events such
as the burning of the Talmud – all of which are commemorated in
the *qinot* of *Tisha B'Av* – the Rav devoted a recognizable and larger
than usual share of his analysis of these texts to the rabbinic figures
who were involved, and to their learning and literary achievements.

III

In doing so, however, it is my contention that with regard to the
German and northern French rabbinic figures from the period of the

---

13. See *The Lord is Righteous in All His Ways*, 298–99; and *KMHK*, 442. As
    I have demonstrated in chapter five of my *The Intellectual History and
    Rabbinic Culture of Medieval Ashkenaz* (375–443), a very large number
    of the *piyyutim* (including *qinot*) that were produced in Ashkenaz were
    composed by Tosafists, although there were also a number of *ḥazzanim* and
    other specialists who composed only *piyyutim* as far as we can tell. See *ibid*,
    22–23 (n. 83), and 442 (n. 333).
14. See *KMHK*, 520. The Rav derived further support for his larger contention
    from the fact that in this second section of the standard Ashkenazic rite of
    the *qinot* in which quite a number of medieval *qinot* begin to appear, these
    are interspersed with *qinot* by Qallir, in much the same way that the *qinot*
    in this section range from those about the destruction of the Temple to the
    impact of the First Crusade, to the suffering of individuals at that time of the
    ḥurban, and then back to the suffering in the communities of the Rhineland
    in 1096. These various authors and themes are thus meant to appear to be
    of equal footing and import. It should be noted that אש תוקד בקרבי appears
    to be of Sefardic origin, even as the identity of its author remains unclear.
    It was, however, included in western European Ashkenazic liturgies for the
    ninth of Av already by the thirteenth century, even as these rites recognized
    (and sometimes even noted) that it came from the Sefardic realm. See e.g.,
    ms. Vatican Ebr. 312, fol. 61r; ms. Parma (de Rossi) 635, sec. 22; and ms.
    Prague (National Library), VI EA 2.

First Crusade and beyond – the Tosafists of the twelfth and thirteenth centuries and other *Ḥakhmei Ashkenaz* to whom he refers in his comments on the *qinot* – the Rav displays an almost uncanny awareness, owing to his unparalleled mastery of the talmudic literature from this period, of certain phenomena and aspects of the intellectual history of the period, including a series of important works that are no longer extant. As we shall see below, the existence and impact of these works and their authors have been highlighted by contemporary scholarship and academic literature and research only within the last thirty five years or so (and much of it only in the last two decades), long after the Rav first put forward his interpretations of the *qinot*. For someone who did not always seem to be particularly interested in the details and specifics of literary history, the Rav, in his comments to the *qinot*, offered some remarkable insights that were very much ahead of their time.

A final introductory comment is necessary, in order to place what follows into its fullest intellectual context and to further highlight what is unique. In his regular shiurim and talmudic analyses, the Rav did not typically search for unusual positions or views that did not appear in the standard, extant canon of medieval talmudic commentary. Following his grandfather R. Ḥayyim (whose library was not known to be particularly extensive, for one of two possible reasons – either because the Brisker practice that required checking each page of a rabbinic tome for ḥameẓ before Pesach would have rendered the possession of a large library as overly onerous and burdensome or, more likely, because the economic situation at that time did not allow for the acquisition of many books beyond the standard volumes that a leading European *talmid ḥakham* absolutely needed to possess – the Rav actually offered both of these reasons himself, although it is clear that the second one is the more compelling), the Rav did not cite variant texts of *rishonim* or little-known (or newly published) texts very often.

As many other leading rabbinic scholars did, the Rav made his case with the "standard *rishonim*" that anyone in early twentieth-century Europe (including his immediate predecessors) might have had available to them.[15] Although this notion of basing talmudic scholarship

---

15. A perusal of the detailed index to *Igrot ha-Grid* illustrates this point quite
    well. In addition to many references to *Gemara, Rashi, Tosafot* (as well

on widely known and available texts rather than on lesser known texts or variants was especially valued with regard to halakhic decision-making (and is sometimes referred to as הכור המבחן של ההלכה), the Rav (and his ancestors) followed this pattern as well with regard to talmudic *ḥiddushim* and other new insights that were beyond matters of practical *halakhah*.[16] In light of its privileged place and the role in the Brisker *derekh* (and perhaps the fact that Maimonides and his followers were always concerned that the most accurate text of this work be available to all), Maimonides' *Mishneh Torah* is virtually the only classical text for which variant (manuscript) readings were welcomed and even sought out.

---

as R. Samson of Sens' commentary to *Zera'im* and *Tahorot*), Rambam (including Rabad's glosses to *Mishneh Torah*), *Arba'ah Turim* and *Shulḥan 'Arukh*, Ramban's talmudic *ḥiddushim* (and his *Milḥamot* commentary on Alfasi's *Halakhot*, as well as his Torah commentary) are frequently cited, as are the *Ḥiddushim* of Rashba, *Hilkhot ha-Rif*, *Pisqei ha-Rosh* and the *Sefer ha-Ma'or* by R. Zeraḥyah *ha-Levi*. There are a handful of references to *Ḥiddushei ha-Ritva* (the Rav once remarked that he did not see a printed version of these *ḥiddushim* until 1959), but any remaining *rishonim* are cited only once or twice. Of the two citations of *Sefer Mordekhai*, for example, the Rav notes that one was cited *la-halakhah* by R. Moses Isserles (Ramo); and the second was cited by the Rav's father, R. Moshe Soloveitchik, to confirm a new interpretation that the Rav had suggested for a *Tosafot* passage. The single Meiri passage cited by the Rav (see above, n. 5) was cited from memory, and he was unsure as to whether it was from Meiri's *Beit ha-Beḥirah* or from Ritva's *ḥiddushim* (והנה בריטב"א או במאירי, ואין הספרים תחת ידי ולא אוכל לדעת על נכון וכו'; this appears to indeed be a citation from *Beit ha-Beḥirh* to *Bezah* 5a). In several additional instances, the words of an otherwise un-cited *rishon* were presented to the Rav by a questioner for his opinion of their interpretation or meaning. In the index to the latest volume of *Harerei Qedem*, ed. M. Shurkin (Jerusalem, 2013), which presents the Rav's *shiurim* to מסכת שבת, the citation patterns of *Ḥiddushei ha-Ritva* and *Sefer Mordekhai* are virtually identical, although there is a bit more usage of Meiri's *Beit ha-Beḥirah*.

16. See the exchange between Rabbi Z. A. Yehudah and Prof. S. Z. Leiman on the attitude of the *Ḥazon Ish* toward the use of manuscripts and newly discovered rabbinic and halakhic works of yore in *Tradition* 18 (1980), 372–78, and 19 (1981), 301–10. One of the few instances in which the Rav cites and discusses the interpretation of a lesser-known *rishon* is his extensive treatment of a passage in the Torah commentary known as *Ḥizzequni* (composed by R. Hezekiah b. Manoaḥ in northern France, c. 1275), regarding the form to be employed for framing the *sefirat ha-'omer*, and its relationship to the counting of the years in the *shemitah* cycle. See *Mesorah* 1 (1989), 11–16.

We now turn directly to the Rav's interpretation of the *qinot*, initially in order to review his theories about the authors of the *qinot* that were composed in medieval Ashkenaz, but ultimately to discuss his comments about the centers of Torah study in Ashkenaz and the literature that was produced in them. The Rav attributes the first *qinah* about the First Crusade found in the standard East European liturgy, החרישו ממני ואדברה, to R. Meir b. Yeḥi'el, "who was, in all likelihood, one of the German Tosafists." There is no independent literary or an-ecdotal evidence to support this suggestion – modern scholarship has generally concluded that this *qinah* was composed anonymously – but the Rav apparently felt that this *qinah* about the events of 1096 was a continuation, in both style and approach, of *Arzei ha-Levanon*, the *qinah* that is found immediately prior in the standard liturgy for the ninth of Av which describes the עשרה הרוגי מלכות, the ten great Torah scholars who were martyred by the Romans, and which was certainly composed by R. Meir b. Yeḥ'iel.[17]

The author of the second *qinah* about that Crusade, מי יתן ראשי מים, "was the famous Qalonymus ben Yehudah, the *payyetan* . . . He was a member of a family of *payyetanim*, an Italian family that settled in Germany." Rashi to *Beizah* (24b, s.v. *ule-'erev*) notes that he received a letter from Worms stating that a great scholar named R. Qalonymus (b. Shabbetai), who was thoroughly knowledgeable in the entire Talmud (בקי בכל הש"ס), had arrived there from Rome; the Rav assumed that the *payyetan* Qalonymus ben Yehudah (*ha-baḥur*) of Worms was a descendant of the R. Qalonymus mentioned by Rashi.[18] Although

---

17. See *KMHK*, 414, 418, 430; *The Lord is Righteous in All His Ways*, 258; and cf. below, n. 23. Alter Velner, '*Aseret Harugei Malkhut ba-Midrash uba-Piyyut* (Jerusalem, 2005), 344, cites *Ozar ha-Gedolim*, which asserts that R. Meir b. Yeḥi'el lived in Halle (סולו, in Saxony) c. 1190, and that *Arzei ha-Levanon* is the only *piyyut* that he composed. Leopold Zunz, *Literaturgeschichte der synagogalen poesie* (Berlin, 1865), 488–89, lists several additional *piyyutim* under his name including a גאולה for parashat Yitro (מלא רחמים כזקן נגלה הורות); an אהבה for *Shabbat Shirah* (מעודד עניס היס בקעת במים רבים); and another *qinah* (משכנותיך א־להים החריבו מחרימי הרג ולא חמל). See also the description of ms. Bodl. 1151, according to the catalogue of the Institute for Microfilmed Hebrew Manuscripts at the Jewish National Library (film #11611): יוצרות בלתי שכיחים לכל השנה כולל מר' חיים פלטיאל, ר' מאיר מסולי, ר' שמואל ממרזבוך, ור' שמואל הכהן. In the context of this group of authors, R. Meir of Halle would seem to have lived somewhat later than 1190.

18. See *The Lord is Righteous in All His Ways*, 258; and *KMHK*, 460.

these two rabbinic figures were both members of the prestigious Qal-onymide clan that originated in Italy and held sway in the Rhineland (and especially in Mainz) during the tenth and eleventh centuries, it is difficult at best to confirm that they were closely or directly related.[19] Qalonymus b. Yehudah (d. 1126) clearly survived the First Crusade, but there is no evidence that he was also a talmudic scholar of note, even as the Rav assumes, as was his wont, that he must have been. Qalonymus b. Yehudah was also the author of the third *qinah* in the standard East European liturgy about the First Crusade, אמרתי שעו מני בבכי אמרר.[20]

The Rav identifies three distinct tragedies that are recorded and remarked upon in R. Qalonymus b. Judah's *Mi Yitein Roshi Mayym*: (1) the pogroms in קהילות שו"ם (Speyer, Worms and Mainz), which killed thousands of people, among whom were the greatest Torah scholars of the day; (2) the destruction of בתי מדרש ובתי כנסיות, which constituted

---

19. See Avraham Grossman, *Ḥakhmei Ashkenaz ha-Rishonim* (Jerusalem, 1981), 37–38 (n. 44), 348–54, 379–80 (n. 83); and see also Zunz, *Literaturges-chichte*, 164, n. 11. R. Qalonymus of Rome produced materials in the realms of rabbinic and liturgical studies, including several *piyyutim* and a large number of *piyyut* comments; he was apparently killed על קידוש השם in Worms in 1096. See I. Ta-Shma, *Knesset Meḥqarim*, 1:7. *The Lord is Righteous* (above n. 17) maintains that Qalonymus b. Judah "wrote the *piyyutim* מלך עליון and אמרו לא-להים for Rosh ha-Shanah, and many *piyyutim* for Yom Kippur," details that are also not easily confirmed. See the next note.

20. On this *qinah*, see below, n. 64. For R. Qalonymus b. Judah's *seliḥah* for the morning of Yom Kippur, אדברה תחנונים כרש ואבכה, see *Maḥzor le-Yamim Nora'im*, ed. D. Goldschmidt, 2:277; and see ibid, 2:646–47, for his *se-liḥah* for *minḥah*, את הקול קול יעקב נוהם / בידי רשע בהם מתלהם, which is about the events of 1096. For R. Qalonymus' *qinot* on 1096, see also Avraham David, "Zikhronot ve-He'arot 'al Gezerot Tatn"u – bi-Defus ube-Kitvei Yad 'Ivriyyim," *Yehudim mul ha-Ẓelav*, ed. Y. T. Assis et al. (Jerusalem, 2000), 198 (secs. 13, 14, 18); A. M. Habermann, *Gezerot Ashkenaz ve-Ẓarefat* (Jerusalem, 1945), 63–69; and Susan Einbinder, *Beautiful Death: Jewish Poetry and Martyrdom in Medieval France* (Princeton, 2003), 83–84, 163. Qalonymus' unpublished *seliḥah* for the eve of Rosh ha-Shanah (ממעמקי איום קראתיך) is a direct imitation of Rabbenu Gershom b. Judah of Mainz' *Zekhor Brit* composition for that day (with the double refrain, והשב שבות אהלי יעקב/ושוב ברחמים על שארית ישראל); see Daniel Goldschmidt, *Meḥqerei Tefillah u-Piyyut* (Jerusalem, 1980), 341. Qalonymus composed approximately thirty *piyyutim* all told, most of which are penitential or commemorative compositions. See Zunz, *Literaturgeschichte*, 165–66; 255–56; and my *The Intellectual History and Rabbinic Culture of Medieval Ashkenaz*, 391–92.

persecution aimed against the study of Torah as a religious act; (3) and the physical destruction of *sifrei Torah* and books of the Talmud.[21] R. Qalonymus had undoubtedly visited Mainz, Worms and Speyer in the days when there used to be impressive Torah assemblies there. He survived the massacres (of the First Crusade) and came back to the places where just a few years earlier, he had seen much Torah study, many Torah lectures and many *yeshivot*. He visits the same places after the destruction and he asks, "Where are the Torah scholars? What happened to them? Where did they disappear to . . . what happened between my last visit and now? Behold, her place is desolate with none to dwell therein."[22]

The Rav perceptively notes that these *qinot* on the events of 1096 were a thematic continuation of *Arzei ha-Levanon*, the *qinah* for the ten (Tannaitic) martyrs composed by R. Meir b. Yeḥ'iel; the content, idea and basic nature of the catastrophe are the same. In both larger instances, the deaths in reality involved a double disaster, the killing of many Jewish people which included the greatest scholars among them. In the case of the Crusades, in which 'hundreds of thousands' of people were killed, the Crusaders also effectively destroyed Torah scholarship in Germany. In light of the principle of שקולה מיתת צדיקים כשריפת בית א-להינו, if the *Beit ha-Miqdash* was sacred, how much more sacred were entire Jewish communities that consisted of thousands of scholars?[23] The Rav perhaps arrived at these inflated figures through a comparison to the even greater magnitude of the losses during the Holocaust; he notes elsewhere in his *qinot* commentaries that *Ḥazal* themselves often mixed historical events and metaphors. Indeed, the Rav asserts early on that "the *payyetan* does not distinguish between the *galut* of the Ten Tribes by Sennacherib, the *galut* of the First Temple by Nebuchadnezzar or the *galut* of the Second Temple by the Romans. The *kinah* (Qallir's שבת סורו מני) is not interested in classifying the events

---

21. See *KMHK*, 464. Note also that the *payyetan* includes here a list of several areas or bodies of Torah study that became desolate: התורה והמקרא והמשנה והאגדה ענו וקוננו זאת להגידה אי תורה ותלמוד והלומדה. It would appear, as expanded upon in the prayer commentary of R. Eleazar of Worms (cited from ms. Paris BN 772, in '*Arugat ha-Bosem le-R. Avraham b.'Azri'el*. ed. E. E. Urbach, vol. 4 [Jerusalem, 1963], 411) that the term *miqra* included in this *qinah* connotes נ"ך as a distinct area of study.
22. See *The Lord is Righteous in All His Ways*, 297–98.
23. See *The Lord is Righteous in All His Ways*, 258–59; and *KMHK*, 430–31.

chronologically; it deliberately moves from event to event and from period to period, spreading an identity of events and destiny over thousands of years."[24] In any case, as the Rav suggests, the death of righteous people is often even more devastating than the destruction of the physical *Beit ha-Mikdash*, and is thus understandably given to conflation as well.[25]

IV

In the course of his interpretations of the *piyyutim* that memorialized the First Crusade of 1096 and its impact, the Rav undertook a lengthy discussion about the locations of Torah study in northern Europe during the twelfth and thirteenth centuries, the period of the Tosafists: "The first center of Torah in Europe was in Germany, not France, and the school of the Tosafists in Germany was older and more numerous than the Tosafists in France. Speyer, Mainz and Worms were densely populated with *Gedolei Yisra'el*. Yet we hardly know any of them. We know that they had traditions from Rabbenu Gershom (Mainz,

---

24. See *KMHK*, 207–08; and below, n. 57.
25. See *The Lord is Righteous in All His Ways*, 260; and *KMHK*, *ibid*. The Rav further noted that the purpose of the *qinot* in describing the deaths of the leading Torah scholars who were known as the עשרה הרוגי מלכות was to fuel and augment the *'avelut* of Tisha B'Av; this was different than describing their deaths during the *selihot* portion of the *Musaf* of Yom Kippur (in the *selihah* אלה אזכרה), which was intended to achieve *kapparah* (as per *Mo'ed Qatan* 28a, מיתת צדיקים מכפרת). As such, the *qinah* for the ninth of Av begins with a very explicit statement about the greatness of these scholars in learning, ארזי הלבנון אדירי התורה בעלי תריסין במשנה ובגמרא, to stress that the loss of these צדיקים is intensified by the strength of their erudition in Torah study. Here again, we find the notion that fully appreciating what the Jewish people once had serves to heighten the *'avelut* at the point of loss. See *The Lord is Righteous in All His Ways*, 255–56; *KMHK*, 418–19; and *Harerei Qedem*, 2:309. In commenting on the fourth and final *qinah* about the First Crusade found in the standard liturgy for the ninth of Av, אבל אעורר אנינות אגרר אויה אויה לי (by R. Menaḥem b. Makhir, a member of another illustrious Ashkenazic rabbinic family of the eleventh century; cf. below, n. 30), the Rav pointed out that "it is noteworthy that there are four *qinot* describing the Crusades, but only one *qinah*, ארזי הלבנון, for the Ten Martyrs." See *KMHK*, 534. On p. 533, a stylistic similarity between this *qinah* and the one before it, אצבעותי שפלו ואשיותי נפלו (by R. Barukh of Mainz) is also noted. Regarding R. Barukh and his *qinah*, see also below, n. 46.

d. 1028), Rabbenu Ḥanan'el (Kairwan, d. 1056) and R. Hai Gaon
(Baghdad, d. 1038), and we know R. Ya'akov b. Yaqar, the teacher
of Rashi [in Mainz, and a direct student of Rabbenu Gershom; Rashi
died in 1105], and Rabbi Yizḥak *ha-Levi* [Rashi's teacher in Worms],
but few other names and teachings have survived. The Torah scholars
of Germany perished at the hands of the Crusaders, and their centers
and many of their writings were destroyed." The Rav pointed to a
passage in *Pisqei ha-Rosh*, מעשה אירע במגנצא בשנת תתק"ה [1145] שתקע התוקע
פעמים תשר"ק ובשלישי תקע ב' שברים, which discusses a "famous controversy"
about blowing shofar that took place in Mainz and "mentions the
names of the *Gedolei Yisra'el* who were involved in the controversy
[R. Elyaqim b. Yosef and his son-in-law R. Eliezer b. Nathan (Raban)
are mentioned, along with other unnamed members of the *qahal*], and
all of them were killed."[26]

It should be noted that Raban, who lived in Mainz, was born shortly
before 1090, and was thus a young lad during the First Crusade.
Nonetheless, he refers to the First Crusade several times in his *Sefer
Raban/Even ha-'Ezer* as הגזירה ("the decree"), which indicates that he
considered this event to be a watershed in terms of both the halakhic
and communal histories of German Jewry.[27] This was perhaps what

---

26. See *The Lord is Righteous in All His Ways*, 260; and *KMHK*, 431, and
    463 (which emphasizes the presence of many early Tosafists in Speyer). The
    reference to the passage from *Pisqei ha-Rosh* is found only in *The Lord
    is Righteous*, where it is identified as *Rosh ha-Shanah*, 4:14. It appears,
    however, that the intended section in *Pisqei ha-Rosh* is 4:11. See also *Harerei
    Qedem*, ed. Shurkin, vol. 1 (Jerusalem, 2000), 34–39 (sections 19–20); and
    Sefer Raban, sec. 61. *Pisqei ha-Rosh le-Rosh ha*-Shanah, 4:14 mentions
    a number of German figures in connection with *Rosh ha-Shanah* rituals
    and practices. These include R. Isaac b. Judah (of Mainz, d. c. 1084–1090)
    and R. Meshullam b. Qalonymus (also of Mainz, d. 1095), concerning the
    reciting of שהחיינו over the *shofar* on the second day of Rosh ha-Shanah,
    which can be covered by intending this blessing for a new fruit as well (a
    solution that was later championed by R. Meir of Rothenburg, d. 1293).
    These figures are then followed by R. Isaac b. Judah and R. Isaac (b. Eli'ezer)
    ha-Levi of Worms (d. c. 1075–1080) regarding the recitation of והשיאנו on
    Rosh ha-Shanah (who in turn are followed by positions in the name of later
    German rabbinic figures, R. She'alti'el and Rabiah, d.c. 1225). This passage
    contains groupings of pre-Crusade German rabbinic scholars who died prior
    to the First Crusade, as well as a smaller number of later German scholars;
    but there is no reference here to any kind of public controversy.
27. See Joseph Hacker, "Li-Gezerat Tatn"u (1096)," *Zion* 31 (1966), 225–26.

prompted the Rav to make the assessment of Raban that he did –
Raban was a German Tosafist who was deeply affected by the First
Crusade, even as he ultimately survived it. As it turns out Raban's
father-in-law R. Elyaqim (who was born around 1070 and was also
one of Raban's main teachers) was already an active rabbinic scholar
in Mainz at the time of the First Crusade, although he too managed
to survive.[28]

In any event, the Rav continues by making the larger point that
when "we come across the names of *Ba'alei ha-Tosafot* in Ashkenaz,
we do not know who they were. They simply died young and their
manuscripts were destroyed. We have only a little quoted by Rashi
and, much later, by the Maharam of Rothenburg and the Rosh. We
have the ראבי"ה [the first part of whose *Even ha-'Ezer* or *Sefer Rabiah*
was published from a Bodleian manuscript beginning only in the late
nineteenth century, with the publication process being concluded only
quite recently], and the *Or Zarua'* [by R. Isaac b. Moses of Vienna, d.
c. 1250, about half of which was first published in Zhitomir in 1862,
and the rest only later], and we have a few statements mentioned by
the ראב"ן and the ריב"ן. But otherwise we have nothing, because they
were destroyed."[29]

Raban composed several *qinot* about the events of 1096, as well as a lengthy
and poignant chronicle. See Urbach, *Ba'alei ha-Tosafot* (Jerusalem, 1980),
1:182–83; my *The Intellectual History*, 396–97; and below, at n. 50.

28. On the date of R. Elyaqim's birth, see Avigdor Aptowitzer, *Mavo la-Rabiah*
(reprinted, Jerusalem, 1984), 48. Raban refers to an episode in 1152, in
which he had a dream involving his recently departed father-in-law and
teacher, R. Elyaqim. See my "Dreams as a Determinant of Jewish Law and
Practice in Northern Europe during the High Middle Ages," *Studies in
Medieval Jewish Intellectual and Social History in Honor of Robert Chazan*,
ed. D. Engel et al. (Leiden, 2012), 112–13. As such, R. Elyaqim died at some
point between 1145 and 1152.

29. See *The Lord is Righteous in All His Ways*, 260–61. R. Judah b. Nathan (ריב"ן)
was a son-in-law of Rashi; he is mentioned by the Rav just below as a representative of the new French center, along with Rashi's grandson Rabbenu Tam
and his great-grandson Ri. It is unclear whether Rivan hailed from Germany,
but he did have access to פירושי רבינו גרשום ומנגצא and may have studied there
as well. See Urbach, *Ba'alei ha-Tosafot*, 1:38–41; and I. Ta-Shma, *Ha-Sifrut
ha-Parshanit la-Talmud*, 1:52:53. Perhaps the reference at this point is to the
early German Tosafist ריב"א, R. Isaac b. Asher *ha-Levi* of Speyer [*ha-Zaqen*] (d.
1133); see Ta-Shma, *ibid*, 1:66–70; my *The Intellectual History and Rabbinic
Culture of Medieval Ashkenaz*, 18–19; and below, n. 42.

The Rav goes on to note that even though the center of Torah in Germany was destroyed, the in-depth study of Torah fortuitously survived because newer centers had already been established in France – "Rabbenu Tam, the Ri and the Rivan were already French scholars, not German. It was an absolute miracle that once Germany was destroyed, France began to emerge as a center of Torah. By that time, people who wanted to study Torah had to go to France." Rashi, who was a student prior to the period of the First Crusade, was forced to travel from France to Germany (owing to the paucity of such opportunities in northern France) to study under the *Hakhmei Ashkenaz*. As noted above, he went to Mainz and Worms to study with R. Ya'akov b. Yaqar and R. Yizhaq *ha-Levi* because "Rabbenu Makhir and Rabbenu Gershom had established a center of Torah there."[30]

Having received excellent training in Germany, Rashi returned to his native northern France "and built it up and established it as a center of Torah ... And then, because of the destruction wrought by the Crusades, the movement began to go in the opposite direction. The Torah centers in Germany were wiped out, and instead of traveling from France to Germany as Rashi did, the generations following Rashi had to leave Germany to go to France ... to study in the *yeshivot* of Rashbam, Rabbenu Tam (d. 1171), Ri (d. 1189) and R. Yehi'el of Paris (d.c. 1260) ... In time, France became the center of Jewish wisdom. We have no *Tosafot* on *Shas* from Germany; *Tosafot Tukh* is all French. By the time of Rabbenu Tam, there was already a strong school in northern France." The Rav concludes his historical survey by noting that "the *Ba'alei ha-Tosafot* in Germany were annihilated during the First, Second, and Third Crusades ... The Second Crusade, in approximately 1146, affected French Jewry as well. Many Jews were killed, but there was no total destruction as in Germany."[31]

---

30. See A. Grossman, *Hakhmei Ashkenaz*, 102–05, 362–64. Rabbenu Gershom had a brother named Makhir who was, in the view of some, the progenitor of the so-called *Bnei Makhir*, a family of important German rabbinic figures during the late eleventh century.
31. See *The Lord is Righteous in All His Ways*, 261–62; and *KMHK*, 431–32. Although the number of Jews killed overall during the Second Crusade was significantly smaller than those who perished during the First Crusade, the Second Crusade nonetheless affected Germany (and particularly the area around Wurzburg) to a larger extent than it did northern France. The Third Crusade (c. 1190) affected English Jewry in the main, but a series of pogroms

The Rav also discussed the burning of the Talmud in 1242 and the implications for Torah study. He linked this tragedy to events that had occurred during the First Crusade – as described by R. Qalonymus b. Yehudah in his *qinah*, מי יתן ראשי מים – in which both *sifrei Torah* and volumes of the Talmud were burnt (וביום נתינתה כמו כן אז חזרה, עלתה לה למרום למקום מדורה, עם תיקה ונרתיקה והדורשה והחוקרה, לומדיה ושוניה באישון כמו אורה). Given that books of Jewish learning during this period existed only in manuscript form and were rather costly to produce, there was a real and imminent danger that Torah knowledge would be lost whenever book burnings occurred. Books could not simply be reproduced via printing, and although there were Jews endeavored to know all of the subject matter contained in them by heart, learning could not continue unabated in the face of the destruction of large numbers of books.[32]

Thus, "the famous Maharam of Rothenburg," whom the Rav notes was the last of the *Ba'alei ha-Tosafot* and the teacher of R. Asher b.

---

and persecutions that occurred in Germany (and to a lesser extent in northern France) before and after 1190 are often referred to as Crusade-related, at least in popular terms. See e.g. Robert Chazan, *Medieval Stereotypes and Modern Antisemitism* (Berkeley, 1997), 53–78; and Judith Baskin, "Rereading the Sources: New Visions of Women in Medieval Ashkenaz," *Textures and Meanings*, ed. L. H. Ehrlich et al. (Amherst, 2006), 299–301 (regarding the wife and daughters of R. Eleazar of Worms who were killed in 1196). Those Tosafists who died 'al Kiddush ha-Shem during the twelfth century (in both France and Germany), can be traced in Urbach's *Ba'alei ha-Tosafot*. See pp. 119 (R. Solomon b. Yosef of Falaise, the brother-in-law of Rabbenu Tam); 142, 145 (two students of Rabbenu Tam, R. Jacob of Orleans and R. Yom Tov of Joigny, both of whom had gone to England and were killed there c. 1190; and see also 149–50 for R. Jacob of Corbeil); 225 (Rabbenu Peter b. Yosef, a student of Rashbam and Rabbenu Tam, who hailed from Austria and died during the Second Crusade); 253 (Ri's son R. Elḥanan, d. 1182); 338 (Ri's student, R. Solomon b. Judah of Dreux; cf. below n. 59); 367, Riva *ha-Baḥur* of Speyer, grandson of Riva *ha-zaqen*, who perished in Wurzburg in 1196, at the same time as R. Eleazar of Worms' family); 375 (for suggestive references to *qiddush ha-Shem* among the Tannaim, as found in *Sefer Yiḥusei Tanna'im va-Amora'im* by Rivaq of Speyer, d. 1199); 388 (R. Uri, a brother of Rabiah, who was burned at the stake in 1216); 432 (a student of R. Barukh of Mainz, d. 1221, who perished 'al Kiddush ha-Shem); and see also below, n. 46. Cf. S. Einbinder, *Beautiful Death*, 55–59, and my *The Intellectual History*, 400 (nn. 104, 106), 408–09 (n. 144), for passages that commemorate the burning of two otherwise unknown rabbinic scholars who may have been Tosafist students of Rashbam and Rabbenu Tam.

32. See *KMHK*, 464.

Yeḥi'el (Rosh), "considered this tragedy [of the burning of the Talmud in 1242] to be a major catastrophe, for without these manuscripts . . . the תורה שבעל פה would indeed be forgotten, or at least would become limited to a very small group of people." As described above (at n. 29), the Rav identified both Maharam and Rosh as among those few Ashkenazic rabbinic scholars who cited material from the virtually un-known *Ba'alei ha-Tosafot* of Germany, whose works were destroyed or otherwise lost.

According to the Rav, one can palpably sense Maharam's fear in his *qinah* for Tisha B'Av, שאלי שרופה באש (which the Rav also pointed out was an imitation of R. Yehudah *ha-Levi*'s ציון הלא תשאלי לשלום אסיריך in terms of both its style and construction),[33] that the Torah might well come to be forgotten. "He and the other Torah scholars of his time considered this to be a catastrophe of a magnitude perhaps far greater and more menacing than the destruction of the Holy of Holies. Ma-haram equated the catastrophe of the burning of the Talmud with the burning of the *Beit ha-Mikdash* – without the תורה שבעל פה, there is no כנסת ישראל. In fact, it was one of the greatest miracles in Jewish history that in spite of the burning of the Talmud, the תורה שבעל פה did survive and was not forgotten." On the contrary, the tragic burning of the Talmud motivated the Jews to renewed commitment and dedication, and they devoted their financial resources and efforts to recopying the lost manuscripts. [34]

V

Is there any evidence for the "lost writings of the German Tosafists" to which the Rav referred – with great concern and poignancy – in his comments on the *qinot*? Recent research has been able to identify and to retrieve isolated passages and even some larger remnants from a number of German *Tosafot* collections that have essentially been lost, or that have survived only in fragmentary form. These include *Tosafot R. Eli'ezer mi-Metz* (d. 1198);[35] *Tosafot R. Yehudah b. Qalo-*

---

33. On these similarities, see above, n. 7; and below, n. 52.
34. See *The Lord is Righteous in All His Ways*, 287–88; *KMHK*, 594. See also J. Woolf, "Historiyyah ve-Toda'ah Historit," (above, n. 1), 336; and my "Al Noshaḥ u-Meqorah shel Tefillah Av ha-Raḥamim," *Yeshurun* 27 (2012), 878.
35. See Simcha Emanuel, *Shivrei Luḥot: Sefarim Avudim shel Ba'alei ha-Tosafot*

nymus (*Rivaq,*) *mi-Shpira* (d. 1199, author of *Sefer Yiḥusei Tanna'im va-Amora'im*);[36] *Tosafot R. Shmu'el b. Natronai* and *Tosafot R. Yo'el ha-Levi* (d. c. 1200);[37] *Tosafot R. Barukh b. Shmu'el mi-Magenẓa* (d. 1221);[38] *Tosafot Rabbenu Simḥah mi-Shpira* (d. c. 1230);[39] *Tosafot R. Mosheh Taku* (d. c. 1235, author of *Ktav Tamim*);[40] and *Tosafot R. Eleazar mi-Vermaiza* (d. 1237, author of *Sefer Roqeaḥ*).[41] As the Rav had theorized, these various German *Tosafot* collections were either destroyed or lost outright, or were at some point discarded or ignored in favor of the *Tosafot* collections from northern France (which further contributed to their near total loss). Indeed, all that remains from the *Tosafot* of R. Isaac b. Asher *ha-Zaqen* (*Riva ha-Levi*) of Speyer (d. 1133), who was arguably the first Tosafist overall, are fragments and some longer passages that are cited by the collections of French *Tosafot* to several tractates of the Talmud.[42]

(Jerusalem, 2006), 293–97. Although R. Eli'ezer (author of *Sefer Yere'im*) was a student of Rabbenu Tam, Metz is a border locale that (moved in and out of the Holy Roman Empire and) often reflected German (or Rhenish) *minhagim*, and R. Eli'ezer's students were, for the most part, of German origin. See Urbach, *Ba'alei ha-Tosafot*, 1:25, 152–64; *Ta-Shma, Ha-Sifrut ha-Parshanit la-Talmud*, 1:82; Emanuel, *Shivrei Luḥot*, 105–08, 127–29; and Avraham (Rami) Reiner, "Rabbenu Tam: Rabbotav (ha-Ẓarefatim ve-Talmidav Bnei Ashkenaz," M. A. thesis, Hebrew University, 1997), 105–13.

36. See Urbach, *Ba'alei ha-Tosafot*, 1:378; and Ta-Shma, *Ha-Sifrut ha-Parshanit la-Talmud*. 2:118.

37. These were both sons-in-law of Raban; see Avigdor Aptowitzer, *Mavo la-Rabiah*, 46–47; Urbach, *Ba'alei ha-Tosafot*, 1:211–12; and Emanuel, *Shivrei Luḥot*, 60–61, 81–86. Emanuel also makes note of the *Tosafot* by R. Yo'el's teacher, R. Moses b. Yo'el of Regensburg, and those composed by R. Moses' son, R. Abraham.

38. See Emanuel, *Shivrei Luḥot*, 112–23.

39. See Ta-Shma, *Ha-Sifrut ha-Parshanit la-Talmud*, 2:116; and Emanuel, *Shivrei Luḥot*, 157.

40. See Ta-Shma, *ibid*; and Emanuel, *Shivrei Luḥot*, 315 (n. 34).

41. See Ta-Shma, *ibid*; and Emanuel, *R. Eleazar mi-Vermaiza—Derashah le-Pesaḥ* (Jerusalem, 2006), 50–51. For the *Tosafot* of R. Meir of Rothenburg, much of which are no longer extant, see Urbach, *Ba'alei ha-Tosafot*, 2:563–64; Emanuel, *Shivrei Luḥot*, 41–43; and Binyamin Richler, "Kitvei Yad shel ha-Tosafot 'al ha-Talmud," *Sefer Zikkaron li-Prof. Y. M. Ta-Shma*, ed. M. Idel et al. (Alon Shvut, 2011), 789 (secs. 55–56).

42. See my *The Intellectual History and Rabbinic Culture of Medieval Ashkenaz*, 2–9; Yaakov Lifshitz, "Mavo le-Tosafot ha-Riva," *Sanhedrei Gedolah le-Massekhet Sanhedrin*, vol. 1, ed. Y. Lifshitz (Jerusalem, 1968), editor's

Moreover, a series of voluminous halakhic works composed by German Tosafists during the late twelfth and early thirteenth centuries have also been lost in large measure. Among these no longer extant German compendia are *Sefer Arba'ah Panim* by R. Ephraim of Regensburg (d. 1175);[43] *Sefer ha-Ḥokhmah* by R. Barukh of Mainz;[44] and *Seder 'Olam* by R. Simḥah of Speyer (d. 1230).[45] As the Rav had suggested, these are extensive, in-depth works from outstanding German *talmidei ḥakhamim* whom we barely know for the most part, even though they too were bona fide Tosafists who were considered to be of great importance in their own day.

In addition, the Rav's firm sense about the authors of the *qinot* from the medieval period, that many of them were *Ba'alei ha-Tosafot* (and Germany Tosafists at that), can also be confirmed in this context. Found within the standard East European *qinot* liturgy for Tisha B'Av are selections by R. Barukh b. Samuel of Mainz, the author of *Sefer ha-Ḥokhmah*, who also served as a leading *dayyan* on the Mainz *beit din* – his *qinah,* אצבעותי שפלו ואשיותי נפלו אויה, בני ציון גלו וכל אויבי שלו

---

introduction, 16–29; and above, n. 29.

43. See Emanuel, *Shivrei Luḥot*, 289–91. Cf. below, n. 53.

44. See *ibid*, 123–39.

45. See *ibid*, 158–66. A number of pieces from *Seder 'Olam*, along with material by R. Simḥah's student, R. Samuel b. Abraham of Worms (known as R. Bonfant), were published in *Teshuvot u-Pesaqim me'et Ḥakhmei Ashkenaz ve-Ẓarefat*, ed. E. Kupfer (Jerusalem, 1993), from ms. Bodl. 692. An extensive collection of halakhic rulings and other comments following the order of the portions of the Torah, by another of R. Simḥa's students, R. Avidgdor b. Elijah Katz of Vienna (found in ms. British Library 243 and ms. Hamburg 45) was published only in 1996 in Jerusalem (by Machon Harerei Qedem), under the title *Perushim u-Pesaqim le-Rabbenu Avigdor Ẓarefati*. These works can be contrasted with two of the very few large-scale German works of this period that have survived, *Sefer Rabiah* and *Sefer Or Zaru'a* (both as noted by the Rav above, at n. 29), whose author, R. Isaac b. Moses of Vienna was also a student of R. Simḥah of Speyer (and of Rabiah in Germany, although R. Isaac *Or Zaru'a* also studied extensively in northern France with R. Yehudah Sirleon and R. Samson of Coucy). See also *Sefer Assufot*, noted in the next paragraph. Awareness of these many (lost) German Tosafist works, which began to emerge in the revised edition of Urbach's *Ba'alei ha-Tosafot* published in 1980, was significantly heightened (and expanded) by Ya'akov Sussmann's in-depth review of Urbach's work that appeared twenty years ago. See Sussmann, "The Scholarly Oeuvre of Professor Ephraim Elimelech Urbach," [Hebrew], *E. E. Urbach: A Bio-Bibliography* [Supplement to Jewish Studies 1] (Jerusalem, 1993), esp. 39–40 (n. 63), 47–53.

אוי מה היה לנו, is structured according to Sefardic forms of meter and rhyme[46] – and another by R. Menaḥem b. Jacob of Worms (d. 1203, an uncle of R. Eleazar of Worms and the head of the *beit din* there, who is cited extensively in *Sefer ha-Assufot*, a lengthy halakhic compendium, extant in only a single manuscript, that was compiled by a student of Eleazar of Worms and of Rabiah).[47] According to the Rav, R. Menaḥem's *qinah*, which begins with the phrase מעוני שמים שחקים יזבלוך, maintains "that the physical destruction of the edifice of the *Beit ha-Miqdash* symbolizes the more tragic destruction of the unique covenantal relationship between God and the Jewish people."[48] As it turns out, both R. Barukh, who may also be the author of the author of the *zemer le-Shabbat*, ברוך א־ל עליון, and R. Menaḥem composed dozens of *piyyutim*, many of which have survived in manuscript and within communal liturgies that were actually recited as well.[49]

However, these leading *dayyanim*, R. Menaḥem of Worms and R. Barukh of Mainz, did not have many students, which may account in part for their seemingly lower profiles as talmudists and halakhists. As has been noted, the lengthy and discursive nature of the German halakhic treatises, which were not as easily preserved – or as utilized – as the northern French glosses or *Tosafot*, appears to have been the most significant factor in this regard, even as the status of these German rabbinic scholars as prolific *payyetanim* has remained relatively intact. Among the other German Tosafists who wrote *qinot* for *Tish'ah be-Av* that focused specifically on the events of תתנ"ו (even as they are not part of our present-day liturgy) were Raban,[50] his son-in-law, R. Yo'el ha-Levi (who was also a leading *dayyan* in Bonn), and his grandson

---

46. See *KMHK*, 525 (editor's note); and my *The Intellectual History and Rabbinic Culture of Medieval Ashkenaz*, 420–23. Among the *qinot* (and *seliḥot*) composed by R. Barukh were a lament for the martyrs at Blois (1171), and for those of Boppard and Speyer (1196), as well as a composition that marked a persecution that occurred in Wurzburg during which R. Isaac b. Asher *ha-Levi ha-baḥur* perished (see above, n. 31).

47. See Aptowitzer, *Mavo la-Rabiah*, 382–84; and my *The Intellecutal History and Rabbinic Culture of Medieval* Ashkenaz, 40–41, 462–63. R. Menaḥem's tombstone reads: לראש צדיק יחיד בדור הוקמה, אשר למד ולימד דת תמימה, רבינו מנחם בן יעקב אבי החכמה, תנא דורש ופייטן אין חסר מאומה, תלמיד רב ובמשנה ידו הרימה, תתקס"ג לפרט ג' באייר נפשו השלימה, עם צדיקים יעמוד ליום נחמה.

48. See *KMVK*, 509.

49. See my *The Intellectual History*, 423–26.

50. See n. 26 above.

Rabiah.[51] R. Eleazar of Worms authored a Zionide *qinah*, ציון הלא תשאלי לשלום עלוביך, which has a similar rhyme scheme and meter to R. Judah *ha-Levi*'s הלא תשאלי ציון (as well as a single rhyme throughout), well before R. Meir of Rothenburg authored his similar-styled ode to the Talmud, שאלי שרופה באש.[52]

Moreover, all of the medieval Ashkenazic *qinot* and *seliḥot* of which we are aware that commemorate the עשרה הרוגי מלכות (in addition to *Arzei ha-Levanon*, which is found in our standard *Tisah B'Av* liturgy as discussed above) were written by German rabbinic scholars. These include a חטאנו that begins with the phrase יקרו רעיך רב מחולל by R. Yo'el *ha-Levi*; a חטאנו that is entitled א-ל א-להים אצעקה, by R. Menaḥem b. Jacob of Worms; another חטאנו, which begins אמנה אנכי חטאתי לה', and the *qinah*, איכה ישבה בדד עגונה, both by R. Ephraim b. Jacob of Bonn (d. 1197), a *dayyan* and halakhist who served in Bonn and in Mainz.[53]

---

51. See my *The Intellectual History*, 40, 403–05.
52. See *ibid*, 416–18. Thirty-five of R. Eleazar's fifty liturgical poems were *qinot* or *seliḥot*. Among other events, his *piyyutim* marked the deliverance of the Worms community from persecution in 1201; the persecution of the Erfurt community in 1221; 'ofanim and *zulatot* for *Shabbat Ḥazon*; an elegy on the death of his wife and daughters who were killed in 1196–97; and an addendum to Qaloymus b. Judah's מי יתן ראשי מים about the events of 1096 which begins, קהלות הקודש הריגתם היום בזכרה. For this addendum (found in ms. Parma [De Rossi] 586), see *Shirat ha-Roqeaḥ*, ed. I. Meiseles (Jerusalem, 1993), 268–69; and my *The Intellectual History*, 418 (n. 183).
53. On these various compositions, see A. Velner, '*Aseret Harugei Malkhut*, 302–42. R. Ephraim of Bonn's wide ranging *qinah* about the ten martyrs directly links them with the events of 1096, while also including references to the destruction of the First and Second Temples. This composition has a triplet form (איכה ישבה בדד עגונה / רבתי עם מקוננת קינה/ הוי אריאל קרית חנה), and each stanza concludes with a portion of a biblical verse; cf. *KMHK*, 497. The section relating to 1096 begins: בשנת תתנ"ו לטבח נתננו / עדת קדושיו לשמר קדשנו / יגענו ולא הונח לנו, and then continues: פשטו צוארם שמע ישראל כהשמיעו / יחד האב והבן בהתחברם / נפגעו / דמים בדמים נגעו. The *qinah* is based overall on a passage in the *petiḥta* of *Eikhah Rabbah* (sec. 24), and was meant to be chanted according to the melody of a *qinah* commemorating the events of 1096 by Raban's teacher, R. Jacob b. Isaac *ha-Levi*, אוי לי על שברי. R. Ephraim also offered an elegy for those who were killed in Halle (קינה על קדושי סולי), לבי חללי לי). He composed other *qinot* for the ninth of Av, as well as those that marked various persecutions which occurred in his lifetime. And of course, he composed his *Sefer Zekhirah* which commemorated in narrative form a series of persecutions that occurred throughout northern France, Germany and Austria during the twelfth century. On R. Ephraim's work as a *dayyan* and *payyetan*, see my *The*

As part of his larger conception of the history of the *rishonim* and the *ḥakhmei ha-masorah*, the Rav sensed that the Germans began the Tosafist movement in the late eleventh century, and that Rashi and his northern French descendants, students and successors then took this enterprise over in light of the destruction visited by the First Crusade and beyond on the rabbinic scholars of Germany.[54] This awareness impacted his interpretation of the *qinah*, החרישו ממני ואדברה, in a rather fascinating way. In assessing the loss of great Torah scholars during the First Crusade, the author of this *qinah* laments: מי יפליא נזירות ומי יפליא נדרים. Since these are typically not such pressing halakhic issues – who will articulate [the effectiveness of] Nazirite vows and who will assess the value of your pledges (even as *hatarat ve-hilkhot nedarim* certainly requires the input of great Torah scholars) – the Rav suggested that this phrase refers instead to the talmudic tractates of *Nazir* and *Nedarim*, two particularly difficult tractates for which we do not possess the authentic commentary of Rashi himself. Indeed, to fill this gap, the *Tosafot* to *Nazir* serve as a direct commentary, and do not play the more familiar roles of posing questions and contradictions from other talmudic *sugyot*, and of offering and marshaling responses to these various questions.

Since many German Tosafists were killed, the Rav reasoned that we were left without the dialectical analysis that they normally would have provided, and thus the *qinah* is mourning these various losses. Had the massacres in Mainz, Worms and Speyer (*qehillot Shu"m*) not taken place, a great Torah scholar would have been able to provide an extensive commentary in place of Rashi, and the *Tosafot* and (the Tosafists) would have been left to do their usual job as well. The Rav notes that he and his father once attempted to study *Nedarim* with the existing pseudo-Rashi, but were unsuccessful. They were able to

---

Intellectual History, 24–25, 399–403; and cf. R. Chazan, above, n. 31. R. Yo'el *ha-Levi*'s חטאנו for the ten martyrs appears in the standard Ashkenazic editions of the *seliḥot* for the fast of Gedalyah shortly after an '*akedah* (אם אפס רובע הקן) by another German Tosafist (and author of more than thirty *piyyutim*), R. Ephraim b. Isaac of Regensburg. Ephraim of Regenburg studied with both R. Isaac *ha-Levi* of Speyer and Rabbenu Tam. On his *piyyutim*, see my *The Intellectual History*, 376–77; and see also above, n. 43.

54. On the development of nascent Tosafist dialectic in Germany during the late eleventh century, see e.g., A. Grossman, *Ḥakhmei Ẕarefat ha-Rishonim*, 439–54; my *The Intellectual History*, 89–103; and I. Ta-Shma, above, n. 29.

proceed only by relying on the fourteenth-century ר"ן (Rabbenu Nissim b. Reuven), who provided both the interpretation that was usually provided by Rashi, and the analysis usually provided by the Tosafists.[55]

All of this, however, raises another larger question. How did the Rav know about the disappearing German Tosafists, and how did he develop this overarching theory? Did he simply extrapolate from the fact that the standard *Tosafot ʿal ha-Shas* are almost exclusively French (in point of fact, the only complete tractates whose standard printed *Tosafot* are of German origin are *massekhet Sotah*, and the relatively brief *massekhet Horiyyot*),[56] and that many of the *qinot* and related compositions that we have (such as *seliḥot*) were composed by German Torah scholars, suggesting that they were no strangers to these kinds of tragedies, and had apparently suffered from more of them – and in more extensive ways – than their French counterparts did? There are few known German talmudists from the death of Rabiah (d. c. 1225) through the days of R. Meir of Rothenburg (d. 1293). In northern France, on the other hand, one can easily name (and identify the comments or rabbinic writings of) a series of northern French Tosafists throughout this period, such as R. Samuel b. Solomon of Falaise, the brothers of Evreux (Rabbi Samuel, Moses and Isaac b. Shne'ur), R. Moses b. Jacob of Coucy, R. Yeḥi'el b. Joseph of Paris, R. Tuvyah b.

---

55. See *KMHK*, 434–35; and see also *Harerei Qedem*, 2:310: כלל ישראל שבאותו הזמן היו מצפים שראשונים אחרים יכתבו פירושים על נדרים ונזיר במקום רש"י ותוספות (שאין לנו פרש"י כלל, וגם התוספות אינם כמו כמו התוס' בכל הש"ס כידוע). אלא שבעוה"ר נהרגו ונטבחו ונעקדו הראשונים על קידוש השם ... וע"ז סובבת קינת המקונן. The Rav also noted that *Nedarim* was not studied so thoroughly already during the Geonic period (as expressed by Rav Hai in one of his responsa), a limitation that went all the way back to an instruction of R. Yehudai Gaon. There are also a number of Geniza documents that confirm this situation; see, e.g., Robert Brody, *The Geonim of Babylonia and the Shaping of Medieval Jewish Culture* [New Haven, 1997], 45). I would add that the standard *Tosafot* to tractate *Nazir* are *Tosafot Evreux*, which do not always provide the full range of dialectical questions and responses that typified other *Tosafot* collections (see, e.g., my *Jewish Education and Society in the High Middle Ages* [Detroit, 1992], 75–79), ואכמ"ל.

56. See Urbach, *Baʾalei ha-Tosafot*, 1:428–29, 2:637–39, 660–61; and my *The Intellectual History*, 4 (n. 9), for German-based *Tosafot* that are classified as "addenda" to the main *Tosafot* (and are often referred to as *Tosafot Yeshanim*, or as some other form of marginal composition or *gilyonot*). To that listing should be added the *Tosafot Ḥadashim* to tractate *Keritot* which (partially) cover only the first fifteen folios; see Urbach, 2:672.

Elijah of Vienne, and R. Isaac b. Joseph of Corbeil, whose existence points to a more stable environment for ongoing Torah study.

I would suggest that in accordance with his strong commitment toward remembering and commemorating the losses of Torah scholarship and Torah scholars, the Rav also followed and embraced an approach in his study of the *qinot* that he did not typically follow in his talmudic learning and analysis, which further stimulated his awareness of the Tosafist losses suffered in Germany. Not only was the Rav preoccupied much more than usual with specific historical details, incidents and patterns,[57] but he perhaps also capitalized on his keen awareness of how some leading *'aharonim* operated. Unlike R. Aryeh Leib Gunzberg (d. 1785) in his שאגת אריה or R. Jacob Joshua Falk (d. 1756) in his פני יהושע, R. Aryeh Leib Heller (d. 1803), in his קצות החושן (following R. Shabbetai b. Meir *ha-Kohen*'s ש"ך commentary to the *Shulḥan 'Arukh* as a model), made extensive use of the *Sefer Mordekhai* (whose compiler, R. Mordekhai b. Hillel died a martyr's death in Germany in 1298), in order to locate and make use of 'lost' or otherwise unknown earlier *shitot* of talmudic and halakhic interpretation. Through the *Sefer Mordekhai* (and the so-called *Haggahot Mordekhai*, as well as other related collections of the views of the

---

57. We would not, however, expect the Rav to be concerned about whether Rashi in fact composed the commentary to *Divrei ha-Yamim* that bears his name. The Rav cites this commentary (on II Chron. 35:25, s.v. ויתנום לחוק) as further support for his point that Tisha B'Av is the designated day to mourn for any and all Jewish tragedies of moment. See *KMHK*, 430–31; *The Lord is Righteous in All His Ways*, 213; and cf. J. Woolf, "Historiyyah ve-Toda'ah Historit," 332–33; and J. J. Schacter, "Remembering the Temple: Commemorations and Catastrophe in Ashkenazi Culture," *The Temple of Jerusalem: From Moses to the Messiah*, ed. S. Fine (Leiden, 2011), 278–84. This commentary was composed in Ashkenaz somewhere after 1150; see Eran Vizel, *Ha-Perush ha-Meyuḥas le-Rashi le-Sefer Divrei ha-Yamim* (Jerusalem, 2010), 303–33. The Rav also suggested that Rashi, in his commentary to *Bava Batra* 3b, s.v. *hekh*, refers to Flavius Josephus himself; see *KMHK*, 280, and see also 369. This reference by Rashi, however, is likely to the so-called ספר יוסיפון, which was composed in Italy during the mid-tenth century (although its venerable origins perhaps caused חכמי אשכנז themselves to believe that it had been composed by the historical Josephus). See e.g., I. Ta-Shma, *Knesset Mehqarim*, 1:137–38, 78; A. Grossman, "Bein 1012 le-1096: Ha-Reqa ha-Tarbuti veha-Ḥevrati le-Qiddush ha-Shem be-Tatn"u," *Yehudim mul ha-Ẓelav*, ed. Y. T. Assis et al. (Jerusalem, 2000), 67–70; and cf. above, n. 24.

rishonim), the author of the קצות knew, for example, of the German Tosafist, R. Barukh b. Samuel of Mainz, and of his (no longer extant) *Sefer ha-Ḥokhmah*,[58] just as he knew the view of a Tosafist student of R. Isaac b. Samuel (Ri *ha-Zaqen*) of Dampierre, R. Solomon b. Judah of Dreux (known as הקדוש מדרייש) on issues of שליחות (which does not appear at all in the standard *Tosafot*), from its presence in the *Sefer Mordekhai*.[59] Similarly, the author of the קצות knew of a significant position of R. Avigdor b. Elijah Katz of Vienna (a student of R. Simḥah of Speyer) concerning *qinyanim* from its appearance in a responsum of the Rosh,[60] and he gained access to the *Sefer Or Zarua'* (which was not printed until a half-century after his passing) through its citation in the *Terumat ha-Deshen* of R. Israel Isserlein (d. 1480).[61]

This was not the way that the Rav or R. Ḥayyim Brisker typically worked. They were familiar with the *Sefer Mordekhai* of course, although they did not cite it very much (as noted above). At the same time, however, the Rav knew the קצות החושן quite well, due in no small measure to its excellent reputation among serious לומדים everywhere,

---

58. See e.g., *Qeẓot ha-Ḥoshen* to *Ḥoshen Mishpat*, 92:2 (במרדכי פ' שבועת הדיינין) במרדכי פ"ב דע"ז כת' שהשיב רבינו שמחה); 306:4 (... וכן נראה לרבינו אבי העזרי ולרבינו ברוך) לפי מ"ש המרדכי בשם ספר החכמה בטעמא); 68:1 (לרבינו ברוך דאין אומן קונה אלא לפי השבח) ע"פ שלטי) 46:14 and (וכתב הר"ב בשם ר"ח, ע"פ הגהות אשרי) 157:4 See also (דערכאות הגיבורים); and the next note. Given the attention that he paid to these matters, the *ba'al ha-Qeẓot* (Ḥ. M., 212:4) was also aware of a different R. Barukh (who was a French student of Ri *ha-Zaqen* of Dampierre), as cited in *Tosafot 'Arakhin* 6b, s.v. *'ad*. This reference is to R. Barukh b. Isaac, author of *Sefer ha-Terumah*; see Urbach, *Ba'alei ha-Tosafot*, 2:670.

59. See *Qeẓot* to Ḥ. M., 244:2. Although the name of R. Barukh b. Samuel of Mainz does not appear at all in the standard *Tosafot* on the Talmud, R. Solomon of Dreux is mentioned (in other contexts) a total of twelve times. See Urbach, *Ba'alei ha-Tosafot*, 1:337–40, 344; 2:515–16; and P. Tarshish, *Ishim u-Sefarim ba-Tosafot*, 67 (#254) and 69 (#261). It has been suggested, however, that R. Barukh of Mainz was the (unnamed) compiler of *Tosafot Sotah*; see above, n. 56. Interestingly, *Qeẓot* refers here to another (unnamed) position in the matter at hand, as recorded in R. Moses Isserles' gloss to Ḥ. M. 244:6, based on a passage in *Sefer Mordekhai le-Massekhet Gittin*. This position is attributed in the text of the *Sefer Mordekhai* (*Gittin*, sec. 420) to R. Barukh of Mainz and his *Sefer ha-Ḥokhmah* (הקשה ר"ב ז"ל פ"ב דקידושין בספר החכמה). Cf. my "The Meaning and Significance of New Talmudic Insights," *Why Study Talmud in the Twenty-first Century*, ed. P. Socken (Lanham, Maryland, 2009), 161–76.

60. See *Qeẓot* to Ḥ. M., 241:5 (based on *Teshuvot ha-Rosh* 35:2).

61. See *Qeẓot* to Ḥ. M., 209:10, 370:1, and 382:2.

and he had great familiarity with the work of the ש"ך and cited it often.[62] The Rav would surely have been able to glean from these works quite a bit of information about the German Tosafists and their writings. In developing and presenting his *lomdus*, the Rav did not usually search for or discuss positions of the *rishonim* that had been lost, or that were otherwise not so well-known. But in composing and delivering *hespedim*, and in the recitation and study of *qinot*, he did, for the reasons that were enumerated at the beginning of this study.

VI

In several places in his interpretation of the *qinot*, the Rav takes up a critical issue involving martyrdom that is raised by a number of passages, which indicate that individuals committed suicide and even killed their children in order not to be forced to worship idolatry (through conversion to Christianity). The Rav points out that the question is raised in *Tosafot* to *Sanhedrin* (74a, s.v. והא אסתר) as to why Jews felt obligated to kill themselves (and each other) in circumstances of forced baptism, since if they were physically taken and baptized completely by force without any action on their part, they were not committing any transgression of their own volition, and therefore were not obligated to take their own lives. "The answer is that in fact, they were not obligated to do so, but they considered even an involuntary gesture to idolatry as requiring them to suffer death rather than to submit."

After noting that there is a dispute among the *Rishonim* as to

---

62. For citations of the *Qezot haHoshen*, see e.g., אגרות הגרי"ד, fols. 113a, 285a; and see the index, fol. 312, for references to the ש"ך. In his discussion of the requirement to act לפנים משורת הדין as enunciated in *Bava Qamma* 99b–100a, the Rav noted the comments of ש"ך (*Hoshen Mishpat*, 259:3) and *Qezot ha-Hoshen*, ad *loc.*, which present the view that a level of לפנים משורת הדין can be demanded even in certain standard transactions; see *Reshimot Shi'urim she-ne'emru 'al yedei Maran ha-Grid 'al Massekhet Bava Qamma*, ed. Z. Y. Reichman (New York, 2000), 607. Both ש"ך and *Qezot* write that this is the position of Raban and Rabiah, as cited by *Sefer Mordekhai le-Bava Mezi'a* (sec. 257), although Rabiah's formulation does not appear in the extant *Sefer Rabiah* (*Avi ha-'Ezri*). Cf. R. Aharon Lichtenstein, "Does Jewish Tradition Recognize an Ethic Independent of Halakhah," *Modern Jewish Ethics* (Columbus, 1975), 74–75 (and n. 56); and below at n. 65, regarding Rabiah's no longer extant *Sefer Avi'asaf*.

"whether parents have the right to sacrifice their small children in order to prevent them from being converted to Christianity," the Rav asserts that the author of the *qinah*, החרישו ממני ואדברה (R. Meir b. Yeḥie'el), "apparently approved of this practice," and the Rav then presents two justifications for committing suicide and killing the children in such cases. The first is from the (positive) midrashic approach to King Saul's request to his aide to kill him before he could be captured, since he feared the impact of torture. "Our sages say that if it is certain that one will fall into the hands of the enemy, one is permitted to kill one's children and commit suicide. Second, the Jews did not trust themselves that they would be able to withstand the pressure of converting to Christianity under threat of death . . . Since the Jews were not sure that they would be able to withstand the pressure, they killed one another and themselves to avoid being exposed to temptation . . . the fathers killed them [their children] from fear that if they themselves were killed, the enemy would baptize the children and raise them as Christians."[63] Although no source is provided at this point for the Rav's second reason, it would seem that the Rav had in mind the position of Rabbenu Tam in *Tosafot 'Avodah Zarah* 18a, s.v. ולא יחבול [הוא ב]עצמו, at least with respect to Jews killing themselves under these conditions: "Where they are afraid, however, that they would be compelled to transgress, e.g., via torture that they would not be able to withstand, it is then a *mizvah* for such a person to kill himself," and the passage in *Gittin* 57b (to be discussed immediately below) is cited as a proof text (אור"ת דהיכא שיראים פן יעבירום עובדי כוכבים לעבירה כגון ע"י יסורין שלא יוכל לעמוד בהם אז הוא מצוה לחבול בעצמו כי ההיא דגיטין גבי ילדים שנשבו לקלון שהטילו עצמם לים).

Earlier on, in a *qinah* by Qallir that reflected various מאמרי חז"ל about the atrocities that the Roman legionnaires committed against the בית המקדש and the Jews of Jerusalem, there is explicit reference

---

63. See *KMHK*, 432–33. See also 552, and *The Lord is Righteous in All His Ways*, 264. On the source provided (in *KMHK*) for the dispute among the *rishonim* as to whether parents should sacrifice their children in the face of impending forced conversion, *Responsa Ba'alei ha-Tosafot*, 101 (=*Teshuvot Ba'alei ha-Tosafot*, ed. I. A. Agus [New York, 1954], 189, sec. 101), see the next note. The source given in *KMHK* for the view of "our sages," that it is permitted to sacrifice children if it is certain that they will fall into the hands of the enemy (and also to commit suicide), is *Pisqei ha-Rosh le-Mo'ed Qatan*, 3:94.

to the passage in *Gittin* 57b, which describes the four hundred boys and girls (or young men and women, as described in parallel rabbinic passages such as *Eikhah Rabbah* to *Eikhah* 1:13, ed. S. Buber, 81) who were captured by the Romans and sent by ship to Rome for immoral purposes. Ultimately, all of them threw themselves into the sea before they could reach their destination. The Rav notes that for the Rambam (*Hilkhot Yesodei ha-Torah*, 5:2), there is a question as to whether the *girls* were required to commit suicide, since they might have the halakhic status of קרקע עולם, passive participants. However, the Rav adds, it is quite possible that the purpose of shipping these boys and girls to Rome was not (only) for the purposes of the Romans satisfying their desires, but also for religious conversion. If that was the Romans intent, then the girls as well as the boys were required to sacrifice their lives. The Rav added that martyrdom of this nature occurred with even greater frequency in the Middle Ages and during the Holocaust as well, and he briefly recounts the story of a group of religious young women in Warsaw (or more precisely, Cracow) who were selected by the Germans for immoral purposes and who committed suicide rather than submit.[64]

---

64. See *KMHK*, 371–72. See also 504–05, and *The Lord is Righteous in All His Ways*, 265. Cf. J. T. Baumel and J. J. Schacter, "The Ninety-three Beis Yaakov Girls of Cracow: History or Typology," *Reverence, Righteousness, and Raḥamanut: Essays in Memory of Rabbi Dr. Leo Jung*, ed. J. J. Schacter (Northvale, 1992), 93–130. In discussing a passage in R. Qalonymus b. Judah's second *qinah* about the events of 1096, אמרתי שעו מני, the Rav noted that "one of the leading Ashkenazic rabbinic authorities tells the story of a righteous and pious Jew, who was faced with the Crusaders approaching his house where he and his family were hiding. He killed his wife and three children and was going to kill himself as well, but suddenly a group of soldiers appeared and drove the Crusaders away. The disconsolate survivor then asked whether he is required to do *teshuvah* or not." This material appears in a responsum of R. Meir of Rothenburg that is only partially preserved in *Teshuvot Ba'alei ha-Tosafot*, ed. Agus (cited in the note above). In the full version of this responsum (see *Teshuvot, Pesaqim u-Minhagim le-Maharam mi-Rothenburg*, ed. I. Z. Kahana, vol. 2 [Jerusalem, 1960], 54, sec. 59; and cf. *Teshuvot Maharam mi-Rothenburg ve-Ḥaverav*, ed. S. Emanuel [Jerusalem, 2012], 996, n. 187), this episode is located in Koblenz, "the city of blood" (עיר הדמים), and can be dated to a pogrom that occurred there in the early 1260's. In his response, Maharam emphasizes that expiation (*kapparah*) is not required, since this was indeed the practice of earlier Ashkenazic martyrs, as directed by their rabbinic leadership. For further discussion of

In light of these very sensitive explanations and analyses (which ostensibly could not have been undertaken at all according to the approach of Rambam in chapter five of *Hilkhot Yesodei ha-Torah*), one can only wonder about how the Rav would have reacted to the following rather remarkable passage, firmly attributed to Rabiah, and emanating in all likelihood from his lost halakhic work, ספר אביאסף. This passage is found in several manuscripts of the so-called קיצור סמ"ג or סימני תרי"ג מצוות, composed *circa* 1265 by R. Abraham b. Ephraim. R. Abraham was a student of R. Yeḥiel of Paris' close colleague, the French Tosafist R. Tuvyah of Vienne, and he preserves nearly ten other pieces from this no longer extant work of Rabiah in his *Qizur Semag* as well: ואותם הקדושים ששחטו עצמם הם וזרעם שהיו יראים לבא לידי ניסיון כמו שאמרו באבות, אל תאמן בעצמך עד יום מותך. והיו יראים שיהיה שם שמים מחולל על ידם בפרהסיא. כולם יש להם חלק לעולם הבא כמו ששנינו בספרי אך את דמכם לנפשותיכם אדרוש כמעשה שאול ת"ל אך. ועוד מצינו פר' הניזקין ארבע מאות ילדים שנשבו והטילו עצמם לים שלא יהא שם שמים מחולל על ידם יצתה בת קול ואמרה כולכם מזומנים לחיי העולם הבא ואין להקשות מר' חנניה בן תרדיון וכו' ויודע שלא יהא שם שמים מחולל על ידו. כך פי' באבי העזרי.⁶⁵

In this 'lost' passage, Rabiah (*Avi ha-'Ezri*) justifies and ratifies both suicide and the killing of one's children in instances where there is concern and fear that those involved would not be able to withstand the severe test (of torture) that was in the offing ("and they were fearful lest they come to be tested as the passage in *Avot* states, do not trust yourself until the day of your death, and they were fearful that they

---

this responsum and its place in the rabbinic thought of medieval Ashkenaz, see the next note.

65. See *Qizur Sefer Mizvot Gadol*, ed. Y. Horowitz (Jeursalem, 2005), 31. See also the two earliest (thirteenth-century) manuscripts of this work, ms. Paris BN 392, fol. 5*r*; and ms. Paris BN 1408, fol. 175*v*; and *Haggahot Rabbenu Perez le-Sefer Mizvot Qatan*, *mizvah* 3, sec. 5. On Rabiah's *Sefer Avi'asaf*, see S. Emanuel, *Shivrei Luḥot*, 86–100. For the citation by *Qizur Semag* of passages from *Sefer Avi'asaf*, see my "Returning to the Community in Medieval Ashkenaz: History and Halakhah," *Turim: Studies in Jewish History and Literature Presented to Dr. Bernard Lander*, ed. M. Shmidman, vol. 1 (New York, 2007). 86 (n. 34). For the halakhic, literary and historical contextualization of the Rabiah passage (as well as the responsum of Maharam), see my "Halakhah and Meẓi'ut (Realia) in Medieval Ashkenaz: Surveying the Parameters and Defining the Limits," *Jewish Law Annual* 14 (2003), 193–224 (and esp. 201–16). Cf. Haym Soloveitchik, "Halakhah, Hermeneutics and Martyrdom in Medieval Ashkenaz," *JQR* 94 (2004), 98–104.

would cause the desecration of the Divine Name to occur.") Rabiah concludes that those who took this course of action are destined to be welcomed into the world to come, as further indicated by the cases of Saul and the four hundred young people who had been taken captive by Rome. In an irony of Jewish learning, history and life, the very passage that largely adumbrates the Rav's thoughts on this crucial matter of martyrdom appears to have originated in one of the lost works of a leading German Tosafist.

DANIEL RYNHOLD

Science or Hermeneutics? Rav Soloveitchik's Scientific Method Revisited

Whether reading *Halakhic Man* with its comparison of the eponymous hero to a mathematician, *Lonely Man of Faith* and its discussion of the dignity to be found in technological advancement, or *U-vikkashtem mi-Sham* with its talk of the role scientific endeavor plays in the journey of the *Ish ha-Elohim*, it is clear that science looms large in the work of Rabbi Joseph B. Soloveitchik. But there are various strands of his general admiration for science that ought to be distinguished. The strands that I have in mind here are as follows:

(1) His use of scientific analogies in describing the world view of halakhic man
(2) His attitude towards science itself, as a substantive discipline
(3) His insistence on the use of scientific method in the realm of Jewish philosophy, most notably in *The Halakhic Mind*

The first has been treated at length in discussions of *Halakhic Man*[1] and the second often crops up in discussions of *Lonely Man of*

---

* The following abbreviations are used in this paper for quotations from the following works: HMD: Joseph B. Soloveitchik, *The Halakhic Mind* (New York: The Free Press, 1986); and HM: Soloveitchik, *Halakhic Man*, tr. L. Kaplan (Philadelphia: Jewish Publication Society, 1983)
1. See, for example, Lawrence Kaplan, "Rabbi Joseph B. Soloveitchik's Philosophy of Halakhah," *The Jewish Law Annual* vol. 7 (1988), 139–197; Avi Sagi, "Rav Soloveitchik and Professor Leibowitz as Theoreticians of the Halakhah," (Hebrew) *Daat*, 29/1, (1992), 131–48; and Dov Schwartz, *Religion and Halakha: The Philosophy of Rabbi Joseph B. Soloveitchik*, Volume 1 (Boston, MA: Brill, 2007), esp. chapters 5 and 8.

Faith.[2] But it is the third strand, Soloveitchik's admiration for scientific *method* that has long been an obsession of mine, and scratching that particular itch yet again has led me to the philosophical point that I wish to present in this essay. And that point is as follows:

Much has been made in the scholarship – and rightly so – of the Neo-Kantian origins of Soloveitchik's admiration of science. The influence of Hermann Cohen and the Marburg school, for whom mathematics and the physical sciences were the apotheosis of objective knowledge, can clearly be seen in Soloveitchik's work. I have argued previously that strands of thought that bear comparison to those we find in more hermeneutically inclined thinkers are also very much in evidence, most notably in Soloveitchik's methodological reflections in *The Halakhic Mind*.[3] What I wish to argue here, however, is that a careful analysis of the claims he makes for the scientific nature of his method in that work actually lead, conceptually speaking, to a method that, depending upon one's rhetorical leanings, either (a) does not distinguish his scientific method from that used in all manner of other disciplines, including most notably ethics and literary interpretation; or (b) barely deserves the title "scientific" at all. Ultimately, I will argue, his version of scientific method slides inexorably into a more hermeneutic vision such that what he terms scientific method turns out to be closer to the *critique* of the very notion of scientific method presented by philosophers of science such as Paul Feyerabend and Michael Polanyi. These claims regarding scientific method in turn have a number of implications for how we ought to understand Soloveitchik's use of key notions such as objectivity and rationality that are significant both for how we read Soloveitchik, and for suggesting future directions of substantive interest for the philosophy of halakhah. What I intend to do in what follows, therefore, is briefly outline a key element of scientific method as classically understood, then turn to Soloveitchik's own presentation of his so-called scientific

---

2.   The most sustained and comprehensive synoptic treatment of the issue is in David Shatz, "Science and Religious Consciousness in the Thought of Rabbi Joseph B. Soloveitchik," *Jewish Thought in Dialogue: Essays on Thinkers, Theologies, and Moral Theories* (Boston: Academic Studies Press, 2009), 138–76. The original Hebrew version is in Avi Sagi (ed.) *Emunah bi-Zemanim Mishtanim* (Jerusalem: World Zionist Organization, 1996).
3.   See my *Two Models of Jewish Philosophy: Justifying One's Practices* (Oxford: Oxford University Press, 2005), chapter 2.

method, before dealing with the ramifications of this for our reading of Soloveitchik's thought and more briefly for certain aspects of philosophy of halakhah going forward.

1. ON SCIENTIFIC METHOD

Soloveitchik's insistence on the use of a scientific method in the formation of a Jewish philosophy is the explicit focus of *The Halakhic Mind*, though a similar view is also expressed in more general terms in *Halakhic Man*, where Soloveitchik writes that

> It is preferable that religion should ally itself with the forces of clear, logical cognition, as uniquely exemplified in the scientific method, even though at times the two might clash with one another . . . . (*HM*, 141, note 4)

But what is the nature of such a scientific method? Soloveitchik himself notes that in the natural sciences

> Knowledge . . . is not concerned with content but form, not with the "what" but with the "why" and "how." It does not investigate A and B, but attempts to determine the interdependencies of these relata. (*HMD*, 31)

Or again

> The method applied by the scientist in his interpretation is the so-called explanatory method, which is concerned primarily with the interrelations and interdependencies of successive phases in the objective order. (*HMD*, 63)

What Soloveitchik here presents is a standard view of the aims of science. As Ernest Nagel describes it, it is the purpose of science to "discover and to formulate in general terms the conditions under which events of various sorts occur, the statements of such determining conditions being the explanations of the corresponding happenings."[4] What the scientist looks to do is explain phenomena by looking at

---

4.   Ernest Nagel, *The Structure of Science* (Indianapolis, Ind.: Hackett, 1979), 4.

what Soloveitchik calls the interdependencies and interrelations – or what Nagel terms the "repeatable patterns of dependence"[5] – between the relata being studied. We explain the relevant phenomena by subsumption, bringing individual phenomena under universal laws, the holy grail of the scientist wishing to be able both to explain past phenomena of this class, or predict and control future ones.

This concept of scientific explanation was first presented in a systematic philosophical fashion by Carl Hempel[6] who presents two basic types of scientific explanation – deductive-nomological (D-N) and inductive-statistical (I-S) - both of which attempt to explain or predict a particular event E through a combination of the particular facts (C_1. . . . C_n) antecedent to E, and empirically well-confirmed general laws ($L1$ . . . L_n) linking these conditions to E in a law-like manner. While a D-N argument differs from an I-S argument in a number of ways – most obviously in the strictly universal nature of the laws invoked in the former as opposed to the probabilistic nature of the laws invoked in the latter – both nonetheless have the same explanatory objective, an objective that was seen by many to define the scientific enterprise. As Hempel puts it, what we are interested in is the deductive (or inductive) "subsumption of the explanandum [the thing being explained] under principles which have the character of general laws."[7] The theory is thus known more colloquially as the covering law theory of explanation, since an explanation has to state the law that "covers" the explanandum.

Of particular interest for our purposes is the epistemic nature of Hempel's account. Hempel basically sees his notion of explanation as a form of philosophical argument – a deductive one in the case of D-N explanations – that gives us reason to believe why an event

---

5.   Nagel, *The Structure of Science*, 4.
6.   He first presented his views in a set of articles in the 1940s when *The Halakhic Mind* was written but there is no evidence that Soloveitchik would have been aware of his work at the time. Hempel was, however, giving a more philosophically sophisticated account of a view that had been around since John Stuart Mill and thus we will use Hempel to illustrate a philosophically developed version of the *type* of account that Soloveitchik appears to be invoking. All of the key articles are reprinted in Carl G. Hempel, *Aspects of Scientific Explanation and Other Essays in the Philosophy of Science* (New York: Free Press, 1965).
7.   Hempel, *Aspects of Scientific Explanation*, 337

has (or will) occur by invoking facts that will include a law (the nomological element). As he puts it, an explanation "may be regarded as an argument to the effect that the phenomenon to be explained ... was to be expected in virtue of certain explanatory facts."[8] So an explanation is an argument that appeals to a law of nature. This is to be distinguished from ontic accounts of explanation that go beyond arguments that give us reasons to believe an event has occurred (or will occur) by invoking those entities to which our explanatory premises refer. According to Wesley Salmon, for example, we must show how events "fit into the causal structure of the world,"[9] while Hempel, wary of "metaphysical" interpretations of such concepts as causation, made no appeal to causation in accounting for his laws. We need not enter into detailed discussion of the philosophy of explanation. The covering law theory has been subjected to all manner of objections and refinements, and whether or not one can fix the various issues that arise for it – and whether a causal account will do so – is a question that has engendered a vast literature. But the point for us of invoking the Hempelian view is that it models a *type* of explanatory approach to phenomena that Soloveitchik takes to be characteristic of the natural sciences. Moreover, it remains influential among some of Soloveitchik's readers, who take the specifically *deductive* account of scientific explanation beyond the world of natural science and apply it in the realm of halakhah. Thus, there are those who apply this scientific model to the halakhic realm, understanding the halakhah on the model of a deductive system, based on scientific analogies that Soloveitchik draws between science and halakhah.[10]

There is no doubt that this type of explanatory method was, for a long time, taken to be central to the notion of scientific method, and is "one of the cornerstones of contemporary empiricism,"[11] according

---

8. Hempel, *Aspects of Scientific Explanation*, 336
9. Wesley Salmon, "A Third Dogma of Empiricism," in Robert Butts and Jaako Hintikka (eds.), *Basic Problems in Methodology and Linguistics* (Dordrecht: D. Reidel, 1977), 149–66, 162.
10. Hempel too believes that his method could be applied to all manner of other disciplines, most notably, in his opinion, to history.
11. Paul Feyerabend, "How to be a Good Empiricist: A Plea for Tolerance in Matters Epistemological," *Knowledge, Science, and Relativism: Philosophical Papers Volume 3* (Cambridge: Cambridge University Press, 1999), 78–103, 82.

to Paul Feyerabend. Indeed, hand-in-hand with the claims made on behalf of the scientific theory of explanation goes the idea that such a method, bound as it is to the observation of empirical facts, is therefore *the* rational and objective way to gain knowledge of reality, "that science has finally found the correct *method* for achieving results,"[12] one that avoids the fantastical or irrational excesses of the human imagination. The natural sciences and their methods were seen to be the apotheosis of objectivity and rationality. Little wonder, it might be thought, that Soloveitchik, and so many others, are keen to nail their colors to this particular flag when attempting to work theoretically in their own disciplines.

2.   SOLOVEITCHIK ON SCIENTIFIC METHOD

Let us now turn to Soloveitchik's own appropriation of scientific method as he applies it to the practice of Jewish philosophy. The bare bones of his method of descriptive reconstruction as outlined in *The Halakhic Mind*, are as follows:

(1) In order to do Jewish philosophy we must reconstruct our theory out of "objective data," which in this case, as he emphasizes time and again, would be halakhic data. For Soloveitchik, any attempt at a "sympathetic fusion with an eternal essence," (*HMD*, 62), simply looking into the mind of God, so to speak, and claiming that one can "intuit" the essence of the religious experience, is dismissed as "a frank admission of defeat for reason" (*HMD*, 51). The reliance instead on empirical halakhic data saves our theorizing from the arbitrariness to which such sympathetic fusions are liable.

(2) I have argued previously[13] that R. Soloveitchik's method is not simply to utilize this halakhic data in order to construct his conceptual system, but that he engages in a two-way rather than a one-way pro-

---

12. Feyerabend, "How to Defend Society Against Science," *Knowledge, Science, and Relativism*, 181–91, 183.
13. The most detailed account, which further develops earlier discussions, can be found in "Letting the facts get in the way of a good thesis: On Interpreting Rav Soloveitchik's Philosophical Method," *Torah U-Madda* Journal 16 (2012-13), 50-77.

cess that equates to the method of reflective equilibrium utilized most famously by John Rawls in *A Theory of Justice*[14] and subsequently in many discussions of ethical theory. The method involves beginning with settled data, forming a theory, and then allowing that theory to feedback into the interpretation of the data, which in turn may lead to a revision of the theory, and so on and so forth, until we reach a position of reflective equilibrium between the theory and the data. And it is argued that this method is that of the modern quantum scientist, who partly for this reason became a model for the philosopher of religion. As Soloveitchik puts it:

> The understanding of both nature and spirit is dualistic, both mosaic and structural – *but (and this is of enormous importance) the mosaic and structural approaches are not two disparate methodological aspects which may be independently pursued: they form one organic whole.* (HMD, 60, emphasis added.)

My favorite simple example that makes this method more concrete is taken from the Oscar winning movie of 2001 *A Beautiful Mind*, based on the true story of the Nobel prize winning mathematician John Nash. For those who have seen the movie (and for those who have not, I will attempt to avoid explicit spoilers, though some may wish to skip the paragraph), you will recall that as a result of the "mosaic" – or individual scenes – up until about 45 minutes in, you build up a picture – a "whole" – whereby you understand the movie to be an espionage thriller. Suffice to say, at a certain point in the movie something happens that makes you revise that opinion of the whole. And at that point, applying the "structural" approach, your new view of the whole makes you understand all of the "parts" or scenes up to that point very differently from how you had originally understood them. This is precisely the method of reflective equilibrium, more often termed "the hermeneutic circle" in these more artistic contexts, whereby one is continually mutually adjusting one's understanding of the "whole" and the "parts." And unlike a movie, the understanding of a way of life does not have an ending that will put an end to the process (even if individual lives do).

---

14. John Rawls, *A Theory of Justice*, (Oxford: Oxford University Press, 1973).

So while Soloveitchik is aware of the classic explanatory method of the sciences and describes it at various points in *The Halakhic Mind*, the actual "macro" scientific method that he adopts for emulation by the religious philosopher is the method of reflective equilibrium.

It is worth noting that while Soloveitchik's description of this form of scientific method was written in the 1940s, it is not some outdated anachronism. We find, for example, Robert Cummins writing in 1999 that "As a procedure, reflective equilibrium (RE) is simply a familiar kind of standard scientific method with a new name."[15] And Richard Boyd similarly writes that "the dialectical interplay of observations, theory, and methodology which . . . constitutes the *discovery* procedure for scientific inquiry *just is* the method of reflective equilibrium. . . ."[16] So Soloveitchik's adopted scientific method is one that remains current in the philosophy of science.

(3) A disanalogy between the scientist and philosopher might be thought to be that the religious philosopher, unlike the scientist, is concerned with meaning rather than with a purely quantitative universe. The concern is with what Soloveitchik calls the "subjective aspect" – the philosophy that bubbles beneath the surface of the halakhic phenomena rather than with the causal relations between the quantitative phenomena of the scientist, the "what" as opposed to the "why" as the distinction is usually put. But the revolution in quantum science, according to R. Soloveitchik, involved the introduction of such subjective aspects into the *scientific* approach in order to account for the recalcitrant data of the new physics. As Soloveitchik tells us:

> As long as physics operated with a single atomistic approach, its method could not benefit the humanistic sciences, which can ill afford to ignore the subjective aspect. . . . However, as soon as the modern physicist had evolved a subjective

15. Robert Cummins, "Reflection on Reflective Equilibrium," in M. R. DePaul and W. Ramsey (eds.), *Rethinking Intuition: The Psychology of Intuition and Its Role in Philosophical Inquiry* (New York: Rowman & Littlefield, 1998), 113–127, 113.
16. Richard N. Boyd, "How to be a Moral Realist," repr. in Russell Shafer-Landau and Terence Cuneo (eds.), *Foundations of Ethics: An Anthology* (Malden, MA: Wiley-Blackwell, 2007), 163–85, 173. Emphasis in the original.

'cosmos-whole' out of the objective summative universe, the humanist found his mentor . . . (*HMD*, 71).

In philosophy of religion, in order to understand one's "data", it is clear that "the subjective track must be explored" (HMD, 72). Thus "contemporary" scientific method could only be appropriated by the religious philosopher once the physicist similarly had to deal with this "subjective" element. There remains, however, an important disanalogy between the religious philosopher and the scientist that Soloveitchik describes regarding how they approach their respective data, since the philosopher is engaged in an interpretive rather than an explanatory enterprise. As Dilthey notes, this interpretive method "[distinguishes] the human studies radically from the sciences and give[s] the construction of the human studies a character of its own."[17] Interpretation and explanation appear to be importantly different phenomena, and while the Hempelian method might account for the latter, it cannot account for the former. As Soloveitchik recognizes:

> The humanist is concerned not only with the conceptual and universal, but with the concrete particular and individual. Mental reality is characterized by uniqueness and otherness. By reducing spiritual reality to common denominators we *eo ipso* empty it of its content (*HMD*, 32-35).

So when Soloveitchik compares the manner in which the philosopher addresses his data to the manner in which the scientist approaches his, he explicitly notes that while the modern scientist does evolve his "subjective whole" in order to account for his objective data, that subjective whole is not the object of his scientific interest but "an empty phrase, not suitable for portraying nature as such" (HMD, 58). The scientist's interest remains at the level of the causal explanatory relations between his quantitative phenomena, and this is the truth

---

17. Wilhelm Dilthey, *The Construction of the Historical World in the Human Studies* (1910) in H. P. Rickman, *Dilthey: Selected Writings* (Cambridge: Cambridge University Press, 1976), 184. Soloveitchik refers to Dilthey as the godfather of the distinction between the "Hempelian" scientific method and the methods of the humanistic sciences, though Soloveitchik believes that the method, as adopted by modern metaphysicians and applied to the Absolute, was highly problematic.

that endures in the description of scientific method that we cited from
Soloveitchik in the previous section. As Soloveitchik notes, the quanta
and their interrelationships, not the qualia, are the object of the scientist. In contrast, for the religious philosopher, it is the reconstructed
subjective aspect that is of primary interest, since that is what yields
an understanding of the meaning (rather than an explanation of the
occurrence) of his data, and this meaning emerges through the study
of particulars by descriptive techniques that give Soloveitchik's method
its name – descriptive reconstruction.

But the question that therefore arises is whether such a descriptive
approach can be termed scientific? Is this the explanatory method
of the natural sciences that has garnered such universal respect both
within and without the scientific realm? And this is where matters
begin to get complicated. Hempel readily admits that his form of
scientific explanation does not cover examples such as explaining the
meaning of "a complex legal clause or of a passage in a symbolist
poem."[18] Yet the method of reflective equilibrium can be – and is – used
to such effect constantly. And thus, when Soloveitchik appeals to this
difference between the scientist and the religious philosopher – that the
one is approaching his object from a causal explanatory perspective
and the other descriptively – the difference between them seems to
be less at the level of the "macro" method that they use, and more
concerned with the difference in approach to certain levels *within* the
equilibrium that they are most concerned to study. The scientist is
interested primarily in the causally related quantitative phenomena.
The religious thinker is more interested in the subjective aspect that
lies behind, or is correlated with those phenomena. But the difference
between the religious philosopher and scientist does not seem to be
a difference in the macro scientific methodology they use, which in
both cases, at least for Soloveitchik and a number of contemporary
philosophers of science would be that of reflective equilibrium.

3.   HALAKHAH, SCIENTIFIC METHOD, AND THE
     JEWISH PHILOSOPHER

Given the discussion so far, I would argue that it is very clear that
the scientific method of which Soloveitchik speaks when looking at

---

18. Hempel, *Aspects of Scientific Explanation*, 412.

halakhah *as a basis for Jewish philosophy* bears little relation to the subsumptive method characteristic of the classical scientific approach discussed in section 1. His more hermeneutic method would seem to be some distance from the attempt to form some sort of deductive system, whether in application to the way that the subjective aspects relate to each other, or in the way they are formed out of the objective data. Indeed, he points out time and again that the relationship between the two orders in the religious sphere is not to be thought of as causal or as one of "relational necessity" (*HMD*, 95).

However, we have argued that none of this excludes his philosophical method from being scientific, at least if we understand scientific method in the manner of *The Halakhic Mind*. It does, though, mean that we need to be careful when describing what his commitment to scientific method actually amounts to and with the implications that we draw from his lauding of this method. Soloveitchik seems happy to designate his method of "descriptive hermeneutics" as a *scientific* method, and recommends an expansion of what we consider science to be:

> A little magnanimity in interpreting the term "science" is to be recommended. The descriptive method is autonomous and scientific. There is no reason to equate the scientific method with causalistic explanation (*HMD*, 122, n. 68).

But as such, we begin to wonder how useful the continuing use of the term "scientific method" is in this context. Thus James Woodward notes that it is a presupposition of much contemporary philosophy of explanation that "*science sometimes provides explanations (rather than something that falls short of explanation – e.g., "mere description") and that the task of a "theory" or "model" of scientific explanation is to characterize the structure of such explanations.*"[19] While Soloveitchik here seems happy to dignify "mere" description with the appellation "scientific," others might argue that what is really going on here is the far more common everyday process of interpretation

---

19. James Woodward, "Scientific Explanation," *The Stanford Encyclopedia of Philosophy* (Winter 2011 Edition), Edward N. Zalta (ed.), URL = <http://plato.stanford.edu/archives/win2011/entries/scientific-explanation/>. Emphasis added.

by which we understand all manner of things, and not some form of technical specialization unique to science. Indeed, for Soloveitchik, what we actually find appears to be more akin to Feyerabend's dilution of the very idea of scientific method as an independently specifiable method. Instead, Feyerabend simply states with regard to scientific study:

> How does one solve a theoretical problem? . . . One proceeds as a normal person who wants to solve a certain problem, such as a political problem proceeds.[20]

Or, following Feyerabend, as Alexander Bird writes, "There is nothing that can usefully be called *the* scientific method."[21]

> I can find little concurrence as to what it might actually be – the reason being, I conclude, that there is no such thing. If the scientific method is a *method for producing scientific knowledge* then there is nothing that is both a method and has sufficient generality to be called *the* scientific method. [22]

Bird's point is that science uses all sorts of methods – not all of them unique to science, if indeed any of them are. Notably, Shubert Spero similarly writes of Soloveitchik's method of descriptive reconstruction that "to see this approach as a reconstruction rather than just hermeneutics or even as constituting a special methodology is to needlessly complicate matters."[23]

It seems to me then that Soloveitchik's "scientism" regarding method amounts to little more than a wish to contrast his *empirical* method – in which theories are tied to actual data – to the entirely "unscientific" – or non-empirical – methods of more mystically inclined thinkers whose ideas float free of any such "objective" controls. His use of the term "scientific method" is mainly targeted then at

20. Feyerabend, "How to Defend Society Against Science," 183.
21. Alexander Bird, *Philosophy of Science* (Montreal and Kingston: McGill-Queens University Press, 1998), 238.
22. Bird, *Philosophy of Science*, 259.
23. Shubert Spero, *Aspects of Rabbi Joseph B. Soloveitchik's Philosophy of Judaism: An Analytic Approach* (Jersey City, NJ: Ktav, 2009), 125.

mystical attempts to attain unmediated knowledge of the Absolute. So the extent to which it is really a scientific method that applies in any special way to the sciences seems to me limited, to say the very least. Nonetheless, unlike Feyerabend, Soloveitchik seems keen to maintain the language of scientific method, motivated I believe by the associations between science and such exalted notions as objectivity and rationality that have been noted by many scholars. As Kaplan notes, "the system of science provides the halakhah with a model of a system that has a strictly objective and autonomous character but at the same time allows for, indeed is the result of, profound and powerful human creativity."[24]

The point is that the scientific demand, as defined by Feyerabend, was "that science start from observable facts and proceed by generalization" and that "only a system of thought that has been built up in [this] purely inductive fashion can claim to be genuine knowledge."[25] But, as the central argument of *The Halakhic Mind* insists, scientific method in its purest form, as the means of access to some pure and untainted conception of reality – and thus knowledge – is no longer viable in the eyes of many scientists. Not only do they now find the need to deal with the subjective cosmos-whole, but as Soloveitchik notes:

> The claim of the natural sciences to absolute objectivity must undergo a thorough revision . . . The pristine object, when intercepted by the experimenter, is transformed, chameleon like, from transcendent imperviousness to immanent merger with the subject (*HMD*, 25).

We cannot simply read off the data in a manner that is not already indebted to certain prior theoretical commitments. So questions arise regarding what exactly objectivity and rationality amount to once we have moved to a rather less robust concept of scientific method. And it is here that maintaining the language of "scientific method" becomes a double edged sword.

In the realm of Jewish philosophy, Soloveitchik often notes the

24. Kaplan, "Rabbi Joseph B. Soloveitchik's Philosophy of Halakhah,"190.
25. Feyerabend, "How to be a Good Empiricist," 99.

subjective status of his philosophical views. So, for example, he writes in *Lonely Man of Faith*:

> My interpretive gesture is completely subjective and lays no claim to representing a definitive Halakhic philosophy.[26]

Or again, prefacing his philosophy of prayer:

> I acquaint you with my own personal experience. Whether, taking into consideration the differences between minds and the peculiarities of the individual, my experience can be detached from my idiosyncrasies and transferred to others, I do not know. . . . [T]o say that my feeling of certitude carries universal significance would be sheer ignorance.[27]

Now I would argue that he certainly believes that he can argue rationally for his conviction in his theory being correct over and against another, even if there is no logically deductive route to that particular theory. He would, more importantly, show how that theory best coheres with the halakhic data, and in so doing would appeal to his use of his "scientific" method. But any claims to rationality or objectivity cannot amount to much more than that if his method is indeed the one for which we have been arguing. So it is interesting that in this sphere he is happy to speak of his "subjectivity," and thus the "limits" of his scientific method are very much out in the open. But speaking of scientific method in the approach towards halakhah to be taken by the *philosopher* is one thing. Comparing halakhah *itself* to science – and there is no question that Soloveitchik does just this in his works *Halakhic Man* and "Mah Dodekh mi-Dod", where he compares his ideal *a priori* approach to that of the mathematician – is another thing altogether, and here questions of objectivity and rationality start to become rather more vexed.

---

26. Soloveitchik, *The Lonely Man of Faith* (New York: Random House, 2006), 9.
27. Soloveitchik, *Worship of the Heart*, ed., Shalom Carmy (Hoboken, NJ: Ktav, 2003), 2. See also *Out of the Whirlwind: Essays on Mourning, Suffering and the Human Condition* (eds.), David Shatz, Joel B. Wolowelsky, and Reuven Ziegler (Ktav: New York, 2003), 86.

4.   HALAKHAH, SCIENTIFIC METHOD, AND THE HALAKHIST

We have been arguing that, understood correctly, Soloveitchik's appeal to scientific method in *The Halakhic Mind* is not to be seen through the prism of the sort of explanatory or deductive scientific methods prevalent among certain philosophers of science. When it comes to doing Jewish philosophy, this is simply the wrong approach to be taking, though the approach that Soloveitchik does recommend is no less scientific in his eyes. Yet in *Halakhic Man* and "Mah Dodekh mi-Dod", we appear to find portrayals of halakhah as scientific in precisely the sense that we have been arguing Soloveitchik rejects. In *Halakhic Man*, he famously speaks of the *a priori* and ideal nature of halakhah, writing that

> All halakhic concepts are *a priori, and it is through them that halakhic man looks at the world* . . . His world view is similar to that of the mathematician: *a priori* and ideal. Both the mathematician and the halakhist *gaze at the concrete world from an a priori, ideal standpoint* and use *a priori* categories and concepts which determine from the outset their relationship to the qualitative phenomena they encounter (*HM*, 23. Emphasis added).

In his seminal analysis of Soloveitchik's philosophy of halakhah, Lawrence Kaplan has distinguished two senses in which Soloveitchik speaks of halakhah as ideal and *a priori*, noting that in the quote above from *Halakhic Man*, Soloveitchik speaks of the halakhist's approach to the world, whereas in "Mah Dodekh mi-Dod" we find a shift to discussion of "the halakhist's relationship to the *halakhah*"[28]. With regard to the first level of analogy, the halakhic concepts form a certain conceptual prism or perspective that determines "a fundamental mode of orienting oneself to reality."[29] Halakhah yields a particular conceptual orientation to reality which dictates the way that we cognize it, and whether or not best couched in terms such as "ideal" and "*a priori*,"

---

28. Kaplan, "Rabbi Joseph B. Soloveitchik's Philosophy of Halakhah," 142. (Emphasis added).
29. Kaplan, "Rabbi Joseph B. Soloveitchik's Philosophy of Halakhah," 160–1.

this analogy does ring true to many. With respect to the second level of analogy, and particularly germane to our discussion, Soloveitchik portrays the halakhah as a "logical conceptual structure"[30] according to Kaplan (though for reasons that will become apparent, I prefer to use the phrase "rational conceptual structure.") And it is a structure that appears to bear close comparison to the sort of deductive system of the Hempelian scientist. Thus, for example, Soloveitchik speaks of the Brisker revolution wrought in Talmudic study by his grandfather changing the halakhah into "a totally deductive method "[31] Laws were "transformed into abstract concepts and ordered ideas that would join together to form a unified system"[32] wherein we find "a hierarchy of ideas that together form a work of wonderful architectonic."[33]

In this connection, Kaplan notes that Soloveitchik here *explains* mitzvot or halakhot by subsuming halakhic rulings "under highly general, abstract halakhic concepts and principles, concepts and principles of which the specific rulings will be concrete particularizations."[34] Thus "the halakhist introduces unified logical structures, complexes of abstract concepts in order to integrate conglomerations of diverse, seemingly unconnected laws."[35]

Now this certainly sounds like a classical explanatory scientific approach to the halakhic system, and Kaplan identifies it as such, though in truth it has more in common with a more recent philosophical theory of explanation – the unificationist account of Philip Kitcher (among others) – according to which:

> Science advances our understanding of nature by showing
> us how to derive descriptions of many phenomena, using the
> same patterns of derivation again and again, and in demon-

30. Kaplan, "Rabbi Joseph B. Soloveitchik's Philosophy of Halakhah," 148.
31. Soloveitchik, "Mah Dodekh mi-Dod," (Hebrew), in Pinchas H. Peli (ed.), *Besod Ha-Yahid Ve Ha-Yahud* (Jerusalem: Orot, 1976), 189–254, 228. Translations are my own.
32. Soloveitchik, "Mah Dodekh mi-Dod," (Hebrew), in Pinchas H. Peli (ed.), *Besod Ha-Yahid Ve Ha-Yahud* (Jerusalem: Orot, 1976), 227.
33. Soloveitchik, "Mah Dodekh mi-Dod," 228–9.
34. Kaplan, "Rabbi Joseph B. Soloveitchik's Philosophy of Halakhah," 171–2.
35. Kaplan, "Rabbi Joseph B. Soloveitchik's Philosophy of Halakhah," 164.

strating this, it teaches us how to reduce the number of types of facts we have to accept as ultimate (or brute).[36]

We needn't delve into the minutiae of the differences between the D-N model and the unificationist theory, since for our purposes, they share the fundamental features that many would wish to see in the halakhic system – both privilege the notion of a type of argument that is subsumptive and ultimately deductive.[37]

Similarly, Avi Sagi has argued that in certain places Soloveitchik sees the halakhist's theoretical construction as a deductive system, precisely like that of the mathematical scientist. So he writes that for Soloveitchik "The halakhah resembles . . . *a deductive system* whose first principles are the given Sinaitic designs and whose rules are the *a priori* legal system also given at Sinai,"[38] and most significantly that "Halakhic rulings, closely matching deductive-mathematical operations, are conclusions that necessarily follow from the data."[39]

According to this account, it appears as if we would indeed be able to give a classical form of scientific explanation at the halakhic level, at least one whereby a halakhic conclusion could be, as Hempel put it, "expected by reason of certain explanatory facts," which would ideally be halakhic rules and concepts that could be formed into an explanation, whether modeled according to the D-N or unificationist theory. Ultimately, we would have halakhah understood as a formal deductive system such that the conclusion of a halakhic argument, at least when speaking at the level of abstract theoretical study in the Beit Midrash – which is his subject in the quotes from both *Halakhic Man* and "Mah Dodekh mi-Dod" – would be the deductive conclusions of an explanatory argument. The advantage of modeling halakhah this way is that it allows halakhic argumentation to appear rational and indisput-

---

36. Philip Kitcher, "Explanatory Unification and the Causal Structure of the World," in P. Kitcher and W. Salmon (eds.), *Scientific Explanation* (Minneapolis: University of Minnesota Press, 1989), 410–505, 432.

37. Kitcher admits to, and argues for his "deductive chauvinism," ultimately concluding that *"in a certain sense, all explanation is deductive,"* Kitcher, "Explanatory Unification and the Causal Structure of the World," 448.

38. Sagi, "Rav Soloveitchik and Professor Leibowitz as Theoreticians of the Halakhah," 136. Emphasis added. The translation is my own.

39. Sagi, *The Open Cannon: On the Meaning of Halakhic Discourse* (London: Continuum International Publishing, 2007), 44.

able. The conclusion of a deductive argument based on true premises must be true. Once one accepts the basis of halakhah in revelation to be true, a deductive procedure will inevitably yield true results.[40]

All of which raises two key questions: (1) Is this an accurate portrayal of the halakhic system? and, (2) Is this how Soloveitchik understood it? Professor Jacob Taubes, in a remark cited by Kaplan, appears to answer question (2) in the affirmative, but believes that Soloveitchik was wrong to characterize halakhah in these scientific terms.

> R. Soloveitchik's use of the model of mathematics or mathematical physics for explaining how the halakhist understands halakhah is unacceptable. For the fundamental task of the halakhist is to read and interpret texts and there are no two greater opposites than the hermeneutic required for textual interpretation and the construction of mathematical systems.
>
> Unfortunately, R. Soloveitchik when he studied in Berlin went "barking up the wrong tree". He came under the dominant influence of Hermann Cohen when he should have followed the path of Heidegger and later on of Gadamer and Ricouer.[41]

Taubes is arguing here that in looking to portray the halakhist's understanding of the *halakhah*, Soloveitchik mistakenly opted for a scientific model when he should have gone for a hermeneutic one. But given our analysis of Soloveitchik on scientific method, I believe that we can question whether or not Soloveitchik was "barking up the wrong tree." Indeed, wittingly or not, he may have been a rather better arborist than this quote gives him credit for.[42]

Though we will later return briefly to the halakhist-world level of the analogy, the relationship of the halakhist to the halakhah will

---

40. A further aspect of the scientific analogy that should be mentioned is that the Brisker revolution established the autonomy of halakhic reasoning along the lines of the autonomy of scientific reasoning, in order to avoid reductive historical or psychological accounts of halakhic reasoning. See "Mah Dodekh mi-Dod", 224.

41. Kaplan, "Rabbi Joseph B. Soloveitchik's Philosophy of Halakhah," 172–3.

42. The Taubes quote was made prior to the publication of *The Halakhic Mind*, so this should not be seen as a criticism of Taubes, but the quote is instructive since I believe it reflects a scientific bias that continues to influence Soloveitchik scholarship.

be our primary focus, since (a) this is where we find the language of "deduction" and (b) as Kaplan points out, at the halakhist-world level, the analogy amounts to little more than presenting the halakhah as the frame through which the halakhist views his world, and crucially for our purposes it tells us nothing of how we are to proceed with that halakhic structure either when a) theorizing *about* it philosophically – the topic of *The Halakhic Mind* – or (b) studying it as a halakhic system for its own sake, whether for theoretical or practical purposes.

What then of the relationship of the halakhist to halakhah? We should first note that in all of the quotes we have seen from Soloveitchik, it seems as if he is referring to the creative construction of a theoretical system by the scholar in the Beit Midrash. But at this level, even if we wish to call the concepts themselves *a priori* and ideal in the sense of being deliverances of creative reason that are neither based on nor applied to experience, they are certainly not formed deductively. It might be the case that, at least as portrayed in *Halakhic Man*, halakhic cognition is modeled on mathematical cognition.[43] But even so, when the halakhic man is faced with the halakhic data and *creates* his conceptual scheme in order to understand it, he is most certainly not engaged in some deductive enterprise. Indeed, Soloveitchik's description of the nature of this creative process in "Mah Dodekh mi-Dod" points to its origins in some more primordial intuitive realm:

> From my own experience I know that in any halakhic investigation I have always been guided by a dim intuitive feeling which pointed out to me the true path.[44]

Or, as he discusses at length in "Mah Dodekh mi-Dod"

> The creative halakhic act begins not with thought, but with vision; not with formulations, but with unrest; not by the clear light of logic, but in a prelogical darkness.[45]

---

43. For a detailed account of the mathematical method and its application by halakhic man, see Schwartz, *Religion and Halakha*, chapter 5.
44. Soloveitchik, *Community, Covenant, and Commitment: Selected Letters and Communications of Rabbi Joseph B. Soloveitchik* (ed.), Nathaniel Helfgot (Ktav: New York, 2005), 276.
45. Soloveitchik, "Mah Dodekh mi-Dod," 219. The entire section on pp. 218–220 deals with this issue. Again, Soloveitchik's talk of intuition seems

So here, the halakhist is analogous to the philosopher-scientist of *The Halakhic Mind* as regards the relationship between the "objective" or quantitative data of religion and their "subjective" correlates. When the halakhist seeks to understand the halakhah, even as a set of abstract conceptual posits, he does so in a manner that is more interpretive than causal or explanatory. This is not to question the accuracy or sincerity of Soloveitchik's scientific conception of halakhah. But it does show us that what he is willing to include within the realm of the scientific might be rather more than simplistic understandings of his use of the term "scientific" allow.

At a more concrete level, one need simply read his analyses of all manner of specific topics, whether they be *hilkhot aveilut, tefillah,* or *teshuvah,* to see that Soloveitchik is not logically deducing anything in his conceptualization of the data, but rather is trying, it seems, to find a reflective equilibrium between the data and the concepts that is far more reflective of the "method" of descriptive hermeneutics.[46] So while Soloveitchik certainly draws analogies between halakhah and science, viewing halakhic categories as *a priori* and ideal, he nonetheless still seems to be using his conception of scientific method as outlined in *The Halakhic Mind,* which recall was written at the same time as *Halakhic Man,* at least *when theorizing about the halakhic data.* But this seems to undercut the idea that the halakhic man treats his quasi-scientific halakhic system in the manner of a *Hempelian* scientist. What he is in fact doing is using the very hermeneutic approach that Taubes is recommending.

How then are we to understand his references to the halakhah as deductive, when it appears as if the method outlined in *The Halakhic Mind* actually undermines any such account? Dov Schwartz has argued at length that in many ways *Halakhic Man* does not reflect

---

closer to Feyerabend's description of how scientists "invent a new physical theory," (Feyerabend, "On the Limited Validity of Methodological Rules," *Knowledge, Science, and Relativism,* 138–180, 138), and do so through "a more or less irrational act containing the most diverse components." (Feyerabend, "How to be a Good Empiricist," 99). Nonetheless, for Soloveitchik, Feyerabend is wrong to use terms such as "invention" and "irrationality" in speaking of these methods.

46. Shubert Spero discusses such analyses under the rubric of descriptive hermeneutics in his *Aspects of Rabbi Joseph B. Soloveitchik's Philosophy of Judaism,* chapter 5.

Soloveitchik's own views of halakhah, with the mathematical model being one such instance of where the two diverge.[47] The argument of this paper gives further conceptual backing to his argument. Yet some might argue that even if the methodological stipulations of *The Halakhic Mind* apply both to the philosopher and the halakhic scholar, they cannot apply to the halakhic decisor himself, charged with the duty of giving practical halakhic decisions. The philosopher and scholar are concerned at differing levels with the conceptual interpretation of the halakhah, not with practical matters of legal interpretation. Those are the province of the halakhist, and based on Soloveitchik's mention of "deductive methods" above, it might be argued that at the level of actual halakhic decision making, we are to understand the halakhist as having to follow the formal deductive procedures of the Hempelian. Here, one might argue, that just as the scientist is only interested in the causal relationships between his quantitative constructs, and the subjective whole is simply, as noted above "an empty phrase, not suitable for portraying nature as such" (*HMD*, 58), so for the *posek*, what is of importance are the deductive relationships between the data, and the conceptual sphere is a similarly empty vessel.

I would, however, question the legitimacy of making such a claim at a number of levels. Of course, structurally speaking, if Schwartz is correct to argue, as I believe he is, that Part One of *Halakhic Man* is *not* speaking of practical halakhah, and we can make a similar case for "Mah Dodekh mi-Dod", it becomes difficult to maintain the deductive claim for halakhic *pesak*. Moreover, there are also substantive conceptual reasons for questioning whether Soloveitchik himself understands the nature of halakhic pesak in such terms, as Gerald Blidstein has noted in his review of the recent volume collecting a number of Soloveitchik's letters.[48] Thus we find, for example, the following prefacing his engagement with practical halakhic matters:

47. Schwartz, *Religion and Halakha*, 110.
48. See Gerald Blidstein, "Rabbi Joseph B. Soloveitchik's Letters on Public Affairs," *The Torah U-Madda Journal* 15 (2008–9), 1–23. Sagi also notes tensions between a deductive and non-deductive conception in Sagi, "Rav Soloveitchik and Professor Leibowitz as Theoreticians of the Halakhah," 137.

> Since the problem has arisen under unique social circumstances, halakhic formalism and syllogism will not suffice to solve it. Central historical realities with their deep-seated philosophical meaning must be taken into account.[49]

> The halakhic inquiry, like any other cognitive theoretical performance, does not start out from the point of absolute zero as to sentimental attitudes and value judgments. There always exist in the mind of the researcher an ethico-axiological background against which the contours of the subject matter in question stand out more clearly. In all field of human intellectual endeavor there is always an intuitive approach which determines the course and method of the analysis.[50]

Notably for our discussion, this second letter continues:

> Not even in the exact sciences (particularly in their interpretive phase) is it possible to divorce the human element from the formal aspect.[51]

The first of the quotations above could be read as implying that there are areas where halakhic "formalism" and syllogism might be appropriate, though it is worth noting that no formalist would actually accept the caricature of their position as some mechanical form of deduction.[52] But if one were to seek a place for such mechanical deduction, it might be that the place for this is precisely in the Beit Midrash, where once one has formed one's conceptual system one can, in the abstract, see it fitting together in this manner. So even if the conceptual constructs are formed in a more creative intuitive manner as argued above, once so formed, one might indeed be able to derive certain laws or concepts from these theoretical constructs even without understanding the meaning of those constructs. This would

49. Soloveitchik, *Community, Covenant, and Commitment*, 4.
50. Soloveitchik, *Community, Covenant, and Commitment*, 24.
51. Soloveitchik, *Community, Covenant, and Commitment*, 24.
52. For further discussion of the tension between the genuinely formalist and non-formalist moments in Soloveitchik's writings see Yonatan Brafman, "Critical Philosophy of Halakha: The Justification of Halakhic Norms and Authority," (PhD dissertation, Columbia University, 2014), chapter 2.

be to understand the halakhah as an uninterpreted formal system, and while it is possible to engage in some form of classical "lomdus" in this fashion, few who engage in it would be satisfied with the description, and with not knowing the meaning of their constructs.[53]

However, as soon as one has to apply this system to the real world, that structure is bound to be found wanting given the pesky complications of reality. One might speculate that Soloveitchik's repeated protestations in *Halakhic Man* that the ideal constructs may not find their correlate in the real world could be read as saying just this - that once we try to apply the ideal system to the messy and complicated situations of real life, there is no way to achieve some type of simplistic or "deductive" application of the ideal to the real. His ideal that would "subject reality to the yoke of the Halakhah" (*HM*, 29), might well be ideal in the sense of eschatological and thus humanly unrealizable, further reinforcing the gap between the abstract conceptual scheme of halakhah and its real world application.[54] The point we are making then is that even if one wishes to say that in the ideal and *a priori* realm of theoretical halakhic analysis one could find the sort of systematic deductive framework exemplified by Hempelian science, how that system is to be *realized* has nothing more to do with science or scientific method than does the implementation of an ideal political system.

5. CONCLUSION

The argument of this paper can now be summed up as follows. The undoubted success of science has led to its veneration over many other disciplines. Soloveitchik shares this heightened evaluation of science, seeing the natural sciences as "the crowning achievement of civilization" (*HM*, 19). But such statements should not lead to a skewed overemphasis, or misinterpretation, of what Soloveitchik's focus on scientific method implies. For it seems to me that when people see the

---

53. I am grateful to David Shatz for his comments on an earlier draft of this paper that was particularly instrumental in suggesting most of the points made in this paragraph.

54. For a related discussion, see Schwartz, *Religion and Halakha*, 120ff. It is also worth noting here that while Hempel admits that his model of explanation is also an ideal that is not always met by actual explanations, our point is that the deductive halakhic ideal, if it can indeed exist, is inapplicable to reality *in principle*.

term "scientific" applied to some arena – let us call it "P" – in Soloveitchik, they have immediately jumped to the conclusion that P can be understood on the model of science or scientific method exemplified in the types of approach that we have used Carl Hempel or Philip Kitcher to illustrate. This in turn yields correlative notions of objectivity and rationality, such that any questioning of the "scientific" nature of P would be to simultaneously question its objectivity and rationality.

Yet we have argued that for Soloveitchik, with the possible exception of a certain form of abstract halakhic analysis in the beit midrash, being scientific need not mean speaking of some logical derivation of one's halakhic or philosophical constructs from one's data. His version of scientific method is far more expansive than this, and more akin to descriptive hermeneutics, a term that he himself uses. But, our argument has been that to speak of P in this manner need not equate to questioning its scientific nature, since that, for Soloveitchik, is precisely what scientific method is today. Whether at the level of forming our Jewish philosophy, creating our *a priori* (in a suitably qualified sense) halakhic structure, or rendering halakhic pesak itself, it is not at all clear that the old version of the scientific model can be applied. But it is no less rational or scientific for that.

Much of Soloveitchik's argument in *The Halakhic Mind* is that "there is no ideal objectivity" (*HMD*, 66), and that it is only now that science itself has caught up to this notion, with its abdication of the notion of "pristine objectivity" referenced earlier. While the maintenance of a scientific façade used to hold out hope for such ideals, part of what the modern scientist understands is that such ideals of pure objectivity or rationality are simply illusions and always have been.[55] But taking the interpretive approach need not, for Soloveitchik, mean giving up on one's claims to rationality, and it is this that I believe is at the root of Soloveitchik's maintenance of the language of scientific method. Given the identification of his hermeneutic method with scientific method, it seems to me that whether

---

55. When Soloveitchik does speak of objectivity both in *Halakhic Man* and *The Halakhic Mind*, it is usually in the sense that halakhic values have been externalized as concrete practices such as to become a public shared point of departure for study much as physical scientists objectify subjective sense perceptions into mathematical formulae. See, for example, *Halakhic Man*, 59 and *The Halakhic Mind*, 67–9.

he explicitly recognizes it or not, conceptually speaking Soloveitchik would be forced to concur with Feyerabend that ultimately "there is no 'scientific methodology' that can be used to separate science from the rest."[56] But while Feyerabend would say this to undercut scientific notions of rationality, Soloveitchik would do so in order to bolster the rationality of halakhic reasoning at every level. At the end of the day, both scientists and philosophers can often be engaged in similar interpretive enterprises, which are perfectly rational, and yield views that can be held with total conviction, if they provide the best fit with all of the relevant data.

An overemphasis on the "scientific" nature of Soloveitchik's enterprise without understanding precisely how he understands that can lead us to mistaken claims for both the philosophical status of his views and possibly for his, if not our understanding of how to approach halakhah. The question that Soloveitchik's notion of scientific method raises for us is whether it is necessary to understand halakhah in what might be a philosophically untenable fashion in order to maintain the scientific and hence objective nature of our decision making. Do we have to see it as some pristine sphere of objectivity that is somehow insulated from the interpretive conditions of human understanding, such that when we deal with it we somehow miraculously transcend those conditions? Once upon a time we may have had to do this to maintain its "scientific" and hence "rational" nature. Soloveitchik's account of scientific method allows us to maintain a view of halakhic reasoning as eminently human, but no less scientific or rational for that. That might be thought to provide less secure foundations for our conceptual schemes than those promised by classical science. But Soloveitchik, at least implicitly, appears to understand that by the lights of modern scientific method, nothing *could* be more secure than that, yet plenty of things could be less.

---

56. Feyerabend, "How to Defend Society Against Science," 187.

D A V I D   S H A T Z

Contemporary Scholarship on Rabbi Soloveitchik's Thought: Where We Are, Where We Can Go

In memory of my friend and colleague, Charles Raffel z"l,
whose insights and love of the Rav enlightened and inspired me.

My role in this closing chapter is not to consider in detail this-or-that circumscribed issue in the thought of Rabbi Soloveitchik, as other authors in this volume have, but to step back and assess the broader phenomenon of academic scholars, and those wedded to academic methods even if not formally members of the academy, applying the tools of this trade to the Rav. How much attention have scholars paid to his thought? What attracts scholars to the Rav, particularly outside of Modern Orthodox circles? In what directions has scholarship on the Rav moved? What fruits has it yielded? What questions need further exploration?

As we will see, academic scholarship on Rabbi Soloveitchik has followed a natural course for expanded scholarship on any figure: It has become more *contextual*, more *comprehensive*, and more *critically engaged*. Note that this essay is not a review of the literature in all its aspects (an impossible task), but rather a precis of and commentary on *works that exemplify the three categories I consider*. There is no attempt, for example, to review all the many works on *Halakhic Man*, *The Halakhic Mind*, or *The Lonely Man of Faith*, or the question of the unity of the writings, or, say, the Rav's grapplings with the dialectic of autonomy and heteronomy, or the meaning of terms like loneliness and redemption, but only to examine and in many cases merely reference those scholarly books and articles that either (1) promote contextualization, (2) increase the level of comprehensiveness by mining topics in Rabbi Soloveitchik's writings that were neglected until recently, or (3) generate philosophical critique.

This self-imposed limitation should in no way be taken as disparaging any of the fascinating challenges and debates that arise in interpreting the Rav's works but my focus excludes, nor any of the fine works written about his thought that are not referenced here. Rather, in the first instance, the limitation is a means of delimiting and domesticating an otherwise impossible project. However, even though the selective and bird's-eye-view approach I have adopted precludes intricate treatment of particular exegetical questions, the strategy will enable us to detect broad questions and patterns in Soloveitchik scholarship that a micro-examination of interpretive issues might not bring to light. The essay is a synthesis of elements in the literature that generates certain overarching questions and approaches that have not been accorded much treatment. Even given that I have restricted the areas on which I will comment, the massiveness of the literature and constraints of time no doubt have led to oversights. For those I apologize in advance to the relevant authors and to my audience.

Before illustrating these developments and charting future directions, I offer some general observations about the evolution of scholarly interest in the Rav's thought.

I

During the Rav's lifetime, it was a common lament that he had published so little. The lament was repeated so often that it became almost obligatory and ritualistic to offer it. But first of all, in addition to "Ish ha-Halakhah," "Confrontation," and "The Lonely Man of Faith," which the lamenters were well aware of, there were scattered other pieces of philosophical importance, such as "Kodesh ve-Hol" (1945), "Al Ahavat ha-Torah u-Geulat Nefesh ha-Dor" (1960), and *Kol Dodi Dofek* (first published in 1961).[1] Certainly by the late 1970s

---

1. "Kodesh ve-Hol" first appeared in *Hazedek* (May–June 1945): 4–20; *Kol Dodi Dofek*, delivered in Yiddish in 1956, was first published in Hebrew in *Torah u-Melukhah: Al Mekom ha-Medinah ba-Yahadut*, ed. Simon Federbush (Jerusalem: Mossad Harav Kook, 1961); "Al Ahavat ha-Torah u-Geulat Nefesh ha-Dor," which Rabbi Aharon Lichtenstein, the Rav's son-in-law, called "the single best introduction to the Rav's thought," appeared in *Ha-Doar* 40 (1960): 519–23. The latter two were later reprinted in Peli,

the lament was no longer valid (even though people kept repeating it) – not after Pinchas Peli's 1975 collection *Be-Sod ha-Yahid ve-ha-Yahad*, which included authored as opposed to adapted works, not after the five Yiddish *derashot* to Mizrachi appeared in Hebrew (1974) and English (1983), not after the Hebrew and English editions of *Al ha-Teshuvah* (Peli's adaptations of the "teshuvah derashas" of 1960 and 1967–1972) , not after Rabbi Soloveitchik's five articles in *Tradition* Spring 1978, not after *"U-Vikkashtem mi-Sham"* and *"Rayonot al ha-Tefillah"* appeared in Hebrew in 1979/1980. Already in 1966 the Yeshiva University student journal *Gesher* published a translation of "Kodesh ve-Hol," and in 1974 Joseph Epstein, a student, edited a collection of articles and of material based on lectures. (It was expanded in 1994.) [2] A volume of lecture adaptations by Rabbi Abraham R. Besdin became available in 1979; another, similar work by Besdin appeared ten years later.[3] Also in the Rav's lifetime, albeit after he stopped giving *shiurim* due to illness, there appeared adaptations by Moshe Krone (*Yemei Zikkaron* 1986; *Divrei Hashkafah*, 1992). While scholars at times offer caveats about adaptations, such works certainly provide a lot to go on, and in practice many scholars treat them with a presumption of reliability. The publication of *The Halakhic Mind* in 1986 made available a highly significant work authored by the Rav, the most heavily philosophical and science-laden of his writings. And this is to say nothing of the many works of Halakhah published over the decades, works which, while outside my main focus, often bear philosophical import.[4]

Be-Sod ha-Yahid ve-ha-Yahad. Rabbi Lichtenstein's appraisal of "Al Ahavat ha-Torah . . ." appears in "The Rav at Jubilee: An Appreciation," *Tradition* 30, 4 (summer 1996): 55. Noteworthy, too, is "The Synagogue as an Institution and as an Idea," *Rabbi Joseph L Lookstein Memorial Volume*, ed. Leo Landman (New York: Ktav,1980), 321–39.

2. Joseph Epstein (ed.), *Shiurei Harav: A Conspectus of the Public Lectures of Rabbi Joseph B. Soloveitchik* (Hoboken, NJ: Ktav,1974 and 1994). The English version of "Kodesh ve-Hol" is titled "Sacred and Profane: Kodesh and Hol in World Perspectives" (in *Shiurei HaRav*, 1994 edition, 4–32).

3. I will use the title "rabbi" only when referring to individuals whose primary position was/is that of pulpit rabbi or teacher in a rabbinical school or yeshivah. Many people named in this essay were ordained but held academic positions, and are not referred to as "rabbi."

4. A bibliography of published material as well as secondary sources was produced by Zanvel Klein, *Benei Yosef Doverim* (Chicago: Z. E. Klein,

Laments about the scarcity of publications by the Rav in his lifetime were thus exaggerated. What *was* true, however, is that, whereas those of Rabbi Soloveitchik's students who toiled in academia, such as Gerald Blidstein, Shalom Carmy, David Hartman, Lawrence Kaplan, and Rabbi Walter Wurzburger each contributed multiple works about the Rav, writings by academic scholars who were not his students or not associated with Yeshiva University were few and far between. (The primary venue for articles on the Rav, moreover, was the Orthodox journal *Tradition*.) Prominent exceptions prior to the Rav's passing were works by Rabbi Eugene Borowitz of Hebrew Union College analyzing *Halakhic Man*; Pinchas Peli examining the topics of repentance and *derash*; Aviezer Ravitzky comparing *Halakhic Man* and *U-Vikkastem mi-Sham* and elucidating the Rav's uses of Maimonides and Hermann Cohen; Rabbi Jonathan Sacks critiquing *The Lonely Man of Faith* and *The Halakhic Mind*; Avi Sagi examining various aspects of Halakhah and of Rabbi Soloveitchik's relationship to modernity; Dov Schwartz analyzing individual redemption; and Rabbi Elliot Dorff and Michael Morgan reviewing *Halakhic Man*.[5] On

1985, 1988). Most of the listings are halakhic; some of them were written by others, such as the Rav's father, R. Moshe Soloveitchik, with attribution. There are other bibliographies of the Rav, but RAMBI is the bibliography of choice for specifically academic literature. Another valuable tool is Eli Turkel's website, http://www.math.tau.ac.il/~turkel/engsol.html. Regarding adaptations of lecture notes, Daniel Rynhold and Michael Harris have pointed out in their forthcoming book *Halakhic (Over)man? Nietzsche, Soloveitchik, and Contemporary Jewish Philosophy* (Cambridge University Press) that harboring scruples about such sources would have cast into doubt the reliability of works of Aristotle and Hegel.

5. See Eugene Borowitz, "The Typological Theology of Rabbi Joseph B. Solove-itchik," *Judaism* 15, 2 (1966): 203–210; idem, *A New Jewish Theology in the Making* (Philadelphia, 1974), chap. 7; idem, *Choices in Modern Jewish Thought* (New York: Behrmann House, 1983), 222–223; Elliot Dorff, "*Halakhic Man*: A Review Essay," *Modern Judaism* 6, 1 (1986): 91–98 (a critical review); Michael Morgan, "Soloveitchik's Halakhic Platonism," *The Journal of Religion* 66, 2 (April 1986): 194–98 (likewise critical); Pinchas Hacohen Peli, "Repentant Man – A High Level in Rabbi Joseph B. Soloveitchik's Typology of Man," *Tradition* 18:2 (summer 1980): 135–59; idem, "Hermeneutics in the Thought of Rabbi Soloveitchik – Medium or Message?," *Tradition* 23:3 (spring 1988): 9–31; Ravitzky, "Rabbi Joseph B. Soloveitchik on Human Knowledge: Between Maimonideanism and Neo-Kantianism," *Modern Judaism* 6:2 (1986): 157–188; Sacks,"Alienation and Faith," *Tra-

the home front, a massive two-volume collection of essays in honor of the Rav published in 1984 placed eleven of its over eighty essays in the section "Iyyunim be-mishnat ha-Rav," roughly half of which (that is, of the eleven) were by "outsiders" to YU. (The other articles were mostly halakhic and were written in honor of the Rav but were not about him.) These and some other exceptions aside – they will be referenced later in notes – the academic community outside Yeshiva University and outside Modern Orthodoxy was largely distant.[6] The Rav's philosophical works may have been considered of merely parochial interest, lionized by a small circle but unworthy of broader attention. (The Orthodox right obviously did not take interest in the Rav's *mahashavah*, and in fact often disparaged him because of his broad cultural proclivities.[7])

---

dition 13, 4/ 14, 1 (1973): 137–62; idem, "Rabbi J. B. Soloveitchik's Early Epistemology: A Review of *The Halakhic Mind*," *Tradition* 23, 3 (spring 1988): 75–87; several of Sagi's pre-1993 writings, later presented in English in such works as *Tradition vs. Traditionalism: Contemporary Perspectives in Jewish Thought* (Amsterdam and New York: Rodopi, 2008) chaps. 2, 6, 7 and *Jewish Religion After Theology* (Boston: Academic Studies Press, 2009), chap. 5; Schwartz, "Ha-Geulah ha-Individualit be-Mishnato shel Ha-Rav Yosef Dov Soloveitchik," *Alei Shefer* (5750): 175–86, which is the first of Schwartz's extensive contributions to Soloveitchik scholarship. (Again, at the moment I am citing only material that appeared before the Rav's death.) Ravitzky's essay was a translation of a Hebrew article that had appeared in a tribute volume four years earlier: *Sefer Yovel Likhvod Morenu ha-Gaon Rabbi Yosef Dov Halevi Soloveitchik Shlita*, ed. Rabbi Shaul Yisraeli, Rabbi Norman Lamm, Dr. Yitzchak Rafael (Jerusalem: Mossad Harav Kook, New York: Yeshiva University, 1984), vol. 1, 125–15. The film and theatrical producer Zvi Kolitz published *Confrontation: The Existential Thought of Rabbi J. B. Soloveitchik* (Hoboken, NJ: Ktav, 1993).

6. See *Sefer Yovel*, cited in the previous note. It should be mentioned (as Rabbi Sacks does in "Rabbi Joseph B. Soloveitchik's Early Epistemology") that Rabbi Soloveitchik was one of only three American thinkers to whom essays were devoted in Simon Noveck's collection, *Great Jewish Thinkers of the Twentieth Century* (Bnai Brith, 1963), 281–97. Rabbi Lichtenstein authored the essay. In an interview, he describes the circumstances of his deciding to accept the press's invitation. See Chaim Sabbato, *Mevakshei Panekha: Sihot im Ha-Rav Aharon Lichtenstein* (Jerusalem: Yedioth Ahronoth and Chemed, 2011), 150–151.

7. In right-wing Orthodox circles, the Rav was often referred to as "J. B." The odd and offensive obituary in *The Jewish Observer* (1993) is an indicator of a long-standing attitude. In 1984, there appeared a work called *Sefer Kevod*

Rabbi Soloveitchik's passing proved to be a watershed, however.
Beginning three years after Rabbi Soloveitchik's death in 1993, there
has been a torrent of academic studies from many quarters. As of
August 6, 2014, a search of the Rambi data base for "subject=Solove-
itchik," yielded these results: The Hebrew listing has 144 items, of
which 115 appeared after 1993. In English, the main entry has 239
listings, of which 192 are after 1993. That's over 300 items since 1993,
as compared with 66 before that, which would include the fifteen
years when a lot of material by the Rav was already available.[8] Not
all of these works, to be sure, are written by academics, and some
are about his talmudic analyses and his biography, including events
surrounding public policy. But the overall intensification of interest
among academics is clear.[9] One breakthrough book of philosophical
essays was *Emunah bi-Zemannim Mishtannim* (henceforth *EBM*),
edited by Avi Sagi, which appeared in 1996, and another is the 2010
Rav Ba-olam he-Hadash (henceforth *RBOH*), which is based on a
2003 conference at Van Leer Institute).[10] The articles in these books
contribute significantly to the figures from RAMBI, of course, since
combined, the books include forty-five essays. But the fact that they
were written at all is indicative. Moreover, only two authors appear
in both volumes, yielding forty-three different authors with interest in

---

ha-Rav (ed. Moshe Sherman and published through RIETS), a tribute volume
in honor of the Rav's eightieth birthday that included articles by prominent
rabbis who were members of the Moetzes Gedolei Ha-Torah. "Briskers" in
Jerusalem protested in writing against those rabbis and attacked the Rav
with immense vitriol, using epithets like "*okher Yisrael*." See Pini Dunner
and David N. Myers, "A Haredi Attack on Joseph Ber Soloveitchik," *Jewish
Quarterly Review* 106, 1 (Winter 2015): 31-38. I thank Menachem Butler
for mentioning this article. Notwithstanding such attacks from the Orthodox
right, I have the impression that the Rav is now more often quoted positively
by name in religious right-wing publications.

8.   The numbers I presented need tweaking for various reasons, but they are
close enough to establish the picture.

9.   Eli Turkel's web bibliography, http://www.math.tau.ac.il/~turkel/engsol.html,
includes both academic and non-academic works. It too shows a substantial
growth of interest in Rabbi Soloveitchik post-1993. Turkel's list includes
short discussions in books.

10. Avi Sagi (ed.), *Emunah bi-Zemannim Mishtannim* (Jerusalem: World Zionist
Organization, 1996); Avinoam Rosenak and Naftali Rotenberg (eds.), *Rav
Ba-olam he-Hadash* (Jerusalem: Van Leer, 2010).

writing on Rabbi Soloveitchik.[11] Outside the universities, *Tradition*, the journal of the Orthodox group The Rabbinical Council of America, published articles mostly by those in the Rav's circle, resulting in two anthologies, edited by Rabbis Marc Angel and Menachem Genack respectively. [12] I was recently told of a doctoral candidate who spoke to his advisor about writing his thesis on Rabbi Soloveitchik and was asked why he would want to write on a figure about whom so much had already been written – a far cry from the situation not that long ago. The present English and Hebrew volumes add to the literature, of course.

At the risk of sounding hagiographic or triumphalist – I hasten to point out that this essay is not hagiographic, as the last third will be devoted to critiques – I note that, strikingly, a significant number of writers on the Rav are not only from outside the Yeshiva University (YU) circle but are not Orthodox. And some are not Jewish. Doubleday Press and later Random House, major American presses, published *The Lonely Man of Faith* in 1992 and 2006 respectively.[13] The reason for their publishing initiatives is obvious: *Lonely Man*'s message is universal (the text is indeed written mostly in universal terms, though the footnotes are particularistic, i.e., they reference Jewish sources), and the presses hoped it would reach a wide audience.

Here is a sampling from Jewish and Christian scholars and presses

---

11. *RBOH* does not include all the papers presented at Van Leer, so the level of interest among scholars is even higher than the number of published materials would indicate.

12. Marc Angel (ed.), *Exploring the Thought of Rabbi Joseph B. Soloveitchik* (Hoboken, NJ: Ktav, 1996); Menachem Genack (ed.), *Rabbi Joseph Soloveitchik: Man of Halakha, Man of Faith* (Hoboken, NJ, 1998). Rabbi Genack's collection contains contributions by close students, including family members, that originally appeared in an important memorial issue of *Tradition* 30, 4 (Summer 1996), while Rabbi Angel's comprises earlier contributions. Michael Bierman (ed.), *Memories of a Giant* (Boston: Maimonides School, 2003), consists mostly but not entirely of eulogies. Zev Eleff (ed.), *Mentor of Generations: Reflections on Rabbi Joseph B. Soloveitchik* (Jersey City, NJ: Ktav, 2008) is a collection of personal reflections and includes only one article devoted to the Rav's *mahashavah*. Both books are poignant and interesting.

13. In 2012, Maggid Books and OU [Orthodox Union] Press published an edition of *The Lonely Man of Faith* with an introduction by Rabbi Reuven Ziegler and some features missing in previous editions (including the original): transliterations, translations, and full references. The edition also uses the original chapter divisions.

outside the Rav's familiar orbit. Randi Rashkover, a professor of religion at Georgetown University, called *The Lonely Man of Faith*, "One of the most theologically intoxicating essays of the 20th century."[14] Paulist Press published the already mentioned *Soloveitchik on Repentance* (Peli's book). Reinier Munk published a book and some articles on the Rav's thought, dealing with Rabbi Soloveitchik's doctoral dissertation on Hermann Cohen's epistemology.[15] Massimo Giuliani of the University of Trento has written on many Jewish figures, including the Rav.[16] A Jesuit priest, Christian Rutishauser of Switzerland, wrote his dissertation on the Rav, which he turned into an English book produced by the well-known Jewish publisher Ktav.[17] Rusty Reno – the Christian scholar who is editor of the ecumenical journal *First Things* – wrote a laudatory piece on *Halakhic Man* (to which we will return briefly later). Already forty years ago Borowitz, a major Reform thinker, called *Halakhic Man* "a mitnagdic phenomenology of awesome proportions"; and the prominent Reform rabbi Arnold Jacob Wolf, reviewing the *derashot* in Pinchas Peli's *Soloveitchik on Repentance*, wrote, "If I am not mistaken, people will be reading him one thousand years from now."[18] University students have become occupied as well. Universities offer courses on modern Jewish thought where the Rav joins figures like Buber, Rosenzweig, and Levinas in the curriculum. Such public interest is not *entirely* new. Works of the Rav are already translated into French, Russian, German,

---

14. Randi Rashkover," On the Loneliness of Faith," *Cross-Currents* 52, 4 (Winter 2000), 436.

15. Reinier Munk, "Joseph B. Soloveitchik on Hermann Cohen's Logic der reinen Erkenntnis," in *Torah and Wisdom: Studies in Jewish Philosophy, Kabbalah, and Halakhah: Essays in Honor of Arthur Hyman,* ed. Ruth Link-Salinger (New York: Shengold, 1992), 147–63; Munk, *The Rationale of Halakhic Man: Joseph B. Soloveitchik's Conception of Jewish Thought* (Amsterdam: JC Glieben, 1996).

16. For example, Giuliani, "On the Jewish-Christian Dialogue: Halakhic Guidance of Rabbi Joseph B. Soloveitchik," *Keshet* st. 6 n. 1–2 (2008): 69–74.

17. Christian Rutishauser, S. J., *The Human Condition and the Thought of Rabbi Joseph B. Soloveitchik* (Jersey City, NJ, Ktav, 2013).

18. Wolf in *Shma*, Sept. 9, 1975 . Cf. Alan Todd Levenson, "Joseph B. Soloveitchik's *The Halakhic Mind*: A Liberal Critique and Appraisal," *CCAR Journal* 41:1 (1994): 55–63. The leading Conservative thinker Rabbi Elliot Dorff published a highly critical review. See Dorff, "Halakhic Man: A Review Essay," *Modern Judaism* 6, 1 (Feb. 1986): 91–98.

and Czech. Arnold Davidson of the University of Chicago informs me that in Italy, where he teaches half a year, there is great interest in Rabbi Soloveitchik, creating a need for translations into Italian. The phenomena I've described undermine any allegations that Rabbi Soloveitchik's works do not grapple with the modern world enough to engage those outside his circle. [19]

Again risking a hagiographic tone, I believe that we have here an interesting phenomenon, exploration of which will draw out certain general features of Rabbi Soloveitchik's thought. Why is Rabbi Soloveitchik popular among people of persuasions different from, even antithetical to, his?

With regard to Christian thinkers, an obvious explanation is a general rise in interfaith understanding. Across different theistic religions, we find two trends: first, an attempt simply to understand "the Other" because that is desirable in and of itself; second, an attempt to reap theological profit by dint of recognizing common interests, exploring common ideas, and discussing shared challenges in order to negotiate the tensions between religion and modernity. Globalization and global communication not only facilitate but in a way necessitate these trends. Hence a simple explanation comes to mind: the Rav attended to Christian philosophers; Christians, because of our climate, attend to this Jewish philosopher.[20] In addition, the Rav's appropriation of Christian themes (albeit, as we shall see, he often made significant modifications), would inevitably create resonance for his work in

---

19. In an interesting illustration of the broad and at times unexpected appeal of *The Lonely Man of Faith*, the *New York Times* op-ed columnist David Brooks makes the following point in a column critical of sports: that, whereas sports celebrates Adam the first ("assertive, proud and intimidating"), and achievement is measured by eliciting the crowd's admiration, we need that to be in tension with Adam the second, with "redemption, self-abnegation and surrender to God." See Brooks, "The Jeremy Lin Problem," *The New York Times*, February 16, 2012. Brooks not infrequently cites *Lonely Man*, and the contrast between the two Adams of that essay is featured prominently in Brooks's book, *The Road to Character* (New York: Random House, 2015).

20. On the Rav's use of Christian theology, see Alan Brill, "Nitzahon le-Lo Kerav: Gishah Dialektikit le-Tarbut be-Haguto shel Ha-Rav Soloveitchik," RBOH, 118–44; idem, "Elements of Dialectical Theology in Rabbi Soloveitchik's View of Torah Study," in *Study and Knowledge in Jewish Thought*, ed. Howard Kreisel (Beer Sheva: Ben-Gurion University The Negev, 2006), vol. 1, 265–96.

Christian circles. Now, I doubt that the Rav was aiming at "interfaith understanding" per se when he drew upon Christian thought. Rather, he was expanding and enriching his own thought, and, paradoxically, was even polemicizing. Even so, Christians' immersion in his thought may exemplify the motive of interfaith understanding for its own sake.[21]

It is ironic, of course, that non-Jews' interest in Rabbi Soloveitchik has been spurred by interfaith interactions, in light of the fact that Rabbi Soloveitchik opposed interfaith dialogue on theological matters partly on the grounds that a faith commitment cannot be communicated. Famously, that irony also applies to his own adaptation of Christian motifs; in fact, the incommunicability thesis itself derives from Protestant thinkers. To remove or mitigate this anomaly, some point out that intellectual interaction and formal dialogue are different modes of communication. One can intellectually interact with thinkers both dead and alive whom one will never meet, without agreeing to formal dialogue. Receiving intellectual influence is often interaction between individuals; formal dialogue is interaction between communities.[22] Whether this distinction serves to remove the inconsistency between the incommunicability argument and the Rav's practice of learning from Christians (and, note, lecturing to them)[23] is open to question. In any event, Rutishauser's volume includes a back-cover blurb by a Christian cleric that, again ironically, hails his book's potential impact on promoting interfaith dialogue. We should note that the Rav criticized Christianity more explicitly than Christians today criticize Judaism. For the Rav, Christianity is often a foil, the target of a polemic – against its flight from the concrete world (the path of

---

21. Another example of intellectual interfaith interaction is that Orthodox Jewish authors publish in *First Things*.
22. See David Berger, "Emunah bi-Reshut ha-Yahid," *Makor Rishon : Mussaf Shabbat* (Nov 16, 2012); Shalom Carmy, "Orthodoxy and Reticence," *First Things* #150 (February, 2005): 8–10.
23. *The Lonely Man of Faith*, it appears, was first presented in 1962 at a Catholic seminary in Massachusetts, contrary to the impression given by the note in *Tradition* when it was first published. See Ziegler, *Majesty and Humility: The Thought of Rabbi Joseph B. Soloveitchik* (Boston: Maimonides School and Jerusalem: Urim, 2012), 123, n. 6. Other lectures clearly took place in non-Jewish venues, such as Rutgers University and the University of Pennsylvania.

homo religiosus), its negation of the body, its focus on a single emotion (love), and its rejection of the law.[24] By contrast, one finds little polemic against Judaism in contemporary Christian thinkers. The latter fact is probably a result of changed attitudes toward Judaism expressed by The Second Vatican Council. (The Rav's criticisms of Christianity do not appear in *The Lonely Man of Faith*, which was written for a broad audience, but rather in material intended for internal Jewish consumption.)[25]

Especially interesting is that it is not only the universal message of *The Lonely Man of Faith* that some Christians find appealing, but precisely Judaism's nomian elements as expressed especially in *Halakhic Man*. Rusty Reno, cited above, is a good example: "Solove-itchik has helped me see the larger significance of a Jewish pronomian metaphysical dream that sees the Torah as a gift and not a burden." This acquired perspective enables Reno to appreciate an element in Christianity that is nomian. Reflecting critically on Tillich, Bult-mann, and especially postmodernism, Reno writes appreciatively of "a pro-nomian antidote to our antinomian diseases," [26] in particular the collapse of morals. Here a particularist feature of Judaism acquires inter-religious appeal in the contemporary context. Rutishauser tells us that he was originally inspired by his exposure to *Halakhic Man*,

---

24. See *Halakhic Man*, 39ff.; *Family Redeemed*, ed. David Shatz and Joel B. Wolowelsky (New York: Toras HoRav Foundation, 2000), 7, 46, 51–52, 77, 133; *Out of the Whirlwind: Essays on Mourning, Suffering and the Human Condition*, ed. David Shatz, Joel B. Wolowelsky, and Reuven Ziegler (New York: Toras HoRav, 2002), 103, 125–26, 183–84; *And From There You Shall Seek ((U-Vikkashtem mi-Sham)*, trans. Naomi Goldblum (New York: Toras HoRav Foundation, 2008), 54–55, 115–16; *The Emergence of Ethical Man*, ed. Michael S. Berger (New York: Toras HoRav Foundation, 2005), 6–9, 12, 13, 28, 73, 76, 135, 78, 87, 93–94, 125. 137. Of course, Christian anti-Semitism may play a significant role in motivating such polemics; as Heshey Zelcer pointed out, the Rav deemed the Church "indirectly respon-sible" for the Holocaust. See, for example, Rakeffet, *The Rav*, 2:161–163.

25. My thanks to Rabbi Yitzchak Blau for this point. "Confrontation," I should add, does polemicize against the backdrop of classic Christian attitudes to missionizing.

26. Rusty Reno, "Loving the Law: What Christians Can Learn from Jews," in *Rav Shalom Banayikh: Essays Presented to Rabbi Shalom Carmy*, ed. Hayyim Angel and Yitzchak Blau (Jersey City, NJ, 2012), 239–54, also in *First Things* 219 (Jan. 2012).

again suggesting that Rabbi Soloveitchik's stance enables Christians to think about their tradition in new ways.[27]

It is easy to pinpoint one universal aspect of *The Lonely Man of Faith* that could explain, in another way, the Rav's appeal to Christian thinkers like Rutishauser: he addresses the clash between religious and modern sensibilities. In doing so, he captures the complexity of modern religious life, its many sidedness, its self-contradictory character, its antinomies and ambiguities – in short, the dialectic of existence. While Rutishauser had long been interested in Judaism,

> We Jesuits are charged with the vital mission of transposing the Catholic faith and the wider Christian tradition, in an intellectually responsible way, into a form appropriate to modern and postmodern society. It was essential for me to understand how somebody whose background was so different from mine had dealt with the same challenge in respect to his own tradition. . . .[28]

In other words, theological insights about relating to modernity are at least partially transferable among religions.

But some other, less obvious attractions of the Rav's thought should be noted. Admittedly, what follows now are speculations, but I believe them to constitute reasonable explanations of the interest in the Rav we find across a wide spectrum of thinkers – or at least reasonable statements of what his thought can offer to theologians with certain sensibilities and interests.

The first source of attraction is a pattern that Rabbi Reuven Ziegler, in his nearly comprehensive book on the Rav's thought, calls the Rav's groundedness, the "frank acknowledgement of inconvenient facts."[29] Rabbi Soloveitchik's disciple Rabbi Shalom Carmy captures this feature in the following passage:

> What did I learn from the Rav that I could not learn anywhere else? Conventional religion tends to edit reality, to soft-pedal

---

27. See Rutishauser, xi–xii.
28. Rutishauser, xii–xiii.
29. Ziegler, *Majesty and Humility: The Thought of Rabbi Joseph B. Soloveitchik,* 406.

existential conflict, to make the ugly aspects of reality disappear behind a rosy glow. The Rav's memorable and sometimes brutal honesty taught us that religion is no escape from conflict but the ultimate encounter with reality.[30]

Vulnerability, failure, dialectic, complexity, are, as the Rav's late son-in-law Rabbi Aharon Lichtenstein notes, motifs in many of the writings, notwithstanding the portrait of halakhic man as autonomous and bold that we find in *Halakhic Man*. The Rav's legacy is "Not just spellbinding shiurim, magnificent derashos, electrifying hiddushim – but the candid recognition of failure. . . . He has imbued us with a sense of both the frailty of majesty and the majesty of frailty."[31]

In Rabbi Soloveitchik's writings, as in those of existentialists,[32] lies a deep candor, a hard-nosed sense of empirical realities, as opposed to what he probably thought of as the rosy *sub specie aeternitatis* rationales for evil found in, for example, the thought of Rabbi Abraham Isaac Kook. Indeed, in the spirit of the times, he abjures metaphysics to a significant extent, emphasizing instead phenomenology and action. Thus, Rabbi Soloveitchik doesn't paper over evil, nor does he even allow theodicies; rather, he maintains that whatever God's reasons may be for allowing evil, we humans have to treat instances of suffering as absurdities, as monstrosities, as evils, and must fight to overcome them.[33] He appreciates that science and technology and

---

30. Shalom Carmy, "A Three-Part Tribute," in *Memories of a Giant*, ed. Bierman, 142.
31. Lichtenstein, "The Rav at Jubilee," 55–56.
32. Camus figures prominently in Avi Sagi's analyses of recent Jewish thinkers. See the index entries in Sagi, *Jewish Religion After Theology* and *Tradition vs. Traditionalism* (Amsterdam and New York: Rodopi, 2008). As Sagi in effect notes (*Jewish Religion After Theology*, 172), Rabbi Soloveitchik's approach to evil in *Kol Dodi Dofek* is a religious version of Camus's (atheistic) call to ignore metaphysics and instead battle suffering.
33. We also use suffering as an opportunity for repentance and self-improvement. The idea that we should not develop theodicies paraphrases *Kol Dodi Dofek*. The primary reason given there for this position is that it is futile to try to read God's ways. However, "A Halakhic Approach to Suffering" suggests a different consideration, that theodicies encourage moral complacency. In that essay the Rav recognizes the theodic tradition in Judaism more than he does in *Kol Dodi Dofek*. On the differences between the essays, see my "On A Seeming Disconnect Between Halakhah and Theology," in *Mishpetei*

economics and political science and all areas of human endeavor – in sum, all the efforts of Adam the first – contribute to the improvement of human welfare; this, in contrast to a *haredi* worldview that calls for *bittahon* (trust in God) over practical labor. Rabbi Soloveitchik's Zionism famously has a powerful pragmatic thrust too, eschewing messianic metaphysics. The Rav does not delude himself into thinking that his era – marked by antisemitism, secularism, and assimilation – is a time of redemption for his people, even though he may see the return to the land as an opportunity for a dramatic result.[34] In Rabbi Soloveitchik's thought, metaphysics' place is occupied, instead, first by phenomenology and later existentialism (albeit the existentialist phase includes phenomenology).[35] In addition, Rabbi Soloveitchik is realistic in insisting that, *pace* James, religion doesn't automatically bring happiness; rather, it is a "raging, clamorous torrent of man's consciousness, with all its crises, pangs and torments."[36] "Kedushah is not a paradise but a paradox." [37] He is brutally frank and un-apologetic about what Judaism demands by way of sacrifice.

It has often been said, and the Rav himself almost certainly believed this, that demands are less marketable in religions than are promises of happiness.[38] One might therefore project that Rabbi Soloveitchik's philosophy would suffer a cool reception as a result of his stress on obligation. Perhaps this is true at the popular level, but the Rav's high

---

Shalom: A Jubilee Volume in Honor of Rabbi Saul (Shalom) Berman, ed. Yamin Levy (New York: Yeshiva Chovevei Torah Rabbinical School, 2011), 455–57.

34. Gerald Blidstein, *Society and Self: On the Writings of Rabbi Joseph B. Soloveitchik* (New York: OU Press, 2012), 34–35, suggests that in a *Kol Dodi Dofek* passage about "realization of hopes" and "full actualization" that is dissonant with the rest of the work, the Rav "was carried away in his homiletic enthusiasm" (35).

35. See Dov Schwartz, *From Phenomenology to Existentialism: The Philosophy of Rabbi Joseph B. Soloveitchik*, volume 2, trans. Batya Stein (Leiden: Brill, 2013).

36. *Halakhic Man*,142, in the" famous" note 4, which, *inter alia*, contests the American pragmatism of William James.

37. "Sacred and Profane: *Kodesh* and *Hol* in World Perspectives," in Epstein, 8. Pages 4–8 are devoted to this theme.

38. To borrow phrasing from Rabbi Aharon Lichtenstein; see "Bittachon – Trust in God," in *By His Light: Character & Values in the Service of God*, adapted by Rabbi Reuven Ziegler (Jersey City, NJ: Ktav and Alon Shevut: Yeshivat Har Etzion, 2003), 143.

esteem for groundedness and realistic assessment accords extremely well with the anti-metaphysical thrust prevalent in modern Continental philosophy, and can help his philosophy resonate with a segment of the public once they grasp its thrust. To be sure, the absence of metaphysics in his work should not be exaggerated – God *is* a subject of discussion. How can Rabbi Soloveitchik speak of the moment of revelation, for example, as he does extensively in *U-Vikkashtem mi-Sham*, without speaking of God in an "external" way? His stance does not spell rejection of belief in God as it does for other members of the "religion without metaphysics" camp! The most explicit indication of this obvious point is his declaration at the beginning of *The Halakhic Mind* that he does not reject the Absolute.[39] As Schwartz points out, however, often the discussion proceeds by way of images, metaphors and conceptions of God that are part of the *subjective experience* of the believer, or by way of a focus on nature and Torah (this, in the footsteps of Maimonides). The discussion of revelation in *U-Bikkashtem mi-Sham* focuses on the emotions of the person who receives the revelation.[40] As Arnold Davidson pointed out,[41] agreeing with Schwartz, when the Rav does make use of metaphysics, the metaphysical contentions usually have a practical upshot such as Zionism and halakhic behavior – consider the metaphysical flavor of the central image in *Kol Dodi Dofek*, viz., the Beloved knocking in 1948.[42] Indeed, in *The Halakhic Mind* as well, anthropology rather than theology is the means for discussing the Absolute.[43]

It remains accurate, therefore, to attribute to the Rav an anti-metaphysical stance, if we sprinkle this claim with caveats.

---

39. *The Halakhic Mind*, 7–8.
40. See Schwartz, *From Phenomenology to Existentialism*, e.g. chap. 2; see also Schwartz's response to a letter in *Tradition* 40, 1 (spring 2007): 125.
41. In conversation.
42. See also the references to Walfish and Zivan in the section on Religious Zionism below.
43. As Daniel Rynhold puts it in his forthcoming paper, "Perspectivism and the Absolute:" "Soloveitchik believes in transcendence; he believes in God. But he does not believe that we can know this God in any way other than via the only reality through which we can approach him, which is our human reality. And that is a reality that is pluralistic to its very core . . . Soloveitchik's theological writings have been referred to as philosophical anthropology for good reason. Knowledge of the Absolute can only be cashed out in this-worldly human terms."

Other features attractive to contemporary thinkers mark Rabbi Soloveitchik's thought. In our day, self-revelation – disclosure of the personal, the "confessional" as opposed to "apologetic" mode of philosophy – are valued. Rabbi Soloveitchik on occasion writes in the first person, most famously at the beginning of *The Lonely Man of Faith*; and in comments sprinkled through many works he either shares personal experiences or suggests that his presentation merely expresses personal, subjective thoughts and feelings, so that other people may differ.[44] To be sure, much of what the Rav did was designed to defend, indeed argue for, Orthodox Judaism against non-Orthodox Judaism and against Christianity; but even factoring in these polemical thrusts, the confessional mode and the self-attribution of subjectivity are salient.[45]

Another appealing trait of Rabbi Soloveitchik's thought is a strong aversion to corrupted forms of religion, in particular three: (1) extremist forms, which ideally would be neutralized by dialectic; (2) flashy, commercialized forms of religion that are especially conspicuous in America and are criticized in *Lonely Man*; and (3) forms of religion that seek power and personal gain (an Adam the first set of goals). Personal qualities, too, might play a role in the Rav's appeal to an audience beyond his community. Readers can see an unshakeable, indefatigable commitment, one which they can admire without sharing. The wording of Rabbi Soloveitchik's dedication to his wife Tonya in *The Lonely Man of Faith* expresses an axiology: "Great courage,

---

44. See the beginning of *Lonely Man of Faith*; *Worship of the Heart: Essays on Jewish Prayer*, ed. Shalom Carmy (New York: Toras HoRav Foundation, 2002), 1–2; and the end of *Halakhic Man*, 137.

   Among personal experiences the Rav relates are the illness of his wife and his overhearing his father's shiur at his home when he was a little boy. See, respectively, "Majesty and Humility," *Tradition* 17, 2 (spring 1978): 33; *U-Vikkashtem mi-Sham*, section (or chapter) 19. For further analysis, see Reuven Ziegler, "Hidden Man, Revealed Man: The Role of Personal Experience in Rav Soloveitchik's Thought," in *Mah Ahavti Toratekha: Essays in Honor of Yeshivat Har Etzion on the Forty-Fifth Anniversary of Its Founding*, eds. Shaul Barth, Yitzchak Recanati and Reuven Ziegler (Alon Shevut, 2014), 198-219.

45. For elaboration on the self-revelation and the "confessional" as opposed to "apologetic" mode of philosophizing, see especially Sagi, "Ha-Rav Soloveitchik: Hagut Yehudit Le-Nokhah ha-Modernah," in *EBM*, 461–68; *Tradition and Traditionalism*, chap. 2.

sublime dignity, total commitment, uncompromising truthfulness."

At bottom, however, a heavy contributor to interest in the Rav is probably respect for and fascination with an extraordinary mind who penetrated deeply into the religious psyche – not just the Jewish psyche – and described it in both vivid imagery and abstract formulations that strike many readers as exactly on target. It is well worth quoting Arnold Davidson, Distinguished Professor at the University of Chicago in several departments, and a relative newcomer to study of the Rav, who expressed admiration in a personal communication:

> That the Rav is one of the greatest Jewish thinkers of the twentieth century is evident to anyone who opens one of his books. That the Rav is one of the greatest philosophical minds of the twentieth century is no doubt not as evident, in part because his primary readers are not philosophers as such, in part because his philosophical analyses are inseparable from his articulation of Jewish religious experience. Who else, besides the Rav, could refer to Kant's categorical schemata in a discussion of Abraham, introduce Max Scheler while analyzing the Halakhic view of repentance, move in a single footnote from *Genesis Rabbah* and Maimonides to Hume, Kant, Kierkegaard and Anselm of Canterbury, or discuss together Halakhic thinking and N-valued logic? In each case the Rav remains faithful to both the rigors of philosophical examination and the richness and complexity of Jewish *masorah*. From within Judaism he provides a philosophical perspective that helps us to make sense of and give new depth to who we are and what we do. For those outside of the Jewish tradition he allows them to come closer to the specificity and force of Jewish experience and practice in a way that replaces superficial stereotypes with philosophical profundity.

For Davidson, it is the fusion of Judaism and general culture, and in particular the specificity of that fusion, that stands out. Reuven Ziegler calls the Rav "an emblematic figure."[46]

All this said, it may well be the case that interest in Rabbi Soloveitchik's thought is greater in Israel than in North America, even though

---

46. In correspondence.

the Rav philosophized in an American context, framework, and idiom. A number of authors in both venues have raised difficulties, but those emanating from Israel may be sharper in tone. [47]

Unfortunately, students of the Rav at times show far less appreciation of his high assessment of philosophy than academic scholars do. Because the Rav did not teach philosophy in his *shiur*, but did so only for one year at Yeshiva College (1936–37) and again in the Bernard Revel Graduate School of Jewish Studies of Yeshiva University in the late 1940s and the 1950s,[48] many of his students through the decades saw him as a giant in talmudic analysis but either missed or belittled his interest in philosophy. Or, they were intimidated by his technical philosophical vocabulary and didn't put in the effort to comprehend it.[49] Although it must be said – emphatically – that Rabbi Soloveitchik's passion of passions was talmudic learning, he remarked with pain on his students' failure to reflect philosophically, viewing it as manifesting a lack of religious "experience" (which I take to mean a lack of engagement in religious

---

47. See Tovah Lichtenstein, "Reflections on the Influence of the Rov on the American Jewish Religious Community," *Tradition* 44, 4 (Winter 2011): 7–22, esp. 20–22. This article is described as an English expansion of her Hebrew article in RBOH, 535–43. (Dr. Lichtenstein is the Rav's daughter.) She finds the Rav's influence increasing in Israel but declining in the U. S. An example of a sharply worded negative appraisal is that of the Reform thinker Yehoyadah Amir, "Ha-Rav Soloveitchik ke-Sokhen Tarbut: Keri'ah Bikkortit Shel 'Ish ha-Emunah ha-Boded'," in RBOH, 223–44. In the section of this paper on "critical engagement," I survey other criticisms.
48. These dates are based on Rabbi Nathaniel Helfgot's introduction to his volume of communications of the Rav, *Community, Covenant, and Commitment: Selected Letters and Communications*, (New York: Toras HoRav Foundation, 2005), xx. R. Helfgot adds that in the mid-1950s the Rav also taught in the Jewish philosophy department of The Rabbi Isaac Elchanan Theological Seminary.
49. Based on information from students across the decades, Shlomo Zeev Pick relates that the Rav did not integrate philosophy into his halakhic analyses in his *shiur*, whereas he did so in public lectures on topics such as prayer. Moreover, Pick cites Arnold Lustiger's suggestion that, as the years went on, even the public lectures did not introduce philosophy into halakhic analyses, because in those later years the audiences appreciated purely halakhic analyses more than in earlier years. See Pick, "Ha-Rav Soloveitchik: Limmud Madda'i shel ha-Talmud ve-Hashlakhotav," 281–98, esp. 281–87. (Lustiger's suggestion appears on p. 287.)

phenomenology). The failure culminates in "infantile" experience ("they act like children and experience religion like children"). This in turn promotes extremism – and, so Rabbi Soloveitchik tells us, it causes students to view his own philosophical output with suspicion.[50] He blamed himself for the failure, professing inadequacies in conveying *katnut ha-mohin* even while affirming success in conveying *gadlut ha-mohin*.[51] Largely because of the choice he made not to explore philosophy in his Talmud *shiurim* – at a time when some other Yeshiva University *rabbeim*, including his brother (the late Rabbi Ahron Soloveichik) and his son-in-law (the late Rabbi Lichtenstein), devoted some time to what was called "hashkafah" – there was a posthumous controversy: whether the Rav valued general studies and in particular general philosophy. To academics, this debate was virtually absurd; with the posthumous publication of many manuscripts by the MeOtzar HaRav series, the proliferation of adaptations of shiurim that carry philosophical import,[52] and intensified scholarly investigation into the Rav's sources, those who were called revisionists (on the dubious assumption that previously most people appreciated the Rav's positive attitude to the pursuit

---

50. See "Religious Immaturity," in Aaron Rakeffet-Rothkoff, *The Rav: The World of Rabbi Joseph B. Soloveitchik* (Jersey City, NJ: Ktav, 1999), 2: 238–41.

51. See "Al Ahavat ha-Torah u-Geulat Nefesh ha-Dor," in *Be-Sod ha-Yahid ve-ha-Yahad* (Jerusalem: Orot, 1976), 419–20.

52. To cite one example, in "The Kabbalistic Underpinnings of U-Vikkashtem mi-Sham" (*The Torah u-Madda Journal* 17 [2016–17] 174–84), Arnold Lustiger uses a discussion by the Rav of a kabbalistic motif in Nahmanides to shed light on the perplexing thesis of the identity of knower and known in *U-Vikkashtem mi-Sham*. Lustiger has published several books of adaptations and annotations of *derashot*: *You Shall Be Purified: Rabbi Joseph B. Soloveitchik on the Days of Awe*, summarized and annotated by Arnold Lustiger (Edison: Ohr, 1998) and *Derashot ha-Rav: Selected Lectures of Rabbi Joseph B. Soloveitchik*, summarized and annotated by Arnold Lustiger (Ohr, 2003). He has also edited or co-edited *mahzorim for Rosh Hashanah and Yom Kippur*, a *siddur*, and a Hummash, all of which have philosophical value (OU Press and Koren have been involved in the publications.) Among the other individuals who have recently produced adaptations are Rabbis Yosef Adler, Avishai David, and David Shapiro. Noteworthy too are the many volumes of *Noraos HaRav* edited by B. David Schreiber. The essays in these works are often halakhic rather than philosophical.

of general culture) have lost substantial ground even in Orthodox circles, though their ranks are hardly desolate.[53]

II.

But what, specifically, have we learned from academic studies of Rabbi Soloveitchik? And what more do we want to know? Alternatively phrased, what do we know and where should we go? I will not here catalogue the new volumes of manuscripts and tapes that have appeared in recent years, which certainly have added to what we know, but will focus on secondary literature and adduce documentation from primary sources only when it is particularly helpful.

In considering questions about the current and future state of scholarship, we must distinguish between studying philosophy and doing philosophy. In studying philosophy, the scholar interprets and tries to understand the ideas of others, perhaps (but not necessarily) situating them within a social, historical or biographical context, tracing influences that shaped the ideas, locating views they were combatting, and tracing progressions and disparities. When one *does* philosophy, by contrast, one *evaluates* the ideas that have been studied, seeking to determine their truth or plausibility, and/or trying to fashion and establish one's own position. At times, there have been tensions between practitioners of these respective methods. But those have receded as numerous scholars apply their work in their respective specializations to contemporary social problems, and there is recognition that we need to attend both to figuring out what thinkers said and to figuring out whether what they said is persuasive or instead problematic.[54] So, when I say that scholarly work on the Rav has become, as most

---

53. On the sociology involved here, see, besides Tovah Lichtenstein's article cited above, Alan Yuter, "the Nuanced Ambiguities of Rabbi Joseph B. Soloveitchik," in *Review of Rabbinic Judaism* 12, 2 (2009): 221–44, and Dov Schwartz's response, "Personality and Psychology; A Reply to My Critics," in the same issue, 273–84. See also Chaim Waxman," Mahashavah, Tarbut, Hevratit u-Mivneh: Ha-Rav Soloveitchik ke-Manhig Ortodoksiyyah Modernit," in RBH, 363–86. On "Rav revisionism," see Lawrence J. Kaplan, "Revisionism and the Rav: The Struggle for the Soul of Modern Orthodoxy," *Judaism* 48, 3 (summer 1999): 290–312.
54. See my *Jewish Thought in Dialogue: Essays on Thinkers, Theologies, and Moral Theories* (Boston: Academic Studies Press, 2009), xi–xv.

scholarship on a figure does over time, more contextual, more comprehensive, and more critical – the first two categories refer to matters of interpretation; the third to matters of assessment and application.

(1) **More contextual:** The Rav read widely and was unusually eclectic. Skimming the notes in *Halakhic Man* establishes this instantly, and as if there were any remaining doubt, the text and notes of *The Halakhic Mind* are almost astonishing in their scope. Yet, having said that, *how* eclectic he was has emerged only during the past two decades. We've learned much more about intellectual influences on the Rav – both what he appropriated and what he fought against. We also have a greatly expanded sense of what conversations are tacitly going on in the text and notes between Rabbi Soloveitchik and those he engages, whether by name or not – where agreements and disagreements lie.

We have to be careful to distinguish claims of similarities and differences between the Rav and certain thinkers from assertions of causal influence (under which heading I include both acceptance and rejection of particular thinkers whose work he read). Most but not all of the works I'll mention posit causal influence, others explicitly don't. For my part, I think causal influence is likely in several of the cases where authors do not assert it; but the influence may be of the zeitgeist variety, i.e., ideas that are "in the air."

Avi Sagi and Dov Schwartz explicate connections (both resemblances and divergences) to Kierkegaard, Hegel, Camus, and Heidegger. (The references that follow will generally be consolidated in a single footnote.) Both they and Alan Brill display connections to Christian dialectical theologians, such as Brunner and Barth. Schwartz suggests too the potential influence of Maritain and Marcel. (Even the Rav's vocabulary for expressing Jewish ideas includes words derived from Christianity, for example, *kerygma* and charisma.) Elliot Wolfson comments on Rabbi Soloveitchik's relationship to Heidegger. Lawrence Kaplan comments on the influence or possible influence of Cassirer and Leo Baeck, and on the Rav's use of Cohen – similarities and divergences – on suffering, repentance, and prayer. Dov Schwartz significantly expands discussion of Cohen's role in *Halakhic Man* by marking off points of agreement and disagreement and suggesting a new reading of the work as esoteric – with the scientist (*ish ha-da'at*) being greater than halakhic man. We also have Reinier Munk's work, which includes, inter alia, an analysis of Rabbi Soloveitchik's doctoral dissertation on Cohen's epistemology. Avinoam Rosenak argues that a Brisker analysis of *kibbud ve-oneg Shabbat* was modified by the Rav by dint of exposure to Neo-Kantianism.

The Rav cites Max Scheler in *Halakhic Man*, and in *The Halakhic Mind* states that "this work is indebted [to Scheler] in several important points."[55] Rabbi Yitzchak Blau and Eliezer Goldman analyze Rabbi Soloveitchik's use of Scheler as regards repentance. In a 1997 lecture, Mark Gottlieb suggested relating the Rav to Scheler and Karol Wojtyla (Pope John Paul II), who likewise was influenced by Scheler, regarding the value of the body. Recently, Alex Ozar has traced *The Emergence of Ethical Man* to Scheler's *Man's Place in Nature*, showing that *Emergence* borrows heavily from Scheler's work yet disputes it. (The Rav does not quote Scheler in *Emergence*.) Michael S. Berger argues that *U-Vikkashtem mi-Sham* is a response to Buber.[56] A contrast between the Rav and Buber, whom the Rav does not quote by name except in *The Emergence of Ethical Man* but who exerted glaring influence, is developed by Ruth Birnbaum. Dov Schwartz expands on the Rav's use of the I-Thou concept and draws links to Heidegger. William Kolbrener discusses the influence of Paul Natorp's method of reconstruction on *The Halakhic Mind*, while Daniel Rynhold studies the impact of Wilhelm Dilthey, Micha Oppenheim and David Possen that of Kierkegaard, and Reuven Ziegler that of Kant. The point and value of these contextual excursions is not purely historical; rather, often you clarify a thinker's thought by knowing antecedents of his views in other thinkers, by discerning what the author left out and what was selected, and by appreciating the very problems at hand.

Turning to matters of Orthodox ideology, Dov Schwartz traces the Rav's pragmatic, nonmessianic Zionism to Rabbi Yitzhak Yaakov Reines, founder of Mizrachi. Gerald Blidstein locates the roots of *Kol Dodi Dofek*'s distinction between *goral* and *yiud* (and *berit goral/berit yi'ud*) in similar but not identical distinctions in Buber ("people" vs, "nation"), Alexander Altmann, and Heidegger. Rabbi Zev Gotthold reported that the Rav himself traced the origins of *goral* vs. *yi'ud* and

---

55. *The Halakhic Mind*, 120.
56. In an unpublished undergraduate paper in the 1980s, R. Nathaniel Helfgot pointed to the background presence of Franz Rosenzweig as well.

the closely related distinction between *mahaneh* and *edah* (camp and congregation) to the sociologist Ferdinand Tonnies.[57]

Comparisons and contrasts are useful even in the absence of influences. They sharpen certain aspects of our understanding of the Rav by either suggesting similarities or identifying a foil. Moshe Sokol shows that elements of Romanticism (nostalgia, creativity, heroes, emotion) are found in the Rav, though Sokol does not assert causal influence. Hanokh Ben-Pazi, also without claiming causal influence, explicates parts of Rabbi Soloveitchik's thought by means of Freudian concepts and doctrines about sexuality, morality, religion, and anxiety. Dov Schwartz likewise deals with Freud; Roy Mittelman sketches relationships to Bakan and Jung. Zachary Braiterman relates Kant's aesthetics to Rabbi Soloveitchik's understanding of *mitzvah*. Eileen H. Watts uses *Lonely Man of Faith* to analyze Bernard Malamud's stories. As for foils – Daniel Rynhold and Michael J. Harris identify parallels with and divergences from Nietzsche (whom the Rav read), the parallels existing with regard to perspectivist epistemology and world-affirmation. Jonathan Cohen's discussion of the Rav and of Rabbi Eliezer Berkovits identifies significant differences in their treatments of the divine-human encounter. Another example of relating without causally connecting is William Kolbrener's argument that Rabbi Soloveitchik furnishes "a pragmatist defense of theological epistemology which, though authored in 1944, anticipates and overcomes [Stanley] Fish's radical scepticism." Jonathan Cohen relates the Rav to Leo Strauss with regard to their readings of biblical conceptions of the ideal Jew in Genesis. Yoel Finkelman compares the Rav with Rabbis Abraham

---

57. See Ziegler, *Majesty and Humility*, 289. As Gotthold recalled his conversation with the Rav, the Rav stated that he had first developed the idea of two dimensions of Jewish community when he studied political science in Warsaw in the mid-1920s. In private communication, Ziegler informed me that after his book *Majesty and Humility* was published, he learned that Gotthold was talking about Tonnies, who distinguished *Gemenschaft* and *Gesselschaft*. Ziegler wrote to me that "Tonnies' ideas are somewhat remote from the Rav's, but I can see how they would lead him to think in a certain direction." In an interview with Ethan Isenberg, who created the documentary *The Lonely Man of Faith*, Gotthold stated that the Rav told him, prior to writing *Kol Dodi Dofek*, that he was acquainted with Tonnies' teachings. On a Heidegger connection, see Michael Fagenblat, "The Thing that Scares Me Most: Heidgger's Anti-Semitism and the Return to Zion," KD Sol Kierkhttp://www.jcrt.org/archives/14.1/fagenblat.pdf-, 16-17.

Joshua Heschel and Mordechai Kaplan on religion and public life. Shalom Carmy has suggested (in a personal communication) that "It is hard to imagine that when the Rav eventually used the title *U-Vikkashtem mi-Sham*, he was oblivious to Heschel's contrasting title, *God In Search of Man*, especially since the first footnote clearly criticizes Heschel." In the future, Rabbi Soloveitchik's criticism of contemporary religion can be contextualized to the mid-20th century elite critique of popular religion. [58]

---

58. The references in these last four paragraphs are to (alphabetically): Hanokh Ben-Pazi, "Hebeitim Pesikologiyyim-Freudianim be-Mishnato shel Ha-Rav Soloveitchik," in RBOH, 97–117; Michael S. Berger, "'U-Vikkashtem mi-Sham': Rabbi Joseph B. Soloveitchik's Response to Martin Buber's Religious Existentialism," *Modern Judaism* 18, 2 (1998): 93–118; Ruth Birnbaum, "The Man of Dialogue and the Man of Halakhah," *Judaism* 26 (1977): 52–62; Yitzchak Blau, "Creative Repentance: On Rabbi Soloveitchik's Concept of Teshuva," *Tradition* 28, 2 (1994): 11–18; Gerald J. Blidstein, "Biblical Models ," in *Society and Self*, 63–76 (on Barth and *Lonely Man of Faith*; originally published 1994); see ibid., 105–110 on the roots of the *goral/yi'ud distinction*); Zachary Braiterman, "Joseph Soloveitchik and Immanuel Kant's Mitzvah-Aesthetic," *AJS Review* 25, 1 (2000–2001): 1–24 (published before the appearance of Rabbi Soloveitchik, *Worship of the Heart*, which discusses aesthetics); Brill, "Nitzahon be-Lo Kerav" and "Elements of Dialectical Theology"; Jonathan Cohen, "Strauss, Soloveitchik and the Genesis Narrative: Conceptions of the Ideal Jew As Derived from Philosophical and Theological Readings of the Bible," *Journal of Jewish Thought & Philosophy* 5, 1 (1995): 99–143; idem, "Incompatible Parallels: Soloveitchik and Berkovits on Religious Experience, Commandment, and the Dimension of History," *Modern Judaism* 28, 2 (2008): 173–203, also in Hebrew in RBOH, 56–84; Finkelman, "Dat ve-Hayyim Tzibburiyyim: Bein Galut le-Bein Medinah Yehudit be-Hagutam shel Yosef Dov Soloveitchik, Avraham Yehoshua Heschel, u-Mordechai Kaplan," in *Dat u-Medinah be-Hagut ha-Yehudit ba-Me'ah ha-Esrim*, ed. Aviezer Ravitzky (Jerusalem, 2005), 367–407; Eliezer Goldman, "Teshuvah u-Zeman be-Haguto shel Ha-Rav Soloveitchik," in EBM, 175–190; Charles Grysman, "The Self-Actualized Man As Seen Through the Eyes of Rabbi Joseph B. Soloveitchik and Carl Jung," *Jewish Social Work Forum* 16 (1980): 70–74; Aviad Hacohen, "'Mah Nishtannah?': Kavvim le-Heker Shittato ha-Lamdanit shel Ha-Rav Soloveitchik," in RBOH, 299–322; Lawrence J. Kaplan, preface to *Halakhic Man*, vii (on Baeck; see further David Shatz, "A Framework for Reading Ish ha-Halakhah," *Turim: Studies in Jewish History and Literature Presented to Dr. Bernard Lander*; ed. Michael A. Shmidman [New York: Touro College Press, 2008], 208–11; Lawrence Kaplan, "Rabbi Joseph Soloveitchik's Philosophy of Halakhah," *Jewish Law Annual* 7 (1988): 139–97; idem, "Hermann Cohen

The impact of other thinkers is, then, incontrovertible, and so is the

---

and Rabbi Joseph Soloveitchik on Repentance," *Journal of Jewish Thought & Philosophy* 13, 1 (2004): 213–258; William Kolbrener, "No 'Elsewhere': Fish, Soloveitchik, and the Unavoidability of Interpretation," *Literature and Theology* 10, 2 (1996): 171–190. idem, "Towards a Genuine Jewish Philosophy: *Halakhic Mind*'s New Philosophy of Religion," *Tradition* 30, 3 (spring 1996): 21–43; Moshe Meir, "Ha-Rav Soloveitchik ki-Metavvekh bein Haguto shel Hermann Cohen u-bein ha-Ortodoksiyyah," RBH, 85–96; Roy Mittelman, "Agency and Communion According to Bakan and Soloveitchik: Two Perspectives," *Jewish Civilization* III (1985), 209–218; Reinier Munk, "Joseph B. Soloveitchik on Hermann Cohen's 'Logic Der Reinen Erkentiss'"; idem, "La-da'at et HaMakom: Ha-Rav Soloveitchik ve-Hermann Cohen al Mahashavah ve-Trantzendentiyyah," *Da'at* 42 (5759): 97–124 ; Micha Oppenheim, "Kierkegaard and Soloveitchik," *Judaism* 37, 1 (winter 1988): 29–40; Alex Ozar, "The Emergence of Max Scheler: Understanding Rabbi Joseph Soloveitchik's Philosophical Anthropology," *Harvard Theological Review* 109, 2 (April 2016): 178-206; David D. Possen, "J.B. Soloveitchik: Between Neo-Kantianism and Kierkegaardian Existentialism," in *Kierkegaard's Influence on Theology, Tome III: Catholic and Jewish Theology*, ed. Jon Stewart (Burlington, VT: Ashgate, 2012), 189–210; Avinoam Rosenak, "Pilosofiyyah u-Mahashevet ha-Halakhah: Keri'ah be-Shi'urei ha-Talmud shel RYD Soloveitchik le-Or Modellim Neo-Kantianim," in EBM, 275–306 and "Mi-Brisk le-Marburg u-be-Hazarah: ha-Yetzirah ha-Hilkhatit be-Shi'urei ha-Talmud shel ha Rav YD Soloveitchik," *Akdamot* 9 (5760): 9–34 (cf. Hacohen, "Mah Nishtannah" and Shlomo Pick, "The Rav: Biography and Bibliography – A Review Essay," BDD 6 [Winter 1998]: 28–30) ; Ravitzky, "Rabbi Joseph B. Soloveitchik on Human Knowledge"; Daniel Rynhold and Michael Harris, "Modernity and Jewish Orthodoxy: Nietzsche and Soloveitchik on Life-Affirmation, Asceticism, and Repentance," *Harvard Theological Review* 101, 2 (2008): 253–84; Rynhold, "Perspectivism and the Absolute: Soloveitchik's Epistemological Pluralism," forthcoming in *Revue Internationale de Philosophie*, and *Two Models of Jewish Philosophy* (New York: Oxford University Press, 2005), esp. chap. 2; Avi Sagi, "Ha-Rav Soloveitchik: Hagut Yehudit le-Nokhah ha-Modernah," in EBM 461–99; Dov Schwartz, *Religion or Halakha? The Philosophy of Rabbi Joseph B. Soloveitchik* (Leiden: Brill, 2013) and *From Phenomenology to Existentialism* (on Buber and on the existentialists, see chaps. 10–11; on Freud, 276–80; on Heidegger, where the references are more of the "passim" variety, see the index; the phrase about Maritain and Marcel is on 366); Moshe Z. Sokol, "Transcending Time: Elements of Romanticism in the Thought of Rabbi Joseph B. Soloveitchik," *Modern Judaism* 30, 3 (2010): 233–46; Eileen H. Watts, "Keeping the Faith: Aspects of Rabbi Joseph B. Soloveitchik's *The Lonely Man of Faith* in Bernard Malamud's 'The Magic Barrel'," *The Torah u-Madda Journal* 17 (2016–17): 185-201; Elliot R. Wolfson, "Eternal Duration and Temporal Compresence: The Influence of Ḥabad on Joseph

value of relating the Rav's ideas to other thinkers regardless of causal influence. But it is crucial to see that taken as a whole, the scholarship just depicted makes clear, implicitly or explicitly, that an important piece in studying the Rav is to realize that his use of his influences is dynamic and activist rather than passive. To use the Rav's idiom in *Kol Dodi Dofek* and elsewhere: he is, qua interpreter, a subject and not an object. In fact, the Rav's originality lay not in creating his own epistemological or phenomenological or existentialist theories, but in (i) his recruitment of existing philosophical ideas to explicate Jewish tradition and (ii) his ability to subtly or unsubtly transform certain ideas in other thinkers to fit his purposes.[59] It is among his hallmarks not to be slavish toward predecessors, but rather to transform his sources. This point applies in two sorts of cases – one, when he modifies others' ideas without claiming to be interpreting them (at times without citing them), and, two, when he expressly claims to be interpreting them.

Thus, his borrowings from Kierkegaard, Buber, Cohen, and the rest come with alterations, sometimes huge, sometimes subtle.[60] Particularly important is that he places themes like suffering, I-Thou, revelation, and encounter in the context of law and commandment. Drawing upon analyses by Blidstein and Schwartz, we note, for instance, that although Buber and Barth read Genesis 1-3 as dialogic, and served as a source for *Lonely Man of Faith*, the Rav added important elements –

B. Soloveitchik," in *The Value of the Particular: Lessons from Judaism and the Modern Jewish Experience: Essays in Honor of Steven T. Katz on the Occasion of his Seventieth Birthday*, ed. Michael Zank and Ingrid Anderson (Leiden: Brill, 2015), 195-238 (discussion of Heidegger in n. 37 on 208-12); Reuven Ziegler, *Majesty and Humility*, 324–27. Yoel Finkelman (in personal communication) suggested examining critiques of popular religion. In *The Last Rabbi: Joseph Soloveitchik and Talmudic Tradition* (Bloomington and Indianapolis: Indiana University Press, 2016), William Kolbrener examines Rabbi Soloveitchik's thought in the light of numerous philosophers and literary theorists, but the book appeared too late for me to take account of it in this essay. Kolbrener's book relates to several topics referenced here, including feminism , family, psychoanalysis, personal experience, and halakhic interpretation.

59. See also Shatz "A Framework for Reading Ish ha-Halakhah," 230.
60. To add to our list: Arnold Davidson mentioned to me that in *Worship of the Heart*, the Rav invokes Otto's notion of *numen presens* but introduces, too, *numens absens*. See 72, 73, 75, 77, 79.

notably, God as both partner and lawgiver – and that whereas Barth read Genesis 2 as a continuation of Genesis 1, the Rav viewed them as contrasting. Schwartz maintains, in fact, that with regard to reading Genesis, the Rav and Barth "appear rather different and distant . . . the similarity between them is merely formal and hermeneutical."[61] The Rav's stress on redemption as an "inner" phenomenon rather than an external event resembles Christian teaching, but law is for him the *means* of redemption.[62] When Michael Berger construes *U-vikkashtem mi-Sham* as a response to Buber, he argues that for the Rav, as against Buber, encounter and revelation without law and dread are not enough for the religious experience.

Rabbi Blau and Goldman show how the Rav went beyond Scheler with regard to repentance, and Ozar specifies how he diverged from Scheler in *The Emergence of Ethical Man*. Rynhold and Harris have shown that although the Rav adopted certain themes from Nietzsche, he rejected Nietzsche's dismissal of the Absolute and accommodates not only Nietzsche's dominant theme of a life-affirming existence (as in the Rav's analysis of repentance), but also "life-denying" elements of repentance that Nietzsche abhorred. As time went on, the 'life denying" aspects (humility, submission, self-defeat) became more salient, but as Blidstein (quoted by Rynhold and Harris) observes, ". . . almost without exception, man falls solely to rise again with increased strength."[63] I scarcely need to make the parallel point that the Rav adapted Cohen to his purposes. Sagi notes that in presenting a view about evil, he mixed Cohen with existentialism.[64] He also points to a comparison and contrast with Camus, who, like the Rav, stressed the human battle against evil, but unlike the Rav did not see God as involved in history (and did not believe in God!).

The Rav's use of Christian terms like *kerygma* and charisma, and the stress on *inner* redemption, initially may seem surprising.[65] But

---

61. See Blidstein, *Society and Self*, 63–75; Schwartz, *From Phenomenology to Existentialism*, 349–57. The quotation is from p. 357.
62. For other examples of the interiority of religious concepts in Rabbi Soloveitchik's thought, see J. Cohen, "Incompatible Parallels." Alex Sztuden pointed out that The *Emergence of Ethical Man* does speak of redemption in history.
63. Blidstein, "Society and Self," 147.
64. Sagi, *Tradition and Traditionalism*, 162–63, 173.
65. The halakhic status of Christianity in the Rav's opinion is somewhat elusive. Gerald J. Blidstein and Nathaniel Helfgot note his omission of reference to

they make sense when we see them as reflecting the thesis that valuable religious concepts salient in Christianity find a home in Judaism, *but therein are expressed and embedded differently.* The message is that Judaism does not lack any major religious concepts that are of value, because it can incorporate the best of what Christian thinkers have offered while bringing the borrowed concepts to new horizons in a non-Christian and even anti-Christian framework.

We now confront three questions. The first is why Rabbi Soloveitchik does not often cite his sources. The second is why he transforms them, at times interpreting them explicitly in a way that strikes us, once we know from whom he is drawing, as "not peshat." An example is his transformation of Maimonides' concept of providence from fact to norm in *Halakhic Man.*[66] The third question is how aware he was that his interpretations of sources, particularly of Maimonides, at times strayed from *peshat.*

To frame the first question more precisely: in *Halakhic Man,* Rabbi Soloveitchik provides copious references in notes to then-recent figures like Scheler, James and Kierkegaard. He cites both thinkers with whom he agrees and thinkers with whom he disagrees (such as James [n. 4], albeit in *The Halakhic Mind* he approves of James' pluralism). *The*

---

avodah zarah in a responsum about whether an interfaith center for Jewish and Christian worship may use representations of human form (biblical personalities). See Blidstein, *Society and Self,* 41–42; Helfgot, introduction to *Community, Covenant, and Commitment: Selected Letters and Communications,* ed. Nathaniel Helfgot (New York: Toras HoRav Foundation, 2005), xvi–xvii. The letter/responsum appears in *Community, Covenant, and Commitment,* 3–10. Perhaps the Rav omitted the question of *avodah zarah* for reasons of diplomacy. There are conflicting reports from two of Rabbi Soloveitchik's disciples, as summarized by David Berger: "R. Walter Wurzburger reports that R. Soloveitchik once persuaded a wavering Catholic doctor who was treating him not to leave the Church, even as R. Hershel Schachter testifies that the Rav rejected the view that Christian-style *shittuf* is permissible to Noahides." See David Berger, "Covenants, Messiahs, and Religious Boundaries" (a review essay of Irving Greenberg, *For The Sake of Heaven and Earth*), *Tradition* 39, 2 (summer 2005): 66-78. If we try to harmonize the reports, then Christianity is *avodah zarah* even for a gentile, but preferable to atheism. In an unpublished manuscript the Rav seems to regard *avodah zarah* as a flouting of ethics more than doctrinal error. But the matter needs more exploration.

66. *Halakhic Man,* 123–28. Cf., however, Menachem Kellner's article in this volume.

Halakhic Mind is full of references to non-Orthodox and non-Jewish scientists and philosophers. But *The Lonely Man of Faith* and
"Confrontation" are different: there is no reference to, for example,
Barth or Buber (or Cohen) despite obvious and important overlap
and influence. Yehoyada Amir criticizes *The Lonely Man of Faith*
for omitting mention of the liberal Jewish thinkers who preceded
Rabbi Soloveitchik in his analysis of faith, and regards the omissions
as a strategy for selling his ideas to his Orthodox constituents. [67]
There is some logic in this strategy: It is possible that, not necessarily
self-consciously, the Rav was following the model of Maimonides, who
declares in his preface to *Shemonah Perakim* that he will not cite the
sources for his ideas because people might delegitimize an idea once
they know its provenance.[68] In effect, Amir suggests, without invoking
Maimonides, that the Rav did so as well; but he maintains (wrongly, I
think) that the Rav's procedure has attenuated the value of his essay(s).
The reception that the Rav's works have been accorded even outside
Orthodoxy testifies against Amir's claim about value. Moreover, it
was not common practice among theologians to cite others except to
explicitly disagree. Buber did not cite Ferdinand Ebner, whose concept
of dialogue clearly influenced him;[69] nor do Continental philosophers
typically cite sources of their thought.[70] (Strikingly, the Rav does not
even cite himself, i.e., other of his works.) At the same time, based on
Halakhic Man it appears that the Rav preferred to place references in
notes rather than his text. Consequently, it is entirely possible that had
he prepared his manuscripts fully for publication in his lifetime, rather
than merely deliver them orally, references would have been added in
notes. An interesting case is *The Emergence of Ethical Man*, where
names like Buber and the psychologist Gardner Murphy appear in the
text or notes, but Scheler, a clear influence, as Ozar shows, does not.[71]

---

67. See Amir, "Ha-Rav Soloveitchik ke-Sokhen Tarbut."
68. Herbert Davidson has shown that Alfarabi was prominent among the uncited
    sources. See Davidson, "Maimonides' *Shemonah Perakim* and Alfarabi's Fu-
    sul al-Madani," *Proceedings of the American Academy for Jewish Research*
    31 (1963): 33–50.
69. Rabbi Shai Held mentioned this example.
70. This was confirmed for me by Arnold Davidson, a renowned expert on
    Continental philosophy.
71. It is possible that Rabbi Soloveitchik was wary of creating an entire work
    that would be a sustained polemic with Scheler, but this is speculative.

The second question is why the Rav transforms his sources. In cases when he isn't *claiming* to be interpreting a source, it is not problematic or surprising that he simply alters it in whatever way suits him. Many of his adaptations may reflect the Rav's desire to create resonance and relevance for his time and audience, and fidelity to authorial intent is not very relevant if the source is not being interpreted.[72] Another, tantalizing explanation for such a trend invokes his propensity for *hiddush*. As Lawrence Kaplan remarks, "an original thinker does not merely passively absorb 'influences,' but selectively and creatively draws upon and transforms them in the course of his work."[73] How much more so with a thinker who so prized *hiddush*. We may have here a case where talmudic practice impacted upon philosophical practice. Rabbi Soloveitchik's proclivity for *derash* would seem to play a role in his philosophical method as well: an unexpected interpretation of a philosopher bears affinities to *derash*.[74] In some cases the transformation of sources may not be deliberate – do we always know what the Rav understood a particular thinker to be saying? Do we know what he read firsthand and what he learned secondhand, or plucked out of the zeitgeist?[75] That said, it is likely that much of his revision of thinkers was self-conscious.

Besides examples involving interpretations of philosophers, we find creative uses of rabbinic texts. A good illustration is his understanding of Nahmanides' idea that that the lives of the fathers (ancestors) are signs or symbols of the lives of the sons (descendants). (The idea is often paraphrased as *ma'aseh avot siman le-banim*.) The Rav, while accepting the fact that the lives of the sons (descendants) replicate those of the fathers (ancestors), surmounts its deterministic implications by taking a symbol as something that requires free human interpretation and response. "Each event was predetermined by the symbolic acts of the patriarchs. Yet in every generation, how to interpret the event is up to the individual or to the people as a whole. The Jew is free to choose from the many alternative interpretations of the event."[76] In

---

72. See also Ziegler, 370.
73. Kaplan, "Rabbi Soloveitchik's Philosophy of Halakhah," 181.
74. See Ziegler, *Majesty and Humility*, 370 n. 13. On the role of *derash*, see Peli, "Hermeneutics in the Thought of Rabbi Soloveitchik." (See also the article in *Conservative Judaism* 41, 3 (1989): 16–34.)
75. My thanks to Daniel Rynhold for this point.
76. *Abrahams's Journey: Reflections on the Life of the Founding Patriarch*, ed.

some cases, the Rav enlists creative readings of rabbinic texts largely
as literary allusions woven into his prose, without always embracing
the philosophical import of the original. Consider: "R. Jacob says,
this world resembles a vestibule (*prozdor*) before the world to come.
Prepare yourself in the vestibule so you may enter the banquet hall"
(*Avot* 4:21). Whereas the plain meaning of this text denigrates "this
world" by relegating it to a mere vestibule, the Rav alludes to the
images in the statement obliquely, as follows, without claiming to
interpret the text: "The ontological approach serves as the vestibule
whence he may enter the banquet hall of normative understanding.
Halakhah cognizes the world in order to subordinate it to religious
performances."[77] This obviously homiletic rendition ignores the an-
ti-worldly sense of the *peshat*, and allows the Rav to retain his strong
this-worldly stress.[78] (He mutes the sequel: "Better one hour of bliss in
the world to come than the whole life of this world.") Such deviations
from rabbinic texts in *Halakhic Man* must be explained by viewing
the recruited phrases as (mere) literary allusions. Eugene Korn pointed
out[79] that in one passage the Rav asserts there is a natural yearning "in
every human being, Jew and gentile alike . . . to come as possible to
Master of the Universe." The Rav then refers to a specific passage in
the *Tanya* that calls this drive "ahavah tiv'it."[80] However the passage
in Tanya states "this only applies to Jews, not non-Jews." He thus used
the Tanya to get at the idea of *ahavah tiv'it* but felt no obligation to
accept the rest of the Tanya's discussion. However, we should separate
this phenomenon of de-contextualized allusions from the phenomenon
of misquotation. The latter is puzzling, and doubly so because the Rav
did not correct the quotation errors when the English translation of
Halakhic Man was being prepared.[81]

David Shatz, Joel B. Wolowelsky, and Reuven Ziegler (New York: Toras
HoRav Foundation, 2008), 11. The idea of a symbol is discussed on pages
7–11 of the book.
77. *Halakhic Man*, 63.
78. See Dorff, 93.
79. In correspondence.
80. The passage is *Abraham's Journey*, 59. Cf. *Tanya, Likkutei Amarim* chaps.
    12, 19, 38.
81. On *Halakhic Man*, 30, the Rav cites *Avot* 4:17 as "[R. Jacob says] Better is
    one hour of Torah and *mitzvot* in this world than the whole life of the world
    to come" (*Avot* 4:22), benignly replacing "repentance and good deeds" with

The third question has to do with self-consciousness. To what extent was he cognizant that his representations of ideas of other thinkers weren't *peshat*? What was the Rav really doing when he portrayed Maimonides as an existentialist?[82] In his own mind, is that *peshat* or *derash*? Ziegler notes that Rabbi Soloveitchik at one point in *U-Vikkashtem mi-Sham* indicates that he is consciously transmuting philosophic proofs of God's existence into experiences of God, but later in the same work presents an experiential reading of the cosmological proof given at the outset of *Mishneh Torah*, as capturing Maimonides' original intent.[83] Is he engaging in *peshat* or *derash*? In two letters to Simon Rawidowicz, he cites a non-experiential reading.[84] In some cases, specifically those involving German thinkers who published prior to the Rav's years in Berlin, it would be helpful to know exactly what his professors in Berlin taught, both about themselves and about other figures. That would illuminate how the Rav understood those German thinkers who influenced him and whom he cites – and apparently alters for his own purposes. [85]

"Torah and *mitzvot*." This discrepancy between the text as cited and the original was pointed out to me by Arnold Davidson. A misquotation of the Vilna Gaon appears on page 57. On its significance, see my "Science and Religious Consciousness in the Thought of Rabbi Joseph B. Soloveitchik," *Jewish Thought in Dialogue*, 142.

82. See especially the grouping of Maimonides *Hil. Teshuvah* 10:3 with Kierkegaard in *Out of the Whirlwind*, 196. Another example of interpreting Maimonides in an unconventional way is one that Wolfson addresses, for other purposes, at 198-99, n. 7, involving the imputation of acosmism to Maimonides.

83. See also Heshey Zelcer, "The Mystical Spirituality of Rabbi Joseph B. Soloveitchik," *Hakirah* 11 (2011): 143–44.

84. See *Community, Covenant and Commitment*, 279–84 together with Ziegler, Majesty and Humility, 369–71 and 373–74, "Further Reference" #5. The differing presentations are in "And From There You Shall Seek," 11–15 and 158–59. See also the footnote in *LMF*, 51–52 , which uses the experiential reading.

85. Scholars seem to have a special interest in relating the Rav to Heidegger, both with regard to his in-person exposure to Heidegger and with regard to connections between parts of their philosophies despite the chasm between their outlooks. See Schwartz, *Religion or Halakha?*, esp. 20-25, and Wolfson, 208-12, n. 37. See also Michael Fagenblat "The Thing that scares me most: Heidgger's Anti-Semitism and the Return to Zion," KD Sol Kierkhttp://www.jcrt.org/archives/14.1/fagenblat.pdf-, 16-17, and the brief blogpost by Gil Student, "Rav Soloveitchik and Heidegger," http://hirhurim.blogspot.com

Interestingly, there has been much less scholarship on the Rav's relationship to rabbinic sources and Jewish philosophy than on his relationship to general philosophy. Possibly, this is because in the case of rabbinic texts and Jewish philosophy the task looks relatively easy. There is no need for a scholar to hunt for sources, since they are quoted explicitly (even if at times a quote or phrase is presented without an author's name). Exploring the connections to rabbinic sources is nonetheless a good project for the future; we do now better understand his relationship to Maimonides. Warren Zev Harvey, Lawrence Kaplan, Menachem Kellner, Michael Nehorai, Aviezer Ravitzky, Daniel Rynhold, Dov Schwartz, Phillip Stambovsky, Shira Weiss, and Walter Wurzburger have examined this relationship with regard to a variety of areas, notably ethics, epistemology, intellect and experience, the religious ideal, creativity, *imitatio Dei*, and providence.[86] Shira Weiss elaborates on the Rav's relationship to Halevi and Maimonides.[87] Eliezer Goldman wrote a more general assessment of the difference between medieval philosophy (in particular its attempt to derive God

---

/2006/10/rav-soloveitchik-and-heidegger.html.

86. Harvey, "He'arot al ha-Rav Soloveitchik ve-ha-Pilosofiyyah ha-Rambamit," EBM, 95–107; Kaplan, "Maimonides and Rabbi Soloveitchik on the Knowledge and Imitation of God," in *Moses Maimonides (1138–1204): His Religious, Scientific, and Philosophical Wirkungsgeschicte* ed. George K. Hasselhoff and Otfried. Fraisse (Wurzburg:, 2004), 491–523; Nehorai, "Ha-Rambam ve-ha-Rav Soloveitchik al Gevulot ha-Herut," in RBOH, 502–13; Rynhold, *Two Models of Jewish Philosophy* (New York: Oxford University Press, 2005), on *ta'amei ha-mitzvot*; Schwartz, "Peirusho shel Ha-Rav Soloveitchik la-Rambam: Sekhel, Maskil, u-Muskal," *Ha-Rambam be-Nivkhei ha-Sod: Mehuvveh le-Moshe Halamish*, ed. Avraham Elqayam and Dov Schwartz (Ramat Gan: Bar-Ilan University Press, 2009), 301–21; Schwartz, *From Phenomenology to Existentialism*, 135–37 (on Maimon); Phillip Stambovsky, "Rabbi Soloveitchik's Causal Critique of Maimonides As a Religious Philosopher," *Journal of Jewish Studies* 63, 2 (2012): 307–30; Weiss, "Taste and See That the Lord is Good: The Influence of Halevi and Maimonides on the Thought of Rabbi Soloveitchik," delivered at the University of Chicago, February 2014 (available at http://www.spertus.edu/Feb16); Wurzburger. "The Maimonidean Matrix of Rabbi Joseph B. Soloveitchik's Two-tiered Ethics," repr. in Wurzburger, *Covenantal Imperatives* (Jerusalem and New York: Urim, 2008), 161–71, and also Wurzburger, "Imitatio Dei in the Philosophy of Rabbi Joseph B. Soloveitchik," repr. in ibid., 172–90.

87. One of her papers appears in this volume; another is cited in the previous note.

from the cosmos) and a modern experiential approach, with attention to where Rabbi Soloveitchik should be situated.[88] Bahya is another philosopher from whom Rabbi Soloveitchik draws, for example, in the notes to *U-Bikkashtem mi-Sham*; comparisons and contrasts could be interesting since the distinction between physical performance (*ma'aseh ha-mitzvah*) and internal fulfillment (*kiyyum ha-mitzvah*) is prominent in Rabbi Soloveitchik's analysis of *mitzvot*, and Bahya distinguished between duties of the limbs and duties of the heart.

Paul Franks, Aviezer Ravitzky, and Dov Schwartz compare Rabbi Soloveitchik to Solomon Maimon regarding the human intellect and divine intellect and idealism.[89] Regarding Rabbi Soloveitchik's use of Kabbalah, Lawrence Kaplan maintains that the Rav uses Kabbalistic images like *tzimtzum* in contrasting ways, depending on context, and thus does not intend them literally.[90] Numerous comparisons to Rabbi Abraham Isaac Kook have been suggested, though the latter is not cited by the Rav and it is difficult to tell whether he writes with him in mind.[91] Elsewhere I have suggested that the Rav contrasts

---

88. Goldman, "Gilluy ve-Kissuy be-Mishnato shel ha-Rav Soloveitchik," in *Mehkarim ve-Iyyunim: Hagut Yehudit be-Avar u-ba-Hoveh*, ed. Daniel Statman and Avi Sagi (Jerusalem: Magnes Press. 1997), 225–33. See also the previous paragraph concerning proofs.

89. See Ravitzky, "Rabbi J. B. Soloveitchik on Human Knowledge" 162–63, 167–68; Schwartz, *From Phenomenology to Existentialism*, 135–37. Paul Franks deals with Maimon and Rabbi Soloveitchik in a paper delivered at a conference of the University of Chicago and Spertus Institute in February 2014 (available in audio at http://www.spertus.edu/Feb16).

90. See: Kaplan, "Motivim Kabbaliyyim be-Haguto shel Ha-Rav Soloveitchik: Mashma'uttiyyim o Itturiyyim?" in EBM, 75–94; cf. Rivka Horowitz, "Yahaso shel Ha-Rav Soloveitchik la-Havayah ha-Datit u-le-Mistorin," in EBM, 45–74. See also Schwartz, *From Phenomenology to Existentialism*, chap. 4. The article by Lustiger on the place of *U-Vikkashtem mi-Sham*, cited earlier, suggests a more literal reading in the particular context that he analyzes.

91. See Yonah Ben-Sasson, "Mishnat he-Hagut shel ha-RAYH Kuk ve-ha-RYD Soloveitchik," in *Be-Oro*, ed. Chaim Hamiel (Jerusalem, 1986): 419–508; Yuval Cherlow, *Ve-Hayu la-Ahadim be-Yadekha: Mi-Dialektika le-Harmonia be-Mishnato shel Ha-Rav Yosef Dov Soloveitchik* (Alon Shevut: Tenuvot, 2000); Hannah Kehat, "Zugiyyut ve-Shivyon: Bein ha-Rav Kuk le-ha-Rav Soloveitchik," *Massekhet* 4 (5766): 335–48 ; Lawrence J. Kaplan, "Ethical Theories of Abraham Isaac Kook and Joseph B. Soloveitchik," in *The Oxford Handbook of Jewish Ethics and Morality*, ed. Elliot Dorff and Jonathan Crane (New York: Oxford University Press, 2013), 166–85; Eliezer Sariel, "*Ha-Teshuvah be-Hagutam shel Ha-Reayah Kuk ve-ha-GRYD Soloveitchik:*

with Rabbi Eliyahu Dessler.[92] Ziegler suggests that Beit Halevi (Rabbi Soloveitchik's great-grandfather, who bore the same name) and Netziv (Rabbi Naftali Zvi Yehuda Berlin) also were influences.[93]

The role of Hasidic thought in the Rav's philosophy needs clarification. Did the Baal Ha-Tanya and Habad thought have an impact on Rabbi Soloveitchik's philosophy? Elliot Wolfson has explored this issue, primarily with regard to the notion of time.[94] Is the Rav correct in claiming that Hasidim were ascetics, fleeing this world, given evidence that *mitnaggedim* were ascetic while *Hasidim* were this worldly? [95] Was he thinking of particular Hasidic masters or schools when he criticized Hasidism's other-worldliness? Does the notion of *ha'alaat*

Iyyun Mashveh," *Alon Shevut* 155 (5760): 77–103; Dov Schwartz, "Ha-Te-shuvah: Bein Ha-Reayah le-Rav YD Soloveitchik," *Illanot* 1 (5767): 153–61; Ziegler, *Majesty and Humility*, chap. 22 (on repentance; see his index for other discussions in the book). See also the private conversations transcribed in Dov Holzer (ed. Aryeh Holzer), *The Rav Thinking Aloud* (Israel, 2009; self-published), 40, 154–56, 170, 229.

92. "Practical Endeavor and the Torah u-Madda Debate," *The Torah u-Madda Journal* 3 (1991–1992): 98–149. It is possible that when the Rav advocated the scientific activism of Adam the first, he recognized the contrast to Rabbi Eliyahu Dessler's stance, which criticizes human initiative.

93. See Ziegler, "Hidden Man, Revealed Man: The Role of Personal Experience in Rav Soloveitchik's Thought," 46–56.

94. See Wolfson, "Eternal Duration and Temporal Compresence." See also Schwartz, *Religion or Halakha?*, 165-83, 189-90, and *From Phenomenology to Existentialism*, 91, 102-03, 112. See also Yehoshua Glassman's 1997 master's thesis at Bar-Ilan University. The Rav was explicit about his Habad *melammed*'s impact on him (For example, Rakeffet 1: 147-48, 151-52, and the audio tape at http://bcbmmedia.cloudapp.net/Media /RavSoloveitchik/MachshavaOther/Chabad_and_Gaon_19_Kislev_1969 .mp3. In the tape, Wolfson notes, Rabbi Soloveitchik describes himself as a "clandestine Lubavitcher.") A fairly large and interesting popular literature has developed about the personal relationship between Rabbi Soloveitchik and R. Menachem Mendel Schneerson (see the references in Wolfson), but in our present context my focus is on the content of the Rav's philosophy.

95. See Alan Nadler, "Soloveitchik's Halakhic Man: Not a Mitnagged," *Modern Judaism* 13 (1993): 119–147. Also relevant in any analysis of the Rav's appraisal of Hasidut is the story of the Habad shofar blower in *Halakhic Man*, 60–63, a story subject to different interpretations. See also Alex Sztuden, "Why Are There Stories in Halakhic Man?," in *Rav Shalom Banayikh:* (a festschrift for Shalom Carmy), ed. Hayyim Angel and Yitzchak Blau (Jersey City, NJ: Ktav, 2012), 313-29.

ha-guf (elevating the body) found in *U-Vikkashtem mi-Sham* arise, in part, from the Hasidic idea of *avodah be-gashmiyut* (worship through corporeality), or do its origins lie in phenomenologists like Scheler, or both?[96] Does the Rav's focus on *inner* redemption derive from Hasidism, or from Christian theology, or from both? Or, plainly and simply, from reflection on Halakhah? These questions set a potentially fruitful agenda in the attempt to locate the context of the Rav's writings.

Finally, notwithstanding certain literature cited earlier in the notes, there is also room for more work that situates Rabbi Soloveitchik in the context of twentieth century Jewish philosophers such as Buber, Goldman, Hartman, Heschel, Leibowitz, Levinas, and Rosenzweig. An extensive treatment of this area has been produced by Gili Zivan.[97]

In light of the many influences on his thought, how should we interpret the Rav's famous statement that "[T]here is only a single source from which a Jewish philosophy could emerge: the objective order – the Halakhah . . . Out of the sources of Halakhah, a new world view awaits formulation"?[98] How could his procedure be differentiated from the grafting he imputes to the medieval Jewish philosophers in the very same section of *The Halakhic Mind*? One option is to read him as

---

96. On Scheler, see Ozar, "The Emergence of Max Scheler."

97. Works to date in this area (details on Zivan are below) include: Birnbaum, "The Man of Dialogue and the Man of Halakhah"; Hannah Kasher, "Ha-Emunah ke-Bittui Shel ha-Ratzon: Bein Ha-Rav Soloveitchik li-Ye-shayahu Leibowitz," *Proceedings of the American Academy for Jewish Research* 55 (1988): 7–14; Reuven Kimelman, "Rabbi Joseph B. Soloveitchik and Abraham Joshua Heschel on Jewish-Christian Relations," *Modern Judaism* 24, 3 (2004): 251–271; Oliver Leaman, "Jewish Existentialism: Rosenzweig, Buber, and Soloveitchik," in *History of Jewish Philosophy*, ed. Daniel H. Frank and Oliver Leaman (London and New York: Routledge, 1997), 799–819; Avi Sagi, *Tradition vs. Traditionalism*, chaps. 6,7; idem, *Jewish Religion After Theology* (Boston: Academic Studies Press, 2009) chap. 5; Gili Zivan, "*Dat le-Lo Ashlayah: Nokhah Olam Post-Moderni: Iyyun be-Hagutam shel Soloveitchik, Leibowitz, Goldman, ve-Hartman* (Jerusalem: Hartman Institute, Ramat Gan: Bar-Ilan Law School, Tel Aviv: Ha-Kibbutz ha-Meyuhad, 2005); idem, "Me-ha-she'alah 'Lammah?' la-She'elah 'Eikh?': Iyyun be-Divreihem shel Ha-Rav Soloveitchik, Goldman, Hartman, Leibowitz, ve-Levinas," in *Hiddat ha-Yissurin*, ed. Baruch Kahana, Hayutah Doitsh, and Roni Redman (Jerusalem: Beit Morasha and Tel Aviv: Yediot Aharanot, 2012), 207–30. Arnold Davidson informs me that Levinas quotes the Rav only once.

98. *The Halakhic Mind* (New York: MacMillan, 1986), 101–2.

follows: the Halakhah is the touchstone of whether a view drawn from general philosophy should be regarded as authentically Jewish, but Jewish philosophy does not have to be, and perhaps cannot always be, derived strictly from halakhic statements, without the aid of background theories in philosophy.[99]

(2) **More comprehensive.** Rabbi Soloveitchik addressed a large number of topics. If we combine the various works I named earlier and the present English and Hebrew volumes, we find that the range of subjects that have been covered now include such previously uncharted territory as emotion,[100] biblical interpretation,[101] history,[102] ethics,[103]

---

99. See also Shatz, "On A Seeming Disconnect between Halakhah and Theology," 447–48. The procedure would still resemble that of Rambam, who used philosophical knowledge to interpret verses like the Shema. Rabbi Soloveitchik accepts some of these Maimonidean derivations. For further discussion of the idea of Jewish philosophy emerging out of the sources of Halakhah, see Cf. R. Mayer Twersky, "Towards a Philosophy of Halakhah," *Jewish Action* 64, 1 (fall 2003): 49–62; R. Shubert Spero's response, "On the Philosophy of Halakhah," *Jewish Action* 64, 4 (summer 2004): 66–67; and R. Twersky's rejoinder to Spero in the same issue, 68–70. See also Spero, "Rabbi Joseph Dov Soloveitchik and the Philosophy of Halakha," *Tradition* 30, 2 (Winter 1996): 41–64.

100. See Alex Sztuden's essay in this volume and Sztuden, "Grief and Joy in the Writings of Rabbi Soloveitchik" (n. 129 below).

101. See Blidstein, "Biblical Models"; Yuval Cherlow, "Mishkal Pirkei ha-Beri'ah be-Mishnato shel Ha-Rav Soloveitchik u-Mashma 'uto," *Pittuhei Hotam* 2 (5766): 215–25; J. Cohen, "Strauss, Soloveitchik, and the Genesis Narrative"; Aharon Lichtenstein, "Sippur ve-Tzav be-Aspaklariyyat ha-Rav: Le-Darko shel Ha-GRYD Soloveitchik be-Limmud Ha-Mikra ve-Hora'ato" *Alon Shevut* 12 (5758): 53–63; Sagi, *Tradition and Traditionalism* chap. 6 and "*Kitvei ha-Kodesh u-Mashma'utam*," BDD 1 (5755): 49–62; Schwartz, *From Phenomenology to Existentialism*, chap. 11 and 349–57.

102. Samples: Ephraim Kanarfogel, in this volume; Chaim Navon, "Gishato shel Ha-Rav Soloveitchik la-Toda'ah Ha-Historit," *Sinai* 141 (2007-2008): 167–84; Yosef (Jeffrey) Woolf, "Historiyyah ve-Toda'ah Historit be-Mishnato ha-Hilkhatit shel Ha-Rav Soloveitchik," RBOH, 323–38.

103. Daniel Statman, "Hebeitim bi-Tefisato ha-Musarit shel ha-Rav Soloveitchik" in EBM, 249–64; Yosi Turner, "Ha-ma'aseh ha-Dati lefi ha-Rav Soloveitchik: Tzivvuy ha-Kel o Yetzirah Enoshit," in EBM, 383–402.

aesthetics,[104] education,[105] family (marriage, parenthood, sexuality,

---

104. Joshua Amaru, "Prayer and the Beauty of God: Rav Soloveitchik on Prayer and Aesthetics," *The Torah u-Madda Journal* 13 (2005):148–76; Braiterman, "Joseph Soloveitchik and Immanuel Kant's Mitzvah-Aesthetic"; the exchange of letters between Lawrence J. Kaplan and Amaru in *The Torah u-Madda Journal* 15 (2006–07): 247–50; Dov Schwartz, "Estetikah u-Gevulot ha-Tevunah: Gishot be-Hagut ha-Ortodoksiyah ba-Meah ha-Esrim," *Daat* 74–75 (5753): 403–32.

105. Literature on the Rav and education is immense. It includes works on the Rav's philosophy of education, essays on ways to teach some specific *shiurim* or *divrei Torah* of the Rav on particular topics, and ways to teach his philosophy. Although the general thrust of the present essay would make the first category most important, I'll combine works in the various categories – some reflect more than one – and suggest the following non-exhaustive list: Seth Farber, *An American Orthodox Dreamer: Rabbi Joseph B. Soloveitchik and Boston's Maimonides School* (Brandeis University Press, 2003); idem, "Rabbi Joseph Soloveitchik and Co-educational Jewish Education," http://www.jewishideas.org/articles/rabbi-joseph-soloveitchik-and-coeducational-jewish; Yehuda Gelzman, "He'arot al Gishato ha-Hinnukhit shel Ha-GRYD ," *Hagut be-Hinnukh ha-Yehudi* 8 (5768): 243–65; Russell Jay Hendel, "The Educational Pedagogy of the Four Sons," *Shofar* 22, 4 (2004): 94–106; Elie Holzer, "Ha-Te'oriyyah ha-Hermenutit shel Ha-Rav Soloveitchik be-Hibburo *The Halakhic Mind: Iyyun Bikkorti ve-Hashlakhot Hinnukhiyyot*," in *RBOH*, 23–41; idem, ""Pilosofiyyah shel ha-Dat ve-Hinnukh Morim," *Hagut be-Hinukh ha-Yehudi* 53 (2000); Tzvi Pittinsky "The Role of Teacher and Student in Jewish Education According to Rabbi Soloveitchik", *Ten Da'at* 18 (2006): 94–104; Michael Rosenak, "Rabbi Joseph B. Soloveitchik and Aspects of Jewish Educational Philosophy: Explorations in the Philosophical Writings," *Journal of Jewish Education* 75, 2 (2009): 114–129; Michael Rosenak and Avinoam Rosenak, "Ha-Rav Soloveitchik ve-ha-Pilosofyah ha-Hinnukhit ha-Yehudit," in *RBOH*, 397–409; Jeffrey Saks, *Spiritualizing Halakhic Education: A Case Study in Modern Orthodox Teacher Development* (Jerusalem: Mandel Foundation, 2006); Moshe Simkovich, "Teaching Rabbi Soloveitchik's Thought in the High School Classroom" in *Wisdom From All My Teachers: Challenges and Initiatives in Contemporary Torah Education,*" ed. Jeffrey Saks and Susan Handelman. (Jerusalem and New York: Urim Publications, 2003); Moshe Sokolow, "Yetzirat Takhnit Limmudim le-Tefillah be-Hashra'at Haguto shel ha-Rav Soloveitchik," RBOH, 514–534; idem, "Tefillat HaRav: Education for Prayer Utilizing the Writings of Rabbi Joseph B. Soloveitchik: Curricular and Instructional Guidelines," (Azrieli Graduate School of Education, Yeshiva University); http://yu.edu/uploadedFiles/Academics/Graduate/Azrieli_Graduate_School/Research_and_Publications/Sokolow%20Tefillat%20Rav.pdf. (Some other authors suggest curricula on particular topics using Rabbi Soloveitchik's teachings.) Ziegler's *Majesty and Humility* origi-

filial obligations),[106] psychology (in particular, as noted earlier, Freud, Bakan, Jung, and Murphy)[107] community,[108] death,[109] prayer,[110] *dark-hei ha-limmud*,[111] reasons for the commandments,[112] and medical

---

nated in *shi'urim* he gave on the web and represent an educational approach to teaching the Rav's philosophy. See also the review essay about Ziegler's book by Charles M. Raffel, "Reading the Rav: A New Guide," *The Torah u-Madda Journal* 16 (2012–13): 203–14. I thank Rabbi Jeffrey Saks for his assistance in compiling this list. See also the eleven items on the ATID website at http://www.atid.org/journal/journal05/default.asp.

106. See Ziegler, *Majesty and Humility* 203–12; Blidstein, *Society and Self*, 111–20; Lawrence J. Kaplan, review of *Family Redeemed, Judaism* 50 (fall 2001): 491–99; Kehat, "Zugiyyut ve-Shivyon"; Dov Schwartz, "Tefissat ha-Zuggiyut be-Haguto shel Ha-Rav Soloveitchik," *Daat* 57–59 (5766): 333–53.

107. See the articles by Ben-Pazi, Grysman, and Mittelman cited in note 59.

108. See Blidstein, *Society and Self*, 77–104; Ziegler, *Majesty and Humility*, chaps. 2, 13, and *passim* (see the book's index). Blidstein's essay in *Society and Self* is his most recent version of an essay that originally appeared in *Tradition* in 1989, then appeared in Hebrew in EBM.

109. See Blidstein, *Society and Self*, 121–151.

110. Amaru, "Prayer and the Beauty of God"; Shalom Carmy, "Destiny, Freedom, and the Logic of Petition," *Tradition* 24, 2 (1989): 17–37; Lawrence J. Kaplan, review essay on *Worship of the Heart, Hakirah* 5 (fall 2007): 79–114; Elyakim Krumbein, "Im Yesh Bo Davar Asher Tukhal Lekayyemo: Al Hashivuto shel ha-Sefer 'Avodah she-ba-Lev' me-et ha-Rav Y. D. Soloveitchik," *Akdamot* 18 (5767): 141–63; Aharon Lichtenstein, "Ha-tefillah be-Mishnat ha-GRYD Soloveitchik ztl," *Alon Shevut* 149 (5757): 79–91.

111. Elyakim Krumbein, "From Reb Hayyim and the Rav to Shi'urei ha-Rav Aharon Lichtenstein – The Evolution of a Tradition of Learning," in *Lomdus: the Conceptual Approach to Jewish Learning,* ed. Yosef Blau (Michael Scharf Publication Trust of Yeshiva University Press, 2006), 229–97 and the response by Avraham Walfish, "The Brisker Method and Close Reading – Response to Rav Elyakim Krumbein, " in *Lomdus,* 299–321; Rosenak, "Pilosofiyyah u-Mahashevet ha-Halakhah." For broader exposition and critique of the "Brisker derekh" see the essays in Blau (ed.) *Lomdus,* as well as: Chaim Saiman, "Legal Theology: The Turn to Conceptualism in Nineteenth-Century Jewish Law," *Journal of Law and Religion* 21, 1 (2006):39–100; Norman Solomon, *The Analytic Movement: Hayyim Soloveitchik and His Circle* (Atlanta, GA: Scholars Press, 1993) and Marc Shapiro's review of Solomon's book, "The Brisker Method Reconsidered," *Tradition* 31(1997): 78–102, at 78–79.

112. Rynhold, *Two Models of Jewish Philosophy*; Moshe Meir, "*Ta'amei ha-Mitzvot: Gilgulei Rayonot, Hagut Ba-Hinnukh ha-Yehudi*" (5762): 29–50.

ethics.[113]

The present volume deals with the Rav's philosophical oeuvre, but a word is in order about the continuing fascination that his biography inspires and – more significantly for our objectives – about his biography's relevance to understanding his philosophy.

There have been historical articles by Jeffrey Saks on the Rav turning down the chief rabbinate of Israel and on his meeting with Rav Kook, and by Reuven Kimelman and subsequently Yigal Sklarin on the history of the Rav's opposition to theological dialogue; and (in Kimelman's case) on the contrasts between the Rav and Rabbi Abraham Joshua Heschel. Rabbi Aaron Rakeffett-Rothkoff has written considerably on such topics as the Rav's leaving Agudah and defecting to Mizrachi, along with a lengthy biographical précis in the preface to his anthology of excerpts from the Rav's writings and recordings. Seth Farber has written a book on Rabbi Soloveitchik's years in Boston and an article on his appointment as Rosh ha-Yeshivah of the Rabbi Isaac Elchanan Theological Seminary. We also now have a cornucopia of primary sources for a biography – letters of the Rav through the decades.[114] Even so, as the cliché goes, and as Shlomo Pick and Jeffrey

113. See Alan Jotkowitz, "Rabbi Joseph B. Soloveitchik and the Problem of Contemporary Medical Ethics," *Journal of Contemporary Religion* 26, 1 (January 2011): 91–10.

114. See *Community, Covenant, and Commitment* and the additional letters in Helfgot, "From the Rav's Pen: Selected Letters of Rabbi Joseph B. Soloveitchik," in *Rav Chesed: Essays in Honor of Rabbi Joseph Lookstein*, vol. 1, ed. Raphael Medoff (Jersey City, NJ: Ktav, 2009), 315–30. The other articles referenced here are: Reuven Kimelman, "Rabbi Joseph B. Soloveitchik and Abraham Joshua Heschel on Jewish-Christian Relations"; Rakeffet-Rothkoff, *The Rav*, 1–87; Jeffrey Saks, "Rabbi Joseph B. Soloveitchik and the Israeli Chief Rabbinate: Biographical Notes (1959–60)," *BDD* 17 (September 2006) : 45–67; Yigal Sklarin, "'Rushing In Where Angels Fear to Tread': Rabbi Joseph B. Soloveitchik, The Rabbinical Council of America, Modern Orthodox Jewry and the Second Vatican Council," *Modern Judaism* 29, 3 (2009): 351–85; Shaul Farber, "Minnuyo shel Ha-Rav YD Soloveitchik le-Rosh Yeshivat Rabbenu Yitzhak Elhanan Ve-Haga'atah shel ha-Ortidoksyah ha-Amerikanit, *Yeshivot u-Batei Midrashot*" 5757, 417–30. See also Bernard Rosenzweig, "The Rav As Communal Leader," *Tradition* 30, 4 (summer 1996): 210–218; Aharon Yarchi, "Ezer Ke-Negdo: Ha-GRYD Soloveitchik ve-Ishto," *Tzohar* 6 (5761): 139–44; the various books by Rabbi Soloveitchik's renowned student, Rabbi Hershel (Zvi) Schachter, *Nefesh ha-Rav, Divrei Ha-Rav* (Jerusalem: Mesorah: 5770) and *Mi-peninei ha-Rav*

Woolf have urged, a full scale biography remains a desideratum.[115]

We should, however, draw a distinction. Biography and anecdotes, vital as they are, focus – to use "Brisker" terminology – on the *gavra*, the person, not the *heftza* (entity) of thought that he left us. A full scale *intellectual* biography, tracing a progression in the Rav's thought, is also desirable – though much is already understood about, say, the differences between his works in the 1940s (*Ish ha-Halakhah, The Halakhic Mind*, and *U-Vikkashtem mi-Sham*, which was begun in the 1940s) and works in the 1960s (particularly *Lonely Man of Faith*).

An intellectual biography would trace, inter alia, the connections between biography and philosophy.[116] A simple example: A high percentage of Rabbi Soloveitchik's essays on suffering were delivered or composed in the early 1960s, after his battle with cancer, and in the late 1960s after the death of his mother, brother, and his wife over a four-month period in 1967. Of course, his most famous treatment of suffering, *Kol Dodi Dofek*, was delivered earlier in 1956, but it is easy to imagine that in the later periods I mentioned, personal circumstances stimulated a proliferation of works on the theme. Moreover, after these deaths the Rav's writings take on a darker tone. They show greater emphasis on humility, submission, catharsis, and dependence, a far cry from the self-confident autonomous *Halakhic Man* of the 1940s and a more extreme stance than that of Adam the second in *Lonely Man of Faith*. The "action" demanded in *Kol Dodi Dofek* is replaced by submission. The very emphasis on medicine in *The Lonely Man of Faith* may reflect family circumstances and/or Rabbi Soloveitchik's battle with personal illness in 1959-1960. Reuven Ziegler suggests that to understand changes in the Rav's thought we need to look at factors like "age and adversity; the absorption into

---

(Brooklyn: Bet ha-Midrash de-Flatbush (Jerusalem: Reshit Yersushalayim).

115. See Shlomo Pick, "The Rav: Biography and Bibliography – A Review Essay," *BDD* 6 (Winter 1998): 27–44; idem, "The Rav: A Pressing Need for a Comprehensive Biography," BDD 10 (2000): 37–57; Jeffrey Woolf, "In Search of the Rav: The Life and Thought of Rabbi Joseph Soloveitchik in Recent Scholarship," *BDD* 18 (2007): 5–28, esp. 5–12. Pick points to many unanswered questions and mistaken conceptions; see especially "The Rav: A Pressing Need . . . ," 51–57. Bierman (ed.), *Memories of a Giant* and Eleff (ed.), *Mentor of Generations* provide a good amount of history.

116. See, however, the exchanges between Alan Yuter, Shlomo Pick, and Dov Schwartz in *Review of Rabbinic Judaism* 12, 2 (2009): 221–284.

consciousness of historical watersheds like the Holocaust and the State of Israel [the Rav tells us that the Holocaust induced him to shift from Agudah to a pro-Zionist stance – DS]; changes in American Jewry and American society; and so on."[117]

Even when biography did not influence philosophy, biography can *clarify* philosophy. Thus, the dispute over whether the position set forth in "Confrontation" opposing theological dialogue reflects Rabbi Soloveitchik's true position, or whether instead he had a secret one that was more disposed to such dialogue, is deeply affected by Yigal Sklarin's analysis of events before 1965, i.e., the chronological development of the Catholic Church's *Nostra Aetate*, an analysis which suggests that from the very outset of Vatican II the Rav opposed dialogue. Some of the connections between biography and philosophy are completely transparent – such as how his extolling of teaching and *hesed* in *Abraham's Journey* and elsewhere reflects his own personal mission and aspiration of being both a teacher and (following the model of his grandfather Rabbi Hayyim Soloveitchik) a *ba'al hesed*.[118] With the availability now of many letters, we get a fuller sense of historical context that affects interpretations of the philosophy. Thus, as Lawrence Kaplan shows, a comparison of a 1952 letter to Rabbi Emanuel Rackman with a later discussion illuminates the Rav's successive conceptions of the proper role of teleological considerations – or lack of same – in halakhic decision making.[119] In some cases we have to explain why the biography did *not* match philosophical pronouncements – for example, why did he first present *Lonely Man* to a Catholic audience, why was he not active in interfaith coalitions for humanitarian causes as "Confrontation" urges, why did he not visit Israel after 1935.[120]

Another area of biography where more work is needed concerns

---

117. Ziegler, *Majesty and Humility*, 411.

118. See, for example, the stories related by Allen Goldstein, one of the Rav's doctors, in *Memories of A Giant*, ed. Bierman, 173–77.

119. See Lawrence J. Kaplan, "From Cooperation to Conflict: Rabbi Professor Emanuel Rackman, Rav Joseph B. Soloveitchik, and the Evolution of American Modern Orthodoxy," *Modern Judaism* 30, 1 (2010): 46–68. Kaplan identified the addressee as Rabbi Rackman, whose name does not appear in the letter printed in *Community, Covenant, and Commitment*.

120. On his not traveling to Israel, see the letter to Miriam Shiloh in *Community, Covenant, and Commitment*, 227–29.

when and why Rabbi Soloveitchik acquired an interest in philosophy. The origins of and rationales for his immersion in philosophy and larger cultural pursuits are somewhat of a mystery. Elsewhere I have posed a number of conceptual explanations. For example – I argued that, for the Rav, every Jew has a dual identity, Jewish and human; the pursuit of culture reflects our human identity, which complements our Jewish identity even while standing in tension with it.[121] Philosophy, furthermore, when pursued in a phenomenological or existentialist mode (recall, again, Schwartz's distinction), refines and deepens religious experience. Yitzhak (Isadore) Twersky, the Rav's late son-in-law, suggests that philosophy was simply "part of his intellectual capital," and it was simply obvious to him that it could be enlisted in the pursuit of interpreting Torah.[122] Gerald Blidstein has proposed that, for the Rav, the pursuit of philosophy, and of the humanities generally, is justified because they deal with matters of the spirit. By dint of this justification, Blidstein suggests, study of the sciences stands *more* in need of justification than study of the humanities (contrary to what is almost always assumed). The Rav therefore presented justifications for the study of science but not for the study of humanities.[123] Although Adam the first creates broad culture and not only science, which can give some legitimacy to pursuit of the humanities, this point is not blatant in *The Lonely Man of Faith*, and Blidstein's suggestion is plausible even given the expansive and generally positive portrayal of Adam the first. But these theoretical rationales do not provide causes or a biographical timeline of the Rav's interest in philosophy.

---

121. Shatz, "Science and Religious Consciousness," 163.
122. Yitzhak Twersky, "The Rov," *Tradition* 30, 4 (summer 1996): 29–31. See also Blidstein, "On the Jewish People in the Writings of Rabbi Joseph B. Soloveitchik," 20; Shatz, "Science and Religious Consciousness," 164–65 and the slightly different discussion, 333–34 in the earlier Hebrew version in EBM.
123. See *Society and Self* , 81. Blidstein's various versions of his article suggest a progression. See "On the Jewish People in the Writings of Rabbi Joseph B. Soloveitchik," *Tradition* 24, 3 (1989): 20, then some material added in the Hebrew version in *EBM*, 151–52; and then the passage in *Society and Self*, 81. For discussion, see Kaplan's review essay on *Society and Self*, titled "Exposition as High Art," *Hakirah* 15 (Summer 2013): 105–6.

(3) **More critically engaged.** Philosophers do not gain fame by being right; if they had to be right, many great works of philosophy would long ago have been consigned to the dustbin. But in studying the Rav, there's a tension between the impulse of his students to defer to his authority – the rebbi-talmid dynamic – and the critical engagement required when doing philosophy. Some people harbor a stereotype of Modern Orthodox thinkers that they don't criticize "their rabbis." The stereotype is false. It may be true, however, that the new generation, people who did not study with the Rav, feel freer to examine his works critically, albeit within a framework of deep respect.[124] The results of such engagement can often be fruitful. Reflecting on the critiques, one senses that had the Rav been in a department of theology, or attended academic conferences, he would have had input from other theologians and possibly ironed out certain difficulties.[125]

I will deal now with some of the criticisms and with questions of my own about applications of the Rav's philosophy – in other words, "where we can go." I agree with certain critiques, disagree with others. In order to keep the discussion manageable, I will deliberately not scrutinize criticisms of an internal textual nature – the use of an outdated epistemology in the crucial part of *U-Vikkashtem mi-Sham*,[126] contradictions within individual works or the corpus as a whole,[127] the

---

124. A good example is Joshua Amaru, "Prayer and the Beauty of God," who argues that the Rav's view of prayer is not, as the Rav maintains, exoteric and democratic. Rabbi Jonathan Sacks, who did not study with the Rav, penned at age 35 an alternative view to *The Lonely Man of Faith* in *Tradition* 13, 4 (1973): 137–62. Ziegler, author of the most comprehensive study of the Rav in English, did not study with him, and his work enunciates certain difficulties in the Rav's thought. A detailed and somewhat sharply formulated critique by a young scholar is Ira Bedzow, *Halakhic Man, Authentic Jew: Modern Expressions of Orthodox Jewish Thought From Rabbi Joseph B. Soloveitchik and Eliezer Berkovits* (Jerusalem and New York, 2009), esp. 13–78, 125–47. See below, n. 130, for two examples of critiques by older scholars (viz. Hartman and Spero).

125. Cf. Schwartz, "Personality and Psychology."

126. See the criticisms of the thesis of the identity of the knower and the known by Shalom Carmy, David Shatz and Reuven Ziegler which Lustiger cites in the paper mentioned earlier, "Kabbalistic Underpinnings."

127. For a valuable review of proposed methods for handling contradictions, along with suggestions, See Yoel Finkelman, "Theology with Fissures: Contradictions in Rabbi Joseph B. Soloveitchik's Writings," *Journal of Modern Jewish Studies* 13, 3 (2014): 399-421.

difficulties in defining the connection between *ma'aseh ha-mitzvah* and *kiyyum ha-mitzvah*[128] and the like – but rather will discuss critically what the Rav said to the modern world and whether new times call for new messages and applications. My focus is change: what changes have taken place in social realities, including the intellectual and political scene, that might necessitate a reappraisal.[129] Rabbi Yehuda Amital said that scholars want to know what Rav Kook said, but "we" want to know what Rabbi Kook says *to us*. Likewise with the Rav – and the "us" changes from generation to generation, even within a generation. Instructively, Rabbi Amital joked that a new generation comes along every few years.[130]

(i) In 1944, in *Halakhic Man*, the Rav was able to sustain an analogy between Halakhah and science – to wit, between an a priori approach to Halakhah, which is unaffected by social circumstances, and an a priori approach to science that viewed science as likewise unaffected by societal or historical factors. Today the analogy to science would look very different, quite apart from the gap between a Neo-Kantian view of science as *a priori* and a straightforwardly empiricist, *a posteriori* one.[131] In 1961 Thomas Kuhn wrote an iconoclastic and (after an initially harsh reception in some quarters) extraordinarily influential book called *The Structure of Scientific Revolutions*. Kuhn argued that the traditional picture of science as based on straightforwardly inferring hypotheses from data in accordance with set rules, is

128. See Alex Sztuden's three-part article, "Grief and Joy in the Writings of Rabbi Soloveitchik," *Tradition* 43, 4 (2010): 37–55; 44, 3 (2011): 9–32; 45, 2 (2012): 67–79.

129. Books by David Hartman and Shubert Spero, deserve mention among books of critical engagement, but for the most part their probing critiques are not predicated on changing trends, an exception being Hartman on interfaith dialogue. See Hartman, *Love and Terror in the God Encounter: The Theological Legacy of Rabbi Joseph B. Soloveitchik* (Woodstock, VT: Jewish Lights, 2001); Spero, *Aspects of Rabbi Joseph B. Soloveitchik's Philosophy of Judaism* (Jersey City, NK Ktav, 2009).

130. Lawrence Kaplan, in "'Ish ha-Emunah ha-Boded' Le-Rav Soloveitchik be-Mahashavah ha-Ortodoksiyyah-Modernit," RBOH, 147–76, appropriately points to the danger of inaccurately enlisting Rabbi Soloveitchik's thought for one's favored ideology, criticizing David Hartman, Shira Wolosky, and me on this score.

131. Cf. *Halakhic Man*, 146, n. 17, and see Ziegler 306–7.

simplistic and wrong. His study of history showed that scientists hold
on to their paradigms, persisting in believing certain theories despite
contrary evidence. More relevant to us, they may embrace certain
theories because of such factors as peer influence, nationality, age, and
more.[132] Much to Kuhn's chagrin, the book was accused of tarnishing
science as irrational and subjective; and even if that understanding
was not accurate, as Kuhn contended, there is no gainsaying that
views of science have changed dramatically because of Kuhn's work.
Consequently, an analogy between Halakhah and science would fall
apart for the Rav in our times, because even though history of Halakhah has many practitioners, social and historical factors are not *for
him* part of the picture as they are in Kuhnian approaches to science.
Rather, the notion that Halakhah is molded by outside influences was
anathema to him.

In our present intellectual setting, the common analogue to Halakhah is not science but other legal systems – not primarily in the
sense of comparing specific laws in Halakhah to laws of other systems,
but in the sense of understanding the nature of Halakhah as a legal
system by comparison to the nature of other *systems*: for example,
the relationship in the respective systems between law and ethical
considerations, law and social/political considerations, and other
factors.[133] Such comparative endeavors are problematic for the Rav.
Even setting aside the Halakhah-science *analogy* per se, the academic
trend toward historicizing Halakhah undermines the conception of
Halakhah as an a priori system.[134]

Nevertheless, the core analogy in *Halakhic Man* – that a halakhist
imposes categories on the world, that bodies of water become in
halakhic man's noetic framework potential *mikva'ot*, and the like – remains strong and profound as a way of understanding how halakhists

---

132. See also Ziegler, *Majesty and Humility,* 306 n. 12.
133. For a broader discussion of Rabbi Soloveitchik's choice of science over
     law as the apt model, see Kaplan, "Rabbi Joseph Soloveitchik's Philosphy
     of Halakhah," 180–92; Ziegler, 306, n. 13. As Kaplan notes (188–92), other
     Orthodox thinkers formulated analogies between science and Halakhah. In
     his view the Rav was drawn to the Neo-Kantian analogy not for apologetic
     reasons but because it made room for both objectivity and autonomy.
134. Both Jeffrey Woolf and Ephraim Kanarfogel have shown, in different
     ways, that the Rav had a consciousness of history. But he did not think that
     historical factors determine Halakhah.

and for that matter laypersons committed to Halakhah conceive the world.[135] Arnold Davidson discerns in this idea the Kuhnian theme (present in many others too) that perception is theory laden.[136] (In truth, of course the halakhist perceives the world *both* ways, the ordinary and the halakhic.) Furthermore, his depiction of the creativity and sense of freedom of halakhic man remains true to the experience of halakhists even in an age of religious heteronomy and pressures for uniformity on halakhic questions. Finally, as Haym Soloveitchik has pointed out, the jurist's perspective and the historian's perspective are different.[137] Internally, the halakhist may experience his work as insulated from historical circumstances even if in point of fact historical influences operate. Interestingly, the Rav's student Gerald Blidstein, his son Haym Soloveitchik, and his son-in-law Isadore Twersky all dealt with history of Halakhah, albeit not all in the same way.

As Daniel Rynhold notes in this volume, in *The Halakhic Mind*, which is contemporaneous with *Halakhic Man*, we find inklings – or more than that – of a more Kuhnian view of science (pre-Kuhn). In *The Halakhic Mind*, the Rav portrayed scientific method as somewhat less "objective" and more of a humanistic and hermeneutic enterprise, in contrast to the depiction in *Halakhic Man*.[138]

No matter how we slice it, the science-Halakhah analogy no longer holds up in the way the Rav intended in *Halakhic Man*. In assessing

---

135. Kaplan, in "Rabbi Joseph Soloveitchik's Philosophy of Halakhah," traces the Rav's particular conception of the a priori to Ernst Cassirer.

136. In conversation.

137. See Haym Soloveitchik, "A Response to Rabbi Ephraim Buckwold's Critique of 'Rabad of Posquieres: A Programmatic Essay'," *The Torah-Madda Journal* 14 (2006–07): 232–34. A sharp focus for the general issue is the contrast between the "traditionalist" and academic approaches to a "shverer Rambam." See Marc Shapiro, *Studies in Maimonides and his Interpreters* (Scanton and London: University of Scranton Press, 2008), 1–93, esp. 55–93. Shapiro addresses contrasting approaches to Brisker readings in his "The Brisker Method Reconsidered," a review of Norman Solomon, *the Analytic Movement* in *Tradition* 31 (1997): 78–102. Note especially 78–79.

138. See also Kolbrener, "Towards A Genuine Jewish Philosophy," n. 10. Related to this shift is the shift (noted by Kolbrener and Rynhold) in the relative statuses of the religious personality and the scientist. In *Halakhic Man*, the foil to halakhic man, the sharpest contrast, is *homo religiosus*; in *The Halakhic Mind*, the foil is the Newtonian scientist, who was praised in *Halakhic Man* more than was *homo religiosus*.

the Rav's philosophy of Halakhah, thinkers ought also to look at an issue that has stimulated a rich and capacious literature and was alluded to earlier: what is the role of moral intuitions and values in halakhic decision-making? Is halakhic decision-making a matter of formal rules, or should values enter as well? Kaplan showed that although early on the Rav drew upon teleological considerations, he did not do so later.[139]

(ii) A second issue about change is what *The Lonely Man of Faith*, now over fifty years old, implies for today's world.[140] Parts of the essay's critique of contemporary religion remain as strong as ever, and extensions of them can be developed. For example, there is even more tawdry commercialism in the selling of religion than when the Rav wrote. More importantly, certain changes in society make the ideal of Adam the second even more difficult to realize today than in the 1960s. The concept of religious *communities*, so much stressed in *Lonely Man* as essential to Adam the second, is being supplanted by highly individualistic and idiosyncratic forms of belief and practice. Granted, in *Lonely Man* the notion of community can designate a connection between merely two individuals,[141] but the notion of "covenantal communities" requires more than that. I am sure that the Rav would have been unhappy to read The Pew Studies of trends in religion that substantiate the rise of so-called "Nones" who believe in God but have no religious affiliation. The mobility of religious people, the movement from one affiliation to another (or to non-affiliaton) – likewise documented in a Pew study– likewise undermines community.[142] Even among Orthodox Jews, who enjoy a relatively strong sense of community, "breakaway minyanim" typify and virtually symbolize the fragmentation of some communities.

---

139. This emerges in the correspondence with Rabbi Rackman and the examples Rabbi Rackman cites, along with the eventual sequel to the correspondence. See Kaplan, "From Cooperation to Conflict." The examples Rabbi Rackman cites are found in *Community, Covenant, and Commitment.*
140. On the fiftieth anniversary of *The Lonely Man of Faith*, ATID published on its website twelve essays concerning the relevance and impact of *Lonely Man* for individuals and communities. See http://www.atid.org/resources /lmof40.asp.
141. Yoel Finkelman pointed out the need for this qualification.
142. See http://religions.pewforum.org/reports.

Religion has become deinstitutionalized even for a cohort of a young generation of Modern Orthodox Jews, though Orthodoxy is far from bereft of a sense of community.[143]

These are facts, not normative statements; but the above developments show how far contemporary religion falls short of the ideal Adam the second community, and they intensify the problem that the Rav highlights, making his discussion all the more germane today. Another dimension of the contemporary problem surfaces as well. The Rav's message in *Lonely Man* is that, as men and women seeking God, we need both to integrate ourselves into vibrant covenantal communities, and to engage the world. The ideal of engagement surely remains uplifting, but to many Orthodox Jews it seems dangerous and unwise to fulfill in 21st century society. For the gap between religious and secular moralities is now a canyon, an abyss; and so withdrawal from society, from the life of Adam the first, becomes attractive as a strategy for spiritual and ethical survival, to an extent not matched a half century ago. The Rav might have placed this point front and center were he writing the essay today, even if he differed with the withdrawal strategy itself.

In the cases mentioned, recent developments intensify the Rav's critique of religion and therefore ultimately show the validity of his message. However, a facet of *Lonely Man of Faith* that is problematic involves the question: Does religion in our day play too great a role in society? Certainly many think it does. In the form of radical Islam, religion is now a mighty, ubiquitous force, and religious extremism has stimulated from atheists sweeping vilifications of *all* religions.[144] We are witnessing Adam the first's pursuit of victory run amok when it comes to religion. To take a very different sort of example, both America and Israel are deeply, bitterly divided over the propriety of imposing religion on society, Many Americans and Israelis resist letting religious values function in the creation of law. Not only do they fight against legislation that is dictated by religious beliefs, they even object

---

143. See Shmuel Hain (ed.), *The Next Generation of Modern Orthodoxy* (New York, The Michael Scharf Publication Trust of the Yeshiva University Press, 2012). Most explicit about de-institutionalization is the article there by Yehuda Sarna, "The End of the Middle of the Road: Re-envisioning Modern Orthodoxy for the Twenty-first Century," 332–49.

144. I have in mind primarily the "neoatheists," Richard Dawkins, Daniel Dennett, Sam Harris, and Christopher Hitchens.

to "religious reasons" having a voice in the public square at all. This component of liberalism is weakening, but it hasn't vanished. What does *The Lonely Man of Faith* say about this issue? In one reading of the essay, the Rav believed that Adam the second should ultimately guide the endeavors of Adam the first, because Judaism does not divide the world into religious and secular sectors.[145] This assertion seemingly advocates a fusion of religion and state, where political decisions ride on religious considerations. This reading is buttressed by an open letter the Rav penned about the need for different faiths to work together to battle social, moral and religious ills.[146] In that letter, the Rav specifically calls upon religions to apply shared values like *imago Dei* to social problems. We must ask, however: is that proposed goal of religion, that is, influencing society to adopt and implement shared values, workable in America? Or in Israel?

Compounding the difficulty, the Rav's conception of religion as private and incommunicable seems to suggest that religions cannot bring shared values to debates in the public square. I refer the reader to two opposing articles on these tensions, one by Rabbi Meir Soloveitchik and another by Yoel Finkelman. The former argues that for the Rav, religion plays an important role in the public square; the latter sees much tension about the issue, noting that the two Adams cannot communicate. We are presented in those articles with a lively, highly important debate about the place of religion in society – a dispute that reflects dialectical tensions within the Rav's writings.[147] The issue needs to be considered partly in the light of the Rav's positions about separation of religion and state in Israel, which contains aspects of both integration and separation.[148]

---

145. See *The Lonely Man of Faith,* Doubleday edition, 84; Random House edition, 79–80; OU Press edition, 58.

146. *Community. Covenant, and Commitment*, 259–61.

147. Meir Y. Soloveichik, "A Nation Under God: Jews, Christians, and the Public Square," *The Torah u-Madda Journal* 14 (2006–07): 62–83; Yoel Finkelman, "The Rav on Religion and Public Life: A Rejoinder," *The Torah u-Madda Journal* 15 (2008–09): 237–52, and Soloveichik's reply in the same issue, 253–56. See also Finkelman, "Religion and Public Life in the Thought of Rabbi Joseph Soloveitchik," *Jewish Political Studies Review* 13, 3–4 (2001): 41–70, and idem, "Dat ve-Hayyim Tzibburiyyim." Interpreters have perhaps made too much of a footnote in "Confrontation" (24, n. 8) which suggests that there really is no purely secular domain.

148. See *Community, Covenant, and Commitment*, 177–226. On 224–226, he

Lonely Man also did not grapple with moral problems of technology and scientific advance. Although in the 1950s and 1960s, Orthodox rabbis, including prize students of the Rav, stressed from the pulpit the moral challenges of technology, its negative impact on human values and the human psyche,[149] Adam the first doesn't retreat from technology because of moral problems with it, but because (a) it does not satisfy his religious yearnings nor his yearning to understand the world, and (b) he must learn humility. In the heady inaugural days of space travel, technology induced wonder, admiration, and enthusiasm in the Rav (even while some modern Orthodox rabbis criticized it sharply). Today, Adam the first's quest for majesty and dignity, defined in terms of humanity's creative potential, seems more problematic as we confront situations like cloning and designer babies. The ascendance of materialist conceptions of the mind as neuroscience advances creates religiously problematic but scientifically grounded presumptions in the development of medicine (psychiatry being a strong example) and indeed science generally. The Rav rejected materialism in *The Emergence of Ethical Man*, even while affirming to a high degree the biological nature of human beings; but his arguments for that rejection need to be visited in light of present-day science. [150]

Reuven Ziegler makes an important point in this connection: that, although "it is always imperative to view the dialectic in its full-

states, in the course of an interview, "I cannot imagine a secular state." But he then, as in numerous letters where he explains why he turned down an offer of the Chief Rabbinate, criticizes the Chief Rabbinate for its political character, but ends by bemoaning the fact that "the clergy are afraid of their flock." See also *The Rav Speaks*, 78–89, 173–93, 208–09 . Cf. Holzer, 142–43, 175 (noted to me by Heshey Zelcer).

149. See, for example (Rabbi) Norman Lamm, *Festivals of Faith*, ed. David Shatz, Associate ed. Simon Posner (New York: OU Press, 2011), 323–324. On the same theme, see Eliezer Berkovits, *Crisis and Faith* (New York: Sanhedrin Press, 1976), chaps, 1, 2, 4. R. Lamm was a prized student; R. Berkovits did not study with the Rav.

150. Alan Jotkowitz, in "Rabbi Joseph B. Soloveitchik and the Problem of Contemporary Medical Ethics," shows how certain philosophic themes in Rabbi Soloveitchik's writing generate particular stances on issues in medical ethics. Thus, the *Emergence of Ethical Man* argues for a strong biological aspect of the human being, and, according to Jotkowitz, this leads, or should lead, Rabbi Soloveitchik to adopt an aggressive ethic for the treatment of the comatose and terminally ill, and to rule stringently about cases of abortion. Those beings lack conscious awareness – but are still human.

ness," nevertheless, ". . . when one espouses a dialectical philosophy, changing circumstances demand a changing emphasis." Hence, "we must reassess which side of the various dialectics he posits requires strengthening today, even if it is not the same element the Rav felt the need to highlight in his time and place."[151] This might dictate greater stress on humility, in the form of ethical restraint.

The final and perhaps most important change in society, noted by Aviezer Ravitzky, is that Adam the first no longer represents secular humanity. "[T]he image of proud, conquering secular man, filled with majesty and glory, trusting the unlimited rule of reason" has given way: "Today's modernists and secularists are extremely conscious of their deep problematics and fears."[152] Do we have here, asks Ravitzky, "perhaps a third kind of Adam Rav Soloveitchik did not anticipate?"[153]

(iii) *Interfaith dialogue*: The Rav has been criticized widely for arguing in "Confrontation" that religious commitment is incommunicable and theological dialogue is impossible. If commitment were incommunicable, the critics say, nobody could explain his or her faith to anybody, even to other denominations of the same religion and even to people who seemingly belong to the same faith communities. (The Rav himself, however, points out this consequence and embraces it.[154]) Furthermore, the Rav's absorption of ideas from Barth, for example, would have been impossible, including *the idea of Barth and other Christians that faith is incommunicable*. We may add to these points the question: What is the Rav doing when he explicates Judaism to the world?[155] Or when he polemicizes against Christianity and argues for Judaism? If religion is incommunicable, how can he attempt this? Still another question is how the Rav's perspectivist epistemology in

151. Ziegler, 411.
152. "Hadash Min Ha-Torah? Modernist vs. Traditionalist Orientations in
    ' Contemporary Orthodoxy," in *Engaging Modernity*, ed. Moshe Z. Sokol
    (Northvale, NJ and Jerusalem: Jason Aronson, 1997), 46–47. (The Hebrew
    version is in EBM, 445–60.)
153. Ibid., 47.
154. See "Confrontation," 24.
155. See his expression of a desire to explain Judaism to others in Holzer,
    322–325 and Rakeffet 2:168–169. I thank Heshey Zelcer for these refer-
    ences.

"Confrontation" can be rendered consistent with his faith in the truth of one particular perspective.[156]

Arguments have also been advanced that the Rav has a secret position that favors or at least approves of theological dialogue, along with arguments (used by Eugene Korn and Rabbi Shlomo Riskin in setting up an interfaith center) that in today's religious climate of greater understanding and of transformations within Christianity, the Rav would hold differently.[157] Opposing this latter claim, David Berger has contended that the Rav's critical concern over the emergence of pressures for reciprocal concessions in dialogue has turned out to be prescient and would remain decisive for him today, notwithstanding transformations in Christianity.[158] Daniel Rynhold has shown that the argument in "Confrontation" reflects themes already present in *The Halakhic Mind,* suggesting that the Rav's opposition to theological

---

156. See the papers by Rynhold on perspectivism cited earlier.
157. Criticisms of the Rav's position, and/or arguments that he would allow theological dialogue in today's conditions, and/or claims that he held a secret liberal position appear in: Irving Greenberg, *For the Sake of Heaven and Earth: The New Encounter Between Judaism and Christianity* (Philadelphia: JPS, 2004), 13–14; Hartman, *Love and Terror,* 131–65; Eugene Korn, "The Man of Faith and Religious Dialogue: Revisiting 'Confrontation'," *Modern Judaism* (2005): 290–315; David Novak, *Jewish-Christian Dialogue: A Jewish Justification* (New York: Oxford University Press, 1989), 6–9; Shlomo Riskin, "Dialog Yehudi-Notzri : Hashivah Mehudeshet," *Makor Rishon Musaf Shabbat* (Iyyar 5772): 15–21; Marc B. Shapiro, "'Confrontation': A Mixed Legacy," http://seforim.blogspot.com/2009/09/thoughts-on-confrontation-sundry.html. Contrast these with: David Berger, "Response to Eugene Korn," in Berger, *Persecution, Polemic, and Dialogue: Essays in Jewish-Christian Relations* (Boston: Academic Studies Press), 385–91; idem,"Emunah bi-Reshut ha-Yahid," *Makor Rishon* (November 16, 2012); Shalom Carmy,"Orthodoxy and Reticence," *First Things* 150 (February 2005) : 8–10; David Shatz, "Morality, Liberalism, and Interfaith Dialogue," *New Perspectives on Jewish-Christian Relations In Honor of David Berger,* ed. Elisheva Carlebach and Jacob J. Schacter (Leiden: Brill, 2012), 491–519. The Korn and Berger articles originated in a program at Boston College, http://www.bc.edu/content/dam/files/research_sites/cjl/texts/center/conferences/soloveitchik/. Remarks by Aryeh Klapper appear there as well. On how explication and polemicizing can take place within a framework of alleged incommunicability, see my and Daniel Rynhold's tentative suggestions in Shatz, "Morality, Liberalism, and Interfaith Dialogue," 515–16.
158. See Berger, "Emunah bi-Reshut ha-Yahid."

dialogue is strongly motivated philosophically.[159] Elsewhere I have argued that, ultimately, proponents of theological dialogue have to explain their own animus against proselytizing, and that the best grounds for this animus is precisely the appeal to privacy that the Rav invoked in opposing theological dialogue.[160]

Beyond issues about incommunicability and wariness of proselytizing is the fact that, in the current intellectual climate, multiple religions emerge as equally validated. As Abraham Unger points out, "... we are living in a period that presumes a confidence in the authenticity of one's own cultural context, obviating the need to negotiate one's particularistic convictions."[161] Theological dialogue is, this argument suggests, pointless. But dialogues that deal with social and ethical issues that all of society confronts – these the Rav not only permitted but mandated. Unger urges that Jews heed this call, joining with others, in the Rav's words, in confronting "an order that defies us all."[162] It is not clear how differing opinions about ethics in different religious traditions could be resolved in this "permissible" form of dialogue given the idea that particularistic convictions need not or cannot be "negotiated." In practice, Jews, including some organizations on the Orthodox right, sit on coalitions with members of other religions. But they do so out of considerations of Jewish self-interest. One important change between 1964 and now is the rise of radical Islam. There is a new hostile "other" that we confront. Rabbi Jonathan Sacks has called for Jewish-Muslim dialogue, a great shift of emphasis.[163]

(iv) *Religious Zionism*: Dov Schwartz writes that in the past: "The figure of R. Soloveitchik as a *gadol* who was religious-Zionist was a source of admiration and pride. His works were diligently studied in religious-Zionist *yeshivot*. They were not, however, a constitutive component of the religious-Zionist consciousness." He explains, "[t]he rejection of metaphysics in R. Soloveitchik's work relegated it to the

---

159. Daniel Rynhold, "The Philosophical Foundations of Soloveitchik's Critique of Interfaith Dialogue," *Harvard Theological Review* 96, 1 (2003): 101–20.
160. See Shatz, "Morality, Liberalism, and Interfaith Dialogue," esp. 512–19.
161. See Abraham Unger, "A Modern Orthodox Approach to Interfaith Dialogue," *Conversations* 8(2010): 136–142.
162. "Confrontation," 20.
163. See his *The Dignity of Difference* (London and New York: Continuum, 2002).

margins of Israeli religious Zionist consciousness."[164] In other words, while *Kol Dodi Dofek* was regarded, as another writer puts it, as "a classic of Religious-Zionist thought,"[165] its pragmatic, non-messianic Zionism was not able to win many adherents in Israel when it came up against the competition – the fervor of the messianism and metaphysical understanding of history promulgated by the Mercaz ideology of Rabbi Zvi Yehuda Kook. According to Schwartz, however, the current situation is different; the Rav's Zionism is on the ascent – so much so, that "we can safely say that this work has become the unofficial manifesto of the next generation of religious-Zionism."[166] Schwartz attributes this heightened attraction in part to the waning of metaphysics and the "return to 'real' existence in shaping the lives of many religious-Zionists."[167] The work's ascendance as a galvanizing text of religious-Zionism is ironic in light of the point made by Gerald J. Blidstein that religious-Zionism was not at the center of the Rav's thought.[168] (Not all will agree with Schwartz; see anon.)

Of course, to repeat an earlier observation, metaphysics is not altogether absent: the motif of God's "six knocks" obviously entails a metaphysical claim. In fact, Avraham Walfish and Gili Zivan have each pointed out that the Rav's professed eschewing of metaphysics is in conflict with his confident reading of events in 1948. (How, they ask, can he know that God is summoning us, if God's mind is inscrutable?)[169]

---

164. Dov Schwartz, "*Kol Dodi Dofek*: A Religious-Zionist Alternative," *Tradition* 39, 3 (Fall 2006): 68. See also Schwartz's other writings on Religious Zionism, such as *Faith at The Crossroads: A Theological Profile of Religious Zionism*, trans. Batya Stein (Leiden: Brill, 2002), 193–210; and *From Phenomenology to Existentialism*, chap. 8.
165. Avraham Walfish, "When Theology Knocks," *Tradition* 39, 3 (fall 2006):78.
166. Schwartz, 69.
167. Ibid., 69. See also Yuval Cherlow, "Redemption and Responsibility," *Tradition* 39: 3 (fall 2006): 27–30.
168. See Gerald J. (Yaakov) Blidstein, "A Religious-Zionist Thinker?," *Society and Self*, 19–38. In his introduction (12), Blidstein indicates that the title of this essay may have been overstated, so I have cited his more qualified formulation. Other analyses of the Rav's Zionism include: Rabbi Aharon Lichtenstein, "Rav Soloveitchik's Approach to Zionism," *Alei Etzion* 14 (5766): 21–24; the interview in Sabbato, *Mevakshei Panekha*, 187–188; Chaim Navon, "Tefissato shel ha-Tziyyonut ha-Datit shel Ha-Rav Soloveitchik," *Tzohar* 22 (5765): 439–50.
169. Walfish, "Re-Engaging Theology," in *Religious Zionism Post-Disengagement: Future Directions*, ed. Chaim I. Waxman (New York: The Michael

But clearly the work's emphasis is not on metaphysical themes but on human responsibility and opportunity, such as responsibility to settle the land, create solidarity, and most importantly to realize Jewish destiny – all this, along with correlative criticisms of Jews, including the observant, who have evaded their responsibilities.

Walfish does not echo Schwartz's claim of resurgence, but instead offers additional reasons for *KDD*'s limited influence. A stress on benefits and on God's direct activity is a greater attraction than a stress on demands and challenges; the Kook ideology was able to generate more passion. Kalman Neuman suggests that the Rav's view on "land for peace" expressed in 1967 – that whether to surrender land for security's sake is not a rabbinic decision but one for military analysts, even as regards holy places – hurt his standing among Religious Zionists as well. Neuman argues, inter alia, that the Rav's position led Religious Zionists in Israel to construe him as separating the religious from the political – an interpretation seemingly contrary to Religious Zionism. In America, the Rav had many students and his influence was great, and combined with geographic distance from Israel such criticisms of him (argues Neuman) had little traction.[170]

Other questions arise about the power of *Kol Dodi Dofek*: Is its argument too tied to the Shoah, giving it a timebound quality? (Daniel Rynhold suggested to me an analogy to Emil Fackenheim, whose effort to found Jewish identity in consciousness of the Holocaust may lose its

---

Scharf Publication Trust of The Yeshiva University Press, 2008)," 64–67; Zivan, "Me-ha-she'alah 'Lammah' la-She'elah 'Eikh'?: Iyyun be-Divreihem shel Ha-Rav Soloveitchik, Goldman, Hartman, Leibowitz, ve-Levinas," in *Hiddat ha-Yissurin*, ed. Baruch Kahana, Hayutah Doitsh, and Roni Redman (Jerusalem: Beit Morasha and Tel Aviv: Yediot Aharanot, 2012), 213–16. See also Jason Kalman, "Iyyov al Parashat Derakhim: 'Kol Dodi Dofek' u-Mekomo ba-Historiyyah ha-Parshanit shel Sefer Iyyov," in RBH, 177–203. As mentioned earlier, Arnold Davidson observed in conversation that, in this instance, the Rav introduced metaphysics in the service of calling for a practical response, and that perhaps this is why he allowed himself to speak metaphysically.

Another challenge to the Rav's reading of providential history was raised by Hillel Seidman, and the Rav responded. See Helfgot, "From the Rav's Pen," 324–25 (letter to Milton Konvitz).

170. See Neuman, "Bein Ortodoksiyyah Modernit be-Artzot ha-Berit le-Tziyyonut Datit be-Yisrael: Hashpa'at ha-Rav Soloveitchik al Emdot ha-Tzibuur ha-Dati be-Yisrael," in RBOH, 471–89.

visceral quality as time goes on.) Will the memory of 1948 be enough to sustain a sense of religious significance in the future, or even today? Does the discourse deliver too much of an American form of Zionism, appealing for money?[171] The aspects of *Kol Dodi Dofek* that some people find most compelling may well be (a) its treatment of evil, in particular its thesis that we should ask "what?" and not "why?" and (b) its analysis of Jewish identity, in particular the distinction between *berit goral* and *berit yi'ud* – rather than its Zionist thrust.

The absence of messianic motifs and the additional factors just mentioned are reasons why *Kol Dodi Dofek* did not capture the popular imagination as compared to messianic approaches. They are not reasons to impugn the cogency of the work itself. Yet notwithstanding the current importance of *Kol Dodi Dofek* on the Israeli scene, we live in an age of disillusionment with Religious Zionism; a feeling that it cannot be articulated cogently, and that it is even irrelevant.[172] Even among those who do not despair, i.e., Modern Orthodox religious-Zionists, *Kol Dodi Dofek* is thought to have limitations. In a symposium in *Tradition* marking the fiftieth anniversary of *Kol Dodi Dofek*, several critiques emerged in addition to Walfish's. Rabbi Nathaniel Helfgot, in a spirit similar to Blidstein, notes that Rabbi Soloveitchik does not speak about classical Zionist themes like *mamlakhtiyyut*, of Jewish sovereignty per se and of a nation with a government, army, and economic infrastructure.[173] (The Rav's addresses to Mizrachi do contain some reference to these themes, but they are not prominent.) Helfgot also points out that the Rav does not speak of the potential of Israel to be an *or la-goyim*. (I suggest that the reason the Rav rarely

---

171. See Blidstein, "On the Jewish People," 27. As Yoel Finkelman has pointed out, one element lacking in Religious Zionist thought is a theory of Diaspora Zionism. See Finkelman,"Can American Orthodoxy Afford to Have its Best and Brightest (Not) Make Aliya?," in *Religious Zionism Post-Disengagement,* ed. Chaim Waxman (New York: Michael Scharf Publication Trust of Yeshiva University Press, 2008) , 235–60.

172. Yoel Finkelman, "On The Irrelevance of Religious Zionism," *Tradition* 39, 1 (Spring 2005): 21–44; Moshe Koppel, "The Demise of Self-Negating Religious Zionism," in *Religious Zionism Post-Disengagement*, ed. Waxman, 119–32.

173. Nathaniel Helfgot, "On the Shoulders of a Giant: Looking back, Yet Looking Forward," *Tradition* 39, 23 (Fall 2006): 31–-37. But see *The Rav Speaks: Five Addresses on Israel, History, and the Jewish People* [*Hamesh Derashot*] (New York: Toras HoRav Foundation, 2002), 176–-179.

refers to the Jews as an *or la-goyim* is that he wishes to emphasize the obligation of Jews to participate in the larger society as members of humanity, possessed of a human identity as well as a Jewish identity, and not on the Jews being special vis-à-vis fighting the evils of society.)[174] Blidstein observes that, unlike Rav Kook, the Rav does not critique Diaspora life, nor does he highlight the State "as a potential embodiment of the broadest ethical and societal vocation of Judaism . . .," though (Blidstein adds) for many readers the latter theme seems implicit.[175] In a letter to the editor of *Hadoar*, the Rav urged urged methodological caution.[176] Reuven Ziegler likewise describes paths that the Rav did not pursue. Ziegler takes notice of the absence of the themes that a Jew can live a more integrated and organic life in Eretz Yisrael and that there is a special quality to religious observance in the Land, which can be posited even granted the Rav's thesis that *kedushah* of the land is not be understood as a metaphysical property.[177] (In *The Emergence of Ethical Man*, however, we find him affirming that the people are rooted in the soil, which aligns him with Gordon, Hess, and Ahad Haam.[178]) Addressing the motif of *berit goral/berit yi'ud*, Helfgot also argues that the Rav's discussion of *berit goral* and *berit yi'ud* misses the *yi'ud* orientation of many non-Orthodox Jews, their commitment to religious principles and Jewish destiny.[179] Let me add that the Rav's criticism of anti-Zionists (in a *derashah* to Mizrachi) for not believing in "the 14th *ani ma'amin*" – that "Torah, as the eternal Torah, was given for practice within all the social changes and meanderings to which a dynamic society, that is constantly on the move like a mighty stream, is subject"[180] – loses some of its force

---

174. Cf. his use of the phrase in *The Rav Speaks*, 78.
175. Blidstein, "Was the Rav a Religious Zionist Thinker?" 19–36.
176. See *Community, Covenant and Commitment*, 163–66.
177. Ziegler, *Majesty and Humility*, 295–296. See also *Emergence of Ethical Man*, but cf. the next citation.
178. See *The Emergence of Ethical Man*, 62. This passage is noted by Alex Ozar, "The Emergence of Max Scheler."
179. Helfgot, "On the Shoulders of a Giant," 35–36. But in the *derashot* to Mizrachi in *The Rav Speaks,* there are intimations that all Jews have a religious orientation of some sort. See the discussion in Schwartz, "Mishnato shel ha-Rav Y"D Soloveitchik bi-Re'i he-Hagut ha-Tziyyonut ha-Datit: Ha-hillon ve-ha-Medinah," in EBM, 123–145.
180. *The Rav Speaks*, 175–76.

to the extent that Halakhah has not been able to resolve some of the more formidable problems of Israeli society.

Even with these gaps and difficulties in the Rav's thought, we must not obscure the elements of his Zionism that can serve as components of a non-messianic form of Zionist ideology. Specifically, the state's existence has provided physical protection and a place for Jewish refugees from the world over; and it provides a context for seeking fulfillment not only of the responsibilities of Jews for other Jews, but of the responsibilities for keeping the covenant of *yi'ud*.

(v) *Modernity and Traditionalism*: This heading, of course, is the over-arching category under which to subsume items (i)-(iv) in this section – and most of the philosophic themes in Rabbi Soloveitchik's writings. For all that, as Moshe Sokol has pointed out, Rabbi Soloveitchik's project was not that of Maimonides. He did not seek to confront all of the intellectual challenges of his time. His is, rather, as Sokol puts it, a "segmented search." His engagement with modernity is somewhat limited. He did affirm certain values, like autonomy, creativity, and self-expression. But he wrote and spoke only about those issues and challenges to which he felt he could contribute.[181] In support of this restricted view of Rabbi Soloveitchik's aims, it is common to quote the passage at the beginning of *Lonely Man of Faith* in which the Rav states he has "never been bothered" by the challenges of evolution, materialism, and biblical criticism, as well as a dichotomy or dialectic between the adult and "man-child of Torah" (*ish-yeled ha-Torah*) who accepts religious truth with utter simplicity.[182] The aim of *Lonely Man* is phenomenological, not to resolve – to quote the first sentence – "the millennium old problem of faith and reason."[183] Rabbi Jonathan Sacks puts the matter aptly when he states that "it was not secular

---

181. Sokol, "'Ger ve-Toshav Anokhi': Modernity and Traditionalism in the Life and Thought of Rabbi Joseph B. Soloveitchik," *Tradition* 29, 1 (1994): 32–47, repr. in Sokol, *Judaism Examined* (New York: Touro College Press and Boston, MA: Academic Studies Press, 2013), 434–50. The phrase "segmented search" is on p. 436. See also Ziegler, chap. 17.

182. *Lonely Man of Faith*, 7; "Al Ahavat ha-Torah u-Geulat Nefesh ha-Dor," in *Be-Sod ha-Yahid ve-ha-Yahad*, 412–13; "Peleitat Sofereihem," in ibid., 255–94. See Sokol, *Judaism Examined*, 441–45.

183. For discussion of the Rav's approach to intellectual assaults on Judaism, see Ziegler, *Majesty and Humility*, chap. 17.

knowledge . . . that caused Soloveitchik such searing distress, but secular man."[184]

While it is foolhardy to quarrel with the assertion that the Rav's goal is phenomenology and religious anthropology, not intellectual harmonization, we should be careful to acknowledge that Rabbi Soloveitchik has *something* to say about some of modern cognitive challenges to religion. In *The Emergence of Ethical Man*, Rabbi Soloveitchik embraces evolution and applies it broadly. (The work, however, is far from being entirely naturalistic.[185]) The Rav also gestures toward refuting biblical criticism. In fact, a great irony of *The Lonely Man of Faith* is that although he announces that biblical criticism does not "bother" him, the Rav's distinction between the two Adams would, if cogent, refute the critics' contention that Genesis 1 and Genesis 2 trace to different traditions. Elsewhere he explains that Genesis 1 and Genesis 2 reflect the human being from two perspectives: human beings are biologically continuous with the animal kingdom (chapter 1), but they also possess special spiritual and ethical capacities (chapter 2), albeit these are not entirely independent of biological conditions and in fact are related to them.[186] Implicit here is another rebuttal (closer to *peshat*, I believe) of the argument for different creation traditions. He also addresses concerns about the historicity of the Abraham narratives, in two ways: (i) pointing very briefly to archaeological discoveries, and asserting that (ii) just as we need no proof of God's existence, we need no evidence of Abraham's existence because Abraham has become so integrated

---

184. Sacks, *Tradition in An Untraditional Age*, 49. Carl Feit, however, utilizes *The Lonely Man of Faith* in connection with Darwinism. See Feit, "Modern Orthodoxy and Evolution: The Models of Rabbi J. B. Soloveitchik and Rabbi A. I. Kook," in *Jewish Tradition and The Challenge of Darwinism*, ed. G. N. Cantor and Mark Swetlitz (Chicago: University of Chicago Press, 2006), 208–24.

185. See Alex Sztuden, "Naturalism and the Rav: A Reply to Yoram Hazony," *Meorot* 10 (2012). http://www.yctorah.org/images/stories/about_us/%233%20-%20sztuden%20-%20naturalism%20and%20the%20rav.pdf. Sztuden is responding to Hazony's naturalistic reading in "The Rav's Bombshell," *Commentary* (April, 2012): 48–55, and to the exchange about Hazony's article in *Commentary* (September, 2012): 69–76, along with Hazony's post on his blog *Jerusalem Letters* (April 2, 2012), accessible at: http://jerusalemletters.com/jletters/articles/a-bombshell-from-the-rav.

186. See *The Emergence of Ethical Man*, but cf. *Family Redeemed*, chap. 1.

into our historical consciousness.[187] (We might call these the evidential and the existential approaches.) None of these responses to challenges besides the existential are presented as robust refutations, and they are very limited in scope. Still, we may aptly state that, although the Rav's engagement with modernity does not include a substantial rebuttal of the major evidential challenges to religion, he is not totally reticent.

In regard to Talmud criticism, Shlomo Pick demonstrates the Rav's strong opposition to lower criticism, to psychologizing of the Sages, and to historicizing.[188] To be sure, he observes, on occasion the Rav referred to the possibility of a flawed *girsa*, but finding the correct *girsa* of a text by investigating manuscripts was not part of his method, let alone a project. Pick also shows that at times Rabbi Soloveitchik would introduce the historical background of a talmudic text, but not in the way an academic would. Rabbi Walter Wurzburger attributes the Rav's rejection of modern methods to his "modern" post-modernism,[189] but Pick rejects this view. Given the heightened acceptance of the techniques he opposed, the Rav's negative view of academic Talmud study has lost some appeal, particularly for the new generation.[190]

Finally, Aviezer Ravitzky has argued that what qualifies as "modern" shifts. The Rav's philosophy of science, epistemology, and hermeneutics are now outdated. Further, he incorporates the core concepts of modernity of his time – subjectivity, freedom, and alienation – in a Jewish framework and proffers his own treatment of them. But the confrontation with modernity today necessitates confronting other trends.[191]

---

187. See *Abraham's Journey,* ed. David Shatz, Joel B. Wolowelsky, and Reuven Ziegler (New York: Toras HoRav Foundation, 2008), 1–6.
188. Pick, "Ha-Rav Soloveitchik," in RBOH, 281–98.
189. Walter S. Wurzburger, "Rav Joseph B. Soloveitchik As Posek of Post-Modern Orthodoxy," *Tradition* 29, 1 (1994): 7.
190. See, for example, the essay by David Flatto in *The Next Generation of Modern Orthodoxy,* ed. Hain, "Tradition and Modernity in the House of Study: Reconsidering the Relationship Between the Conceptual and Critical Methods of Studying Talmud," (113–36) and Yakov Nagen, "Scholarship Needs Spirituality – Spirituality Needs Scholarship: Challenges for Emerging Talmudic Methodologies," in *Lomdus,* ed. Blau, 137–73.
191. See Ravitzky, "Hadash Min ha-Torah." Feminism is a modern trend that the Rav does not address robustly, though his work contains male vs. female archetypes, studies of biblical women, and more. Shira Wolosky, in "The Lonely Woman of Faith," *Judaism* 52, 1–2 (2003): 3–18, argues that Rabbi Soloveitchik's discussion of Adam the second has implications for feminism

My list of critiques is not complete; more can be said about such topics as relativism and postmodernism and the Rav's thought. Additionally, many of the preceding questions concern the social application of the Rav's philosophy. In his works on suffering, prayer, and the like, by contrast, he explores the private, inner dimension. But I end the examples of critiques here, in the hope that I have explained current discussions about the Rav's relevance and stimulated further critical reflection.

IV

When the Rav passed away, his legions of students expressed the worrisome thought that a younger generation that did not experience his presence – *asher lo yada et Yosef* (Exodus 1:8) – as well as Jews who are distant from Yeshiva University circles, would not take an interest in his life and legacy. Questions sprung to mind, different questions for different groups. For academics who knew the Rav, the questions were: Is the Rav's philosophy doomed to become the province of a small coterie of students and other Modern Orthodox Jews? Will it be treated only hagiographically, or will it be read, interpreted, critically analyzed, and internalized by a larger group of academics and "intelligent readers"? The Rav believes that Halakhah and tefillah are democratic, accessible in some measure to all. Will that prove to be the case with his philosophy? Certainly we have seen a flowering of Soloveitchik scholarship, and his works evoke ever growing interest. Whether his works can serve as an effective voice in working through today's challenges is a complex matter both because of lacunae in his *oeuvre* and because of important changes in society. But it is clear that his writings on halakhic existence and on the human and Jewish experience command respect and have proved resonant. Furthermore, if my analysis is correct, then, while certain themes in his work are dated, some of his perspectives apply even more today than in his time.[192]

---

and shows feminist values to be in accord with Judaism. For critique, see Kaplan, "'Ish ha-Emunah ha-Boded'," 152–55.

192. I thank the following people for their helpful comments and replies to queries: David Berger, Rabbi Yitzchak Blau, Menachem Butler, Shalom Carmy, Arnold Davidson, Yoel Finkelman, Rabbi Nathaniel Helfgot, Arnold Lustiger, Charles Raffel z"l, Daniel Rynhold, Marc Shapiro, Alex Sztuden, Heshey Zelcer, and Reuven Ziegler.

CONTRIBUTORS

SHALOM CARMY teaches Jewish Studies and Philosophy at Yeshiva University. He is editor of Tradition and author of the "Litvak at Large" feature of First Things. He is also editor of R. Soloveitchik's Worship of the Heart and other works on prayer.

EPHRAIM KANARFOGEL is the E. Billi Ivry University Professor of Jewish History, Literature and Law at Yeshiva University. He is Editor-in-Chief of the international journal *Jewish History*, and Secretary of the American Academy for Jewish Research. Among his many books are the award-winning *The Intellectual History and Rabbinic Culture of Medieval Ashkenaz*, and the forthcoming *Brothers from Afar: Rabbinic Approaches toward Apostasy and Reversion in Medieval Europe*.

DANIEL RYNHOLD is Professor of Jewish Philosophy at the Bernard Revel Graduate School of Jewish Studies, Yeshiva University. He is the author of *Two Models of Jewish Philosophy: Justifying One's Practices* (Oxford University Press, 2005), *An Introduction to Medieval Jewish Philosophy* (I.B. Tauris, 2009), and co-author with Michael J. Harris of the forthcoming monograph *Nietzsche, Soloveitchik, and Contemporary Jewish Philosophy* (Cambridge: Cambridge University Press, 2018).

DAVID SHATZ is the Ronald P. Stanton University Professor of Philosophy, Ethics, and Religious Thought at Yeshiva University. He has edited, co-authored, or authored fifteen books and over 80 articles and reviews. A volume devoted to his career and thought appears in the Brill Library of Contemporary Jewish Philosophers, and he is editor of the MeOtzar HoRav series and *The Torah u-Madda Journal*.

197

ALEX SZTUDEN is a Templeton Fellow at the Herzl Institute. He taught philosophy at Fordham University, where he received his M.A. and was awarded a distinguished fellowship, holds a J.D. from Columbia Law School, and received his B.A. from Yeshiva University. Mr. Sztuden has written widely in philosophy and religion, and is the winner of the Joel and Jeanne Novak Prize for Best Essay in Jewish Thought (awarded in 2014). He is the cofounder and director of an online education company.

SHIRA WEISS holds a PhD in Jewish Philosophy from the Bernard Revel Graduate School of Yeshiva University, and is the author of *Joseph Albo on Free Choice: Exegetical Innovation in Medieval Jewish Philosophy* (Oxford University Press, 2017) and *Ethical Ambiguity in the Hebrew Bible* (Cambridge University Press, 2018).